"Park leads the reader on a fasc[...]
apostolic life of Thomas Merto[...]
Merton's life of self-transcend[...]
him to share with fellow contemp[...]
love and intimacy with God. Park's *Thomas Merton's Encounter w[...]
Buddhism and Beyond* is a finely researched work well worth exploring."

> —Joseph Schner, SJ
> Regis College, University of Toronto

"This is the first extensive study to explore Merton's legacy in terms of
how it has shaped the institutional church, through the activities of the
Pontifical Council for Interreligious Dialogue (PCID) and through the
Monastic Interreligious Dialogue (MID), which functions under its aegis.
This is a convincing portrayal of Merton's pivotal importance in the
history of interreligious dialogue."

> —Joe Raab
> Professor of Religious Studies and Theology, Siena Heights
> University
> Coeditor of *The Merton Annual*

"This is a well-researched and readable analysis of Thomas Merton's
understanding of and engagement with Buddhism. The work is enhanced
by an extended consideration of the Christian-Buddhism dialogue from
a monastic perspective. Since the author himself is an Asian monk he
brings a fresh angle to his task. Like the good householder of the Gospel,
Father Park brings forth old things and new."

> —Lawrence S. Cunningham
> The University of Notre Dame

"An intriguing and significant contribution to interfaith encounter. Provides
fresh insight into the way that Merton's evolving sense of contemplation
and his exploration of experiential interfaith dialogue broke new ground.
These explorations, both existential and intellectual, continue to provide
a challenging yet fruitful model for interfaith dialogue that goes beyond
theology and action-orientation to the contemplative core of religious
experience however variously it might be conceptualized or experienced."

> —Wendy M. Wright
> Professor Emerita of Theology, Creighton University

"Park explores Thomas Merton's dialogue with Buddhism getting to the very heart of it as only a fellow monk, steeped in the daily monastic rhythm of prayer and work, could do. Park then builds on Merton's legacy suggesting important ways monastic and contemplative interreligious dialogue can continue to develop in the twenty-first century and beyond."

> —Paul M. Pearson
> Director, Thomas Merton Center, Bellarmine University

"This book delves into the process of Thomas Merton's spiritual transformation through his encounter with Zen and Tibetan Buddhist thought, and his involvement in the dialogue of religious experience with their practitioners. And indeed, because the practitioners of Buddhism emphasize the priority of experience over faith, a fruitful dialogue between Catholics and Buddhists may well be impossible without a dialogue on contemplative prayer."

> —Ovey N. Mohammed, SJ
> Professor Emeritus of Catholicism and Eastern Religions
> Regis College, University of Toronto

"Jaechan Anselmo Park has gifted us with a carefully written, well-organized exploration of Thomas Merton's understanding of inner experience, interreligious dialogue, and inter-monastic/inter-contemplative dialogue. Whether readers have an interest in the work of Thomas Merton, interreligious dialogue, or inter-monastic discourse, they will find this book to be an essential companion."

> —Dennis Patrick O'Hara
> St. Michael's College, University of Toronto

Thomas Merton's Encounter with Buddhism and Beyond

*His Interreligious Dialogue,
Inter-Monastic Exchanges, and Their Legacy*

Jaechan Anselmo Park, OSB

Preface by
BonnieThurston

Foreword by
William Skudlarek

LITURGICAL PRESS
Collegeville, Minnesota

www.litpress.org

© 2019 by Jaechan Anselmo Park, OSB
Published by Liturgical Press, Collegeville, Minnesota. All rights reserved. No part of this book may be used or reproduced in any manner whatsoever, except brief quotations in reviews, without written permission of Liturgical Press, Saint John's Abbey, PO Box 7500, Collegeville, MN 56321-7500. Printed in the United States of America.

1   2   3   4   5   6   7   8   9

Library of Congress Cataloging-in-Publication Data

Names: Park, Jaechan Anselmo, author.
Title: Thomas Merton's encounter with Buddhism and beyond : his interreligious dialogue, inter-monastic exchanges, and their legacy / Jaechan Anselmo Park, OSB.
Description: Collegeville : Liturgical Press, 2019. | Includes bibliographical references.
Identifiers: LCCN 2018050623 (print) | LCCN 2019009331 (ebook) | ISBN 9780814684993 (eBook) | ISBN 9780814684740 (pbk.)
Subjects: LCSH: Merton, Thomas, 1915–1968. | Buddhism—Influence. | Christianity and other religions--Buddhism. | Buddhism—Relations—Christianity.
Classification: LCC BX4705.M542 (ebook) | LCC BX4705.M542 P37 2019 (print) | DDC 271/.12502—dc23
LC record available at https://lccn.loc.gov_2018050623

Contents

Foreword   vii

Preface   xi

Acknowledgments   xvii

List of Abbreviations   xix

List of Tables   xxi

Introduction   xxiii

Chapter 1 Merton's Own Inner Experience
and Interreligious Dialogue   1

Chapter 2 Merton's Pioneering Work
with Buddhist-Christian Dialogue   61

Chapter 3 Merton's Pioneering Work
with Inter-Monastic/Contemplative Dialogue   123

Chapter 4 Merton's Legacy: Beyond His Encounter
with Buddhism   181

Conclusion   243

Bibliography   257

Index   275

Foreword

Since 1996, the North American commission of Monastic Interreligious Dialogue has sponsored meetings of Buddhist and Catholic monks at the Abbey of Gethsemani, Thomas Merton's monastery in Kentucky. The fourth "Gethsemani Encounter," this one on the topic of spiritual maturation, was held in the summer of 2015. One of the presenters was Jaechan Anselmo Park, a Benedictine monk from Korea, who gave a paper entitled "A Christian Contemplative Approach to the Ten Ox-herding Pictures of Zen Buddhism: Interreligious Dialogue as Mutual Self-mediation."

Having recently returned from ten years in Japan, where my efforts to learn Japanese were a never-ending struggle, I was amazed that this Asian monk was able to speak so fluently and with such confidence about a topic as abstruse as "mutual self-mediation." I was even more intrigued when I learned that the focus of his doctoral research at Regis College of the University of Toronto was Merton's intense and transformative experience of contemplative dialogue with Buddhism.

At the closing session of that Gethsemani Encounter, Fr. Anselmo himself recognized how unusual his situation was. He noted that during his seminary studies in Korea he was required to become familiar with Western philosophy and theology. Now, as a doctoral student at a Canadian university, he was studying Eastern religions and examining their impact on a Western Catholic monk. He expressed the hope that his transcultural experiences and studies would prepare him to contribute to the advancement of Buddhist-Christian dialogue in Asia.

The year 2018 marked the fiftieth anniversary of Merton's death in Thailand. On his last night at Gethsemani before embarking on his Asian journey, he wrote, "[I hope] to find something or someone who will help me advance in my own spiritual quest."[1] About a month later, in notes for a talk he gave in Calcutta, he maintained that his principal reason for being so interested in Buddhism—Buddhist monasticism in particular—was not simply to accumulate information about other monastic traditions. Rather, his interest was spiritual. He was concerned about his own monastic calling and dedication, and for that reason he wanted "to drink from ancient sources of monastic vision and experience [in order] to become a better and more enlightened monk."[2]

Much has already been written about Merton's extensive and prophetic interest in other religious traditions and the special appeal that Zen Buddhism had for him. The particular and valuable contribution of Fr. Anselmo to the existing literature is his emphasis on the spiritual motivation of Merton's search, his description of the transformative effect that immersion in Buddhist teaching and practice had on Merton's interior life, and his thoughts on how Merton's approach to Buddhism could help Christian monks in Asia develop a deep spiritual friendship with Buddhist monks that could bring them to "trans-cultural maturity," a retrieving of humanity's original *unity-in-diversity*, which Merton put forth as the goal of contemplative dialogue.

Fr. Anselmo concludes his book noting that his encounter with the writings of Thomas Merton in 2012 changed his academic,

---

1. Thomas Merton, *The Intimate Merton: His Life from His Journals*, ed. Patrick Hart and Jonathan Montaldo (San Francisco, CA: HarperSanFrancisco, 1999), 336ff. The date was September 9, 1968.

2. Thomas Merton, *The Asian Journal of Thomas Merton* (New York, NY: New Directions, 1973), op. cit. Appendix IV, "Monastic Experience and East-West Dialogue (*Notes for a paper to have been delivered at Calcutta, October 1968*)," 312ff. In his journal entry for October 24, 1968, Merton wrote, "I spoke yesterday morning [at the Temple of Understanding Conference in Calcutta], but did not actually follow my prepared text."

spiritual, and monastic life. Now having returned to Korea, he hopes to devote his energies to the promotion of contemplative dialogue between Buddhists and Christians, the form of dialogue that Merton believed must be at the heart of all interreligious dialogue with the great world religions if we are to live together in peace as one spiritual family.

On behalf of Monastic Interreligious Dialogue, I am profoundly grateful to Fr. Anselmo for so clearly articulating Merton's insistence that the core of interreligious dialogue must be spiritual and for his willingness to promote the legacy of this Western and yet universal monk among the Christians and Buddhists of Korea and beyond.

William Skudlarek, OSB
Secretary General
Monastic Interreligious Dialogue
December 10, 2018
Fiftieth anniversary of the death of Thomas Merton

Preface

In the late 1980s and early 1990s when a group of scholars were founding the Society for Buddhist Christian Studies, someone asked, "will you have any Buddhists to talk to?" What the questioner implied was "will you have any *Asian* Buddhists, cultural Buddhists with whom to engage in dialogue?" The implication was that *real* Buddhism was Asian. But while Buddhism arose in a particular place at a specific point in history, its beliefs and practices are not, by definition, the provenance of any ethnic, cultural, or racial group. For example, American Jews can be Buddhists. A Korean can be a Christian and a Benedictine monk. That the author of this book is Asian, Christian, and monastic brings special insight to his study of the well-known Cistercian monk, Thomas Merton, who became enamored of Buddhism and traveled as a pilgrim to Asia.

In his introduction to Merton's essay "Christian Culture Needs Oriental Wisdom," Patrick F. O'Connell provides a helpful comment worth quoting in full. Merton, he explains:

> . . . does not believe that the Christian faith, or Christian doctrine, is somehow incomplete without an infusion from the East, but that the inevitably limited framework of Christian culture, the historical and geographical setting in which faith is embedded, could benefit greatly from an engagement with Eastern wisdom—not the belief system *per se* but the experiential knowledge, the spiritual insights of the great Asian religions.[1]

---

1. Patrick F. O'Connell, ed., *Thomas Merton: Selected Essays* (Maryknoll, NY: Orbis Books, 2013), 103.

While many Western scholars have done serious work on Merton and Buddhism (Dr. Paul Pearson, director of the Thomas Merton Studies Center at Bellarmine University in Louisville, Kentucky, has compiled an extensive bibliography on Merton and Buddhism[2]), and several Asian scholars have written on this and related subjects,[3] Merton readers have awaited a *full* analysis of Merton's dialogue with Buddhism from an Asian perspective. Fr. Park's book provides this analysis as well as descriptions of Merton's encounter with and contribution to both interreligious and inter-monastic dialogue. Fr. Park's insights are those both of an Asian Christian and a Benedictine monk. Being a monk and a Christian (a religion that arose far from his traditional historical, cultural context), Fr. Park sees both Buddhism and Christianity with "baptized eyes." The multifaceted jewel of this cross-cultural seeing is a special gift to Merton studies. His monastic perspective is critical, because if one does not understand monasticism, one cannot really understand or accurately interpret the life and work of Thomas Merton.[4]

Like the pre-Socratic philosopher Heraclitus, Buddhism is skeptical about solid essences; everything is in flux. As Teresa of

2. An example is the collection of essays in *Merton & Buddhism: Wisdom, Emptiness & Everyday Mind*, ed. Bonnie Bowman Thurston (Louisville, KY: Fons Vitae Press, 2007), which includes the work of several scholars and a large section of Pearson's bibliography. And see Robert H. King, *Thomas Merton and Thich Nhat Hanh* (New York, NY: Continuum, 2001), and Alexander Lipski, *Thomas Merton and Asia: His Quest for Utopia* (Kalamazoo, MI: Cistercian Publications, 1983).

3. See, for example, earlier essays by Joseph Chu-Cong, OCSO, "Thomas Merton and the Far East," *Cistercian Studies* 14, no. 1 (1979): 45–58; Kun Ki Kang, "Prayer and the Cultivation of Mind: An Examination Through the Writings of Thomas Merton and Chinul" [unpublished manuscript] (Chonju, Korea: Department of Philosophy, Chonbuk National University); Cyrus Lee, "Thomas Merton and Zen Buddhism," *Chinese Culture* 13, no. 1 (1973): 35–48.

4. For more on this important point see John Eudes Bamberger, OCSO, *Thomas Merton: Prophet of Renewal* (Kalamazoo, MI: Cistercian Publications, 2005), and Lawrence S. Cunningham, *Thomas Merton & the Monastic Vision* (Grand Rapids, MI: Eerdmans, 1999).

Jesus (Teresa of Avila, whom Merton admired) succinctly put it, "*todo se pasa.*" I think Merton's fascination with Buddhism might be summarized by the paradoxical phrase "changing stability," because Thomas Merton was quintessentially two things: a person who changed and a monk. Writing in *The Sign of Jonas* Merton quipped, "I am the impression that will change."[5] It is exactly as Dom Armand Veilleux, OCSO, observed: Merton was "a monk on a spiritual journey, a man in a continual process of growth, whose field of consciousness was always both deepening and opening up to new horizons."[6]

The trajectory of Merton's life and interests followed an evolving trajectory. He understood conversion, not as a single event, but as a process. Christians, and there is no evidence that Merton was ever anything but deeply, committedly Christian, are in the process of conversion, open to conversion in every moment and at every level of life. This *metanoia* summarizes the Benedictine vow of *conversio morum*, conversion of life. Merton's monastic vows *were* his stability. His "changeability" reflected his monastic convictions. Both came together in his openness to Buddhism (and to other religions, in particular, Islam). It is this paradox of monastic stability and *metanoia* that Fr. Park's book illuminates.

Merton's knowledge of Buddhism began (in history of religious fashion) with Hinduism and continued through study of the Mahayana Zen tradition. Then, in response to his experiences in Asia, it turned toward Theravadan Buddhism, represented by the great carved figures at Polonnaruwa and his epiphany there (so eloquently recorded in his *Asian Journal*), and then to Tibetan Buddhism (*Vajrayana* and *Dzogchen*) by means of audience with His Holiness the Dalai Lama and meetings with Tibetan monks

---

5. Thomas Merton, *The Sign of Jonas* (New York, NY: Doubleday/Image Books, 1956), 242.

6. Armand Veilleux, OCSO, "Monk on a Journey," *Cistercian Studies Quarterly* 50 (2015): 99. Originally published in *Thomas Merton/Monk: A Monastic Tribute*, ed. Br. Patrick Hart, OCSO (Kalamazoo, MI: Cistercian Publications, 1983).

and lamas. In notes for a talk he was to deliver in Asia Merton wrote, "I speak as a western monk who is pre-eminently concerned with his own monastic calling and dedication. . . . I come as a pilgrim who is anxious to drink from ancient sources of monastic vision and experience. I seek . . . to become a better and more enlightened monk. . . ."[7]

Merton understood religious dialogue as essential to his vocation as a monk, not defined in terms of "order," but of life orientation. For Merton, "monks" (a gender-inclusive term), whether or not they are in formal, religious orders, are "marginal persons," detached enough from their social and cultural contexts to see them clearly. In an informal talk in Calcutta, October 1968, he noted that " . . . the monk in the modern world is no longer an established person with an established place in society. . . . He is a marginal person who withdraws deliberately to the margin of society with a view to deepening fundamental human experience."[8]

This study brings together its author's own monastic formation and outlook, his knowledge of Asian monasticism (particularly in Korea, his own context), of the Buddhist traditions, and of Thomas Merton. Fr. Park places all this in the context of ongoing contemplative dialogue among monastics and contemplatives of different religious traditions. As do I, Park views Merton as a pioneer of Buddhist-Christian dialogue.[9] His purpose in this book is to examine Merton's "self-transformation through contemplative experience" (chapter 1), to explore his encounter with Buddhism and Buddhist-Christian dialogue (chapter 2), to answer those critical of this endeavor (this he does particularly well at the end of chapter 3), and to present Merton's ongoing legacy in dialogue

---

7. Thomas Merton, *The Asian Journal of Thomas Merton*, ed. N. Burton, P. Hart, and J. Laughlin (New York, NY: New Directions, 1968/1975), 312–313.

8. Ibid., 305.

9. Bonnie Thurston, "Thomas Merton: Pioneer of Buddhist-Christian Dialogue," *The Catholic World* 223 (May/June 1989): 126–128.

and cross-religious encounters especially in the Asian monastic context (chapter 4).

Fr. Park's evaluation of Merton's knowledge of Buddhism is balanced and helpful. He stresses that Merton "realized the dangers of a facile comparison and syncretism" and understood "that Buddhists and Christians must dialogue at a profound spiritual level since those who experienced self-transcendence were no longer in isolation but were able to accept others with openness, freedom, and love, and to dialogue with them at a mature level" (p. 119). Fr. Park's gentle but insistent stress on the necessity of self-transcendence (perhaps Buddhists would say "egolessness") before engaging in and during cross-religious encounter reflects Merton's own position and is absolutely spot on.[10] Merton "saw that the way of self-emptying or self-transformation through self-forgetfulness or self-losing could become the basic principle for Buddhist-Christian dialogue" (p. 79).

To my knowledge, this is the first book-length study in English to evaluate Merton's studies of Buddhism, his dialogue with Buddhists, *and* its relevance for ongoing dialogue. This latter Fr. Park accomplishes by an overview of Merton's influence as represented particularly in the Gethsemani Encounters and inter- and intra-monastic encounters, experiences of "passing over and coming home." Fr. Park expands our knowledge of Merton's life, writing, and travel and its wider influence on the subsequent development of conversations between and among Christians, Buddhists, and monastics.

Each of the book's four chapters opens with a clear statement of its subject and the goal of the chapter; then, in orderly fashion, with pauses for summation, Fr. Park presents his argument and its supporting material. Each chapter's clear organization facilitates

---

10. See also Ryan Scruggs, "Interreligious Dialogue," in *Thomas Merton: Monk on the Edge*, ed. Ross Labrie and Angus Stuart (Thomas Merton Society of Canada, 2012), chapter 7, and Bonnie Thurston, "Waking from a Dream of Separateness: Thomas Merton's Principles of Religious Dialogue," *Cistercian Studies Quarterly* 50 (2015): 83–97.

the reader's understanding of occasionally complex material. Of necessity, there is some repetition of previously covered ground. When Fr. Park revisits earlier material, it is usually from a different perspective, and is rather like looking into the same room from different windows and seeing its contents anew. Parts of chapter 2 (on the more theoretical aspects of Buddhist-Christian dialogue) may be hard going for the general reader (the genesis of this book *was* a doctoral dissertation), but it is critical when the reader comes to chapter 4 on Merton's legacy. Chapter 4 is perhaps Fr. Park's most valuable new contribution, and one hopes he might in the future expand it into a book-length study.

Throughout the book Fr. Park stresses that Merton's "contemplative dialogue was always directed to his inner transformation through engagement with the profound spiritualities of Asian contemplative traditions" (p. 223). In his introduction to Merton's remarks at a meeting in Santa Barbara, California, before the monk departed for Asia, Walter Capps noted, " . . . Merton understood his own engagement with Asian Spiritual pathways to be necessary to his own maturation as both a Christian and a human being. And what he understood as necessary for himself he also understood to be necessary for the world."[11] Indeed. And even more necessary now fifty years later. As Fr. Park's book presents it, Merton's engagement with Buddhism (and, of course, with others of the world's great religious traditions) points us toward the value, indeed, the necessity of openness to a similar "changing stability."

Bonnie Thurston, PhD
Feast of St. Nicholas, 2018
Wheeling, WV

---

11. Walter Capps, ed., *Thomas Merton: Preview of the Asian Journey* (New York, NY: Crossroad, 1989), 30.

Acknowledgments

I am grateful to Regis College for their role in forming my academic vocation. In particular, Prof. Meg Lavin guided me to begin a new academic life, and Prof. Ovey Mohammed, SJ and Prof. John Costello, SJ led me to the discovery of Thomas Merton. Prof. Michael Stoeber taught me about Christian spirituality. Prof. Joseph Schner, SJ helped me to attain a new understanding of human persons through psychology and also directed my Th.M. thesis on spiritual healing through monasticism. Above all, Prof. John D. Dadosky inspired me with the realization of the value of interreligious dialogue in the pluralistic world. He provided me with an insight into the development of inter/intra-monastic dialogue and encouraged me to take part in many conferences that were related to Merton. This book would be impossible without the encouragement, guidance, and patience of my supervisor.

I am also grateful to Prof. Michael Stoeber, Prof. Dennis O'Hara, Prof. Stephen Scharper and Prof. Joseph Q. Raab. They carefully read my writing and gave me invaluable advice. Their deep wisdom and wide knowledge and guidance have been of great value to me. I also appreciate Dr. Bonnie Thurston, who gave me many comments regarding Merton's Buddhist-Christian dialogue for my book. In particular, Fr. William Skudlarek, Secretary General of DIMMID, encouraged me on the monastic interreligious dialogue as well as offered many comments for this book. My sincere gratitude goes to him.

I would like to convey my sincere gratitude to my spiritual family. Kenneth R. Lavin (Meg's husband), a Benedictine Oblate of St. Vincent Archabbey, helped me with my academic English writing and shared his spiritual wisdom with me as my spiritual brother. I would like to use this opportunity to thank my friends, Sr. Ann Delaney (Sisters of St. Joseph), Dr. Marie Dietrich (an Oblate of Benedictine Sisters of Eire), Theresa Shin, Fr. Young-Min Song, Dr. Richard Tetreau and Shirley Tetreau, Fr. Peter Bisson, SJ and Fr. Leonard Altilia, SJ and other members of the Jesuit Community in Toronto, and many Torontonian-Korean parishioners at the St. Andrew Kim Catholic Parish and Sacred Heart of Jesus Parish.

Finally, I would like to acknowledge all of my community brothers in St. Benedict Waegwan Abbey, including a former Abbot, Simon Ri, who died in 2016. A big thank you goes out to my family: my parents and three brothers in South Korea.

List of Abbreviations

Merton's Works

AJ	*The Asian Journal of Thomas Merton*
AT	*The Ascent to Truth*
CFMT	*The Cistercian Fathers and Their Monastic Theology: Initiation into the Monastic Tradition 8*
CGB	*Conjectures of a Guilty Bystander*
CMP	*The Climate of Monastic Prayer*
CWA	*Contemplation in a World of Action*
DQ	*Disputed Questions*
DWL	*Dancing in the Water of Life: Seeking Peace in the Hermitage*
ES	*Entering the Silence: Becoming a Monk and a Writer*
FV	*Faith and Violence*
HGL	*The Hidden Ground of Love: The Letters of Thomas Merton on Religious Experience and Social Concerns*
IE	*The Inner Experience: Notes on Contemplation*
IEW	*Introductions East and West: The Foreign Prefaces of Thomas Merton*
IM	*The Intimate Merton: His Life from His Journals*
LH	*Thomas Merton, Life and Holiness*
LL	*Learning to Love*
L&L	*Love and Living*
MZM	*Mystics and Zen Masters*

NM	*The New Man*
NMI	*No Man Is an Island*
NSC	*New Seeds of Contemplation*
OSM	*The Other Side of the Mountain: The End of the Journey*
PP	*Passion for Peace: The Social Essays*
RJ	*The Road to Joy: The Letters of Thomas Merton to New and Old Friends*
RM	*Run to the Mountain: The Story of a Vocation*
SC	*Seeds of Contemplation*
SCL	*The School of Charity: The Letters of Thomas Merton on Religious Renewal and Spiritual Direction*
SD	*Seeds of Destruction*
SJ	*The Sign of Jonas*
SS	*A Search for Solitude: Pursuing the Monk's True Life*
SSM	*The Seven Storey Mountain*
TMR	*A Thomas Merton Reader*
TTW	*Turning Toward the World: The Pivotal Years*
ZBA	*Zen and the Birds of Appetite*
ZR	"The Zen Revival"

Inter-Monastic Dialogue

AIM	Aide à l'Implantation Monastique
DIM	Dialogue Interreligieux Monastique
DIMMID	Dialogue Interreligieux Monastique/Monastic Interreligious Dialogue
MID	Monastic Interreligious Dialogue
NABEWD	North American Board for East-West Dialogue
PCID	Pontifical Council for Interreligious Dialogue

List of Tables

Table 1: Interreligious Dialogue, Intra-Religious Dialogue, Inter-Monastic Encounters, and Intra-Monastic Dialogue

Table 2: Daily Contents of the Monastery Stay Experience

Table 3: Three Types of the Temple Stay of Buddhism in South Korea

Table 4: Comparison between the Temple Stay and the Monastery Stay

Introduction

In 1968, Thomas Merton (1915–1968), a Trappist monk of the Abbey of Gethsemani, Kentucky, and a well-known American Catholic writer and mystic, took part in the first Congress of Asian and Western monastics in Bangkok, Thailand. No one, including Merton, would have known that this would be his last Congress. The night before his accidental death at the Congress, he told John Moffitt, "Zen and Christianity are the future."[1] His declaration, made with conviction, raises many questions. Why did this Christian contemplative monk mention Zen, despite how impressed he was with the Tibetan Buddhists he had recently encountered?[2] What did he see in the relationship between Zen and Christianity? Did he ignore other religions? What was the future he anticipated for them?

Commenting on his declaration, Moffitt wrote that "Merton held Zen to be not a religion in the usual sense, but essentially a technique for attaining enlightenment; thus it might conceivably be 'included' in Christianity."[3] Although Merton did not consider

1. John Moffitt, *Journey to Gorakhpur: An Encounter with Christ beyond Christianity* (New York, NY: Holt, Rinehart and Winston, 1972), 275.

2. During Merton's Asian journey, he met many Tibetan rinpoches and lamas, and noted, "the Tibetan Buddhists . . . have a really large number of people who have attained to extraordinary heights in meditation and contemplation. This does not exclude Zen. But I do feel very much at home with the Tibetans." See Thomas Merton, *The Asian Journal of Thomas Merton* (New York, NY: New Directions, 1973), 82 (hereafter AJ).

3. John Moffitt, "Memories of Thomas Merton," *Cistercian Studies* 14, no. 1 (1979): 76.

Zen to be a "technique of introversion" when he distinguished Zen from Zen Buddhism, he did regard Zen as "a trans-cultural, trans-religious, trans-formed consciousness."[4] The common spiritual elements of the great world religions that he discovered through the lens of Zen were "a transformation of human consciousness" and a "spiritual liberation" through a contemplative or awakening experience.[5]

As we examine his pioneering works in Buddhist-Christian dialogue, his inter-monastic dialogue, and what he considered to be the center of monastic life, namely, contemplation, we can formulate the following hypothesis: through the lens of Zen, Merton saw the value and possibility of "contemplative dialogue" between monastics or contemplatives of different religious traditions, those men and women who look primarily to a transformation of human consciousness and a spiritual awakening from within their respective traditions. With regard to the future, he hoped that through contemplative dialogue, monastics would strive for "intermonastic communion" and a bonding of the broader "spiritual family" and thus become witnesses of the fundamental unity of humanity to a world that was becoming ever more materialistic and divided.[6]

As an Asian Benedictine monk, I was honored to participate at the celebration of the centennial of Merton's birth organized by the International Thomas Merton Society in Louisville, Kentucky in 2015, the Gethsemani Encounter IV in 2015, and the meeting of the European Dialogue Interreligieux Monastique/Monastic Interreligious Dialogue (hereafter DIMMID) subcommissions 2016 in Norway and 2017 in Ireland. My presence at these events led me to the conviction that Merton's legacy continues to grow

---

4. Thomas Merton, *Mystics and Zen Masters* (New York, NY: Farrar, Straus and Giroux, 1967), 20 (hereafter MZM); Thomas Merton, *Zen and the Birds of Appetite* (New York, NY: New Directions, 1968), 4 (hereafter ZBA).

5. AJ, 333.

6. "Contemplative dialogue," "intermonastic communion," and "spiritual family" are Merton's own terms. See ibid., 316; MZM, x.

and remains worthy of development in Asia. Pending the successful completion of this conviction, I plan to spend the rest of my
career effecting this development specifically in my own Korean
context. The groundwork for that work has already been started
during a multireligious pilgrimage with several scholars in Korea
during the summer of 2016.

The purpose of this book is to examine Merton's role as a pioneer by: 1) delving into the process of Merton's self-transformation
through contemplative experience; 2) exploring his encounter with
Zen and Tibetan Buddhists and his pioneering engagements in
Buddhist-Christian dialogue; 3) presenting and responding to the
criticisms of those who raise questions about Merton's understanding of Buddhism; 4) studying his inter-monastic exchanges
with Buddhists at the level of contemplative dialogue; and 5) presenting the ways in which Merton's pioneering legacy continues
in the ongoing Gethsemani Encounters and monastic exchange
programs as well as in *intra*-religious dialogue in an Asian monastic context.

The book will articulate and analyze the influences of Buddhist
theory and practice on Merton's contemplative spirituality and the
influence of Merton's legacy on inter-monastic and interreligious
dialogue. To this end, I will examine some specific questions about
how contemplative dialogue and inter-monastic exchanges influenced Merton's life and thought and also influenced the development of such dialogue. Some specific questions will be explored:
1) What motivated Merton as a practicing Christian monastic to
turn to Buddhism in the first place? 2) To what degree did Merton
integrate his inner experience and interreligious dialogue on his
journey of self-transcendence? 3) In the dialogue between the
nondual experience of Buddhism and the theistic mystical experience of Christianity, what did Merton discover that was useful
for Buddhist-Christian dialogue? 4) What were the limitations in
Merton's knowledge of Buddhism? 5) Why did Merton emphasize
experiential dialogue and "intermonastic communion," and what
was the relationship between these different levels of dialogue

and Merton's understanding of Buddhism? 6) What developments were inspired by his pioneering example, and how can they continue, particularly in an Asian monastic context?

The Pontifical Council for Interreligious Dialogue (hereafter PCID) asserts that monastic interreligious dialogue operates at a profound level: "Interreligious dialogue does not merely aim at mutual understanding and friendly relations. It reaches a much deeper level, that of the spirit, where exchange and sharing consist in a mutual witness to one's respective religious convictions."[7] Such a spiritual exchange occurred in 1996 when Buddhist and Christian monastics and lay contemplatives gathered at Gethsemani Abbey, where Thomas Merton spent his monastic life, for a dialogue on the spiritual life and inter-monastic communion. This vision of interreligious dialogue was one that Merton himself had suggested. He was convinced that Christian contemplative monastics who were striving for inter-monastic communion could easily become dialogue partners with Buddhist monastics and suggested that interreligious dialogue between East and West could benefit from these different perspectives on monastic experience.

Through his encounter with Buddhists/Buddhism, Merton's inner experience and his interreligious dialogue contributed to a dynamic evolution of his religious awareness.[8] In his Louisville

---

7. Pontifical Council for Interreligious Dialogue, "Dialogue and Proclamation," in *Interreligious Dialogue: The Official Teaching of the Catholic Church from the Second Vatican Council to John Paul II (1963–2005)*, ed. Francesco Gioia (Boston, MA: Pauline Books, 2006), 1170.

8. Merton used the term "the inner experience" to express both the Buddhist enlightenment experience and Christian contemplative experience. See Thomas Merton, *The Inner Experience: Notes on Contemplation*, ed. William H. Shannon (San Francisco, CA: HarperCollins, 2003), 6–18 (hereafter IE). Joseph Raab claims that this inner experience is an awakening of the inner self and "the subsequent *affirmation* of the *primary unity* between consciousness as intentional and the reality of its transcendental ground and goal *in love and freedom*. . . . Merton and Suzuki call [this experience] 'the inner experience.'" See Joseph Q. Raab, *Openness and Fidelity: Thomas Merton's Dialogue with D. T. Suzuki*

Epiphany of 1958, which occurred years after he had initially *fled* the world and lived a cloistered monastic life for almost seventeen years, Merton turned with an open heart and mind to the world and to other religions, including Zen.[9] He had come to know Zen from his voracious reading and through personal contacts with such experts as Dr. D.T. Suzuki. Dialogue and friendship with Buddhists changed his outlook on Asian religions and classical Christian contemplation. Beyond intellectual discussion, he proposed that there be contemplative dialogue and spiritual communion between monastics of other religions. Just what these notions mean will be explained more fully in this book. His encounters with monks and lamas of the Tibetan diaspora on his Asian trip in 1968 reflected his growing interest in such dialogue up to the end of his life.

Merton's dialogue with Buddhist traditions reached its high point in his transformative experience at Polonnaruwa in Sri Lanka near the end of his life: "everything is emptiness and everything is compassion."[10] This powerful *satori*-like experience represented a bridge between Buddhism and Christianity, a bridge rooted in his own religious experience. Although his knowledge of Buddhism was limited, Merton found, in the light of this inner experience, the fundamental source and method for Buddhist-Christian dialogue. Given that he died shortly after this experience, we cannot be certain about directions in which he would have gone or how he would have subsequently interpreted the experience. There is some evidence that he was preparing to delve more deeply into Tibetan Buddhist practices under the tutelage of a famous and

---

and Self-Transcendence (PhD diss., Toronto School of Theology, 2000), 170 (emphasis in original).

9. As an example of his openness to Buddhism subsequent to his Louisville Epiphany of 1958, it can be noted that in order to explain his new understanding of contemplation, Merton began using Buddhist terminology in his book *The Inner Experience*, which was largely written in 1959, and in his letters to D.T. Suzuki, which he began writing in March 1959.

10. AJ, 235.

reclusive rinpoche.[11] Still, he believed that contemplative dialogue at the level of inner experience could lead to a mutual acceptance and affirmation of the wisdom of both traditions. In a "state of trans-cultural maturity," he believed that "we are already one" and that contemplative dialogue could help to retrieve our original *unity-in-diversity*.[12]

Today, Eastern and Western monastics have appropriated Merton's insights as they engage in dialogue with one another in various monastic exchange programs, such as those organized by DIMMID. DIMMID is presently trying to promote Merton's legacy in Asia and in Africa. Thus, I, as an Asian monk, will show the urgent need for the development of monastic interreligious dialogue in Asia. Finally, I will suggest ways to develop his example and the model he proposed in an Asian context.

In Merton's contemplative life, spiritual transformation through inner experience was deeply connected to his understanding of interreligious dialogue and the method he proposed for engaging in it. Thus, chapter 1 will begin with an examination of Merton's biographical data to determine the relationship between his inner experiences and the transformation of his consciousness. These led to a greater openness to others that was complemented by openness to and dialogue with other religions, especially Buddhism. This, in turn, brought him to a deep inner experience of other religious traditions and to a deepened appreciation of contemplation in the Christian tradition. In this dynamic progress, Merton experienced the presence of God in the church, among people, and

11. See ibid., 143–144; Judith Simmer-Brown, "The Liberty That Nobody Can Touch: Thomas Merton Meets Tibetan Buddhism," in *Merton & Buddhism: Wisdom, Emptiness and Everyday Mind,* ed. Bonnie Thurston (Louisville, KY: Fons Vitae, 2007), 73–85; Bonnie Thurston, "Footnotes to the Asian Journey of Thomas Merton," in *Merton & Buddhism,* 229–233. "Rinpoche" is the deferential title given to spiritual masters in Tibetan Buddhism.

12. Thomas Merton, *Contemplation in a World of Action* (Notre Dame, IN: University of Notre Dame Press, 1998), 206 (hereafter CWA); AJ, 308.

through other religions, and came to believe that final integration was a state of transcultural maturity. In order to express and interpret his inner experience of contemplation, Merton made use of various concepts taken from Buddhist spirituality. He realized that Buddhists and Christians could be mutually enriched by exchanging their different ways of expressing contemplative experience. His religious experience in Polonnaruwa is a striking example of the fruits of dialogue at the level of cross-cultural religious experience. This chapter will conclude with an evaluation of Merton's writings on inner experience and of the self-transformation that took place on his spiritual journey, which was key to his view of Buddhist-Christian dialogue.

The purpose of chapter 2 is to explore how Merton paved a new way for Buddhist-Christian dialogue by identifying the strengths and limitations he brought to his dialogue with Buddhists. To this end, the chapter will first explore his encounters with Buddhism and Buddhists. His growing acquaintance with Buddhism moved him from intellectual dialogue to experiential dialogue and then to integrated dialogue at a deeper spiritual level. His attitude toward Buddhists also changed from naively seeing them as pagans to regarding them as teachers, friends, and brothers. Second, the chapter will present Merton's understanding of Buddhism intellectually, experientially, and spiritually to demonstrate that his knowledge of Zen and Tibetan Buddhism was advanced for his time and was developed primarily at the level of contemplative experience and spiritual communion rather than doctrine.[13] His dialectical and ongoing involvement in Buddhist-Christian dialogue on contemplation revealed that his limited knowledge of Buddhism could be transcended by his transcultural perspective. Third, the chapter will explore the three types of interreligious dialogue that led Merton to Buddhist-Christian dialogue: the dialogue

13. Further evidence of his broader knowledge of Buddhism can be found in his acquaintance with Buddhist masters, such the XIV Dalai Lama, Thich Nhat Hanh, and Chatral Rinpoche.

of theology, religious experience, and action. He realized that since Buddhists focused more on experience and practice, inner experience had to become the primary topic for dialogue between the two religions. His lasting contribution was to make contemplative dialogue the goal of interreligious dialogue for monastics. Finally, in order to go beyond Merton's personal encounters with Buddhists, the chapter will discuss his limited exposure to Buddhism as a spiritual/philosophical system, his notion of transcendent identity, and his monastic approach to Buddhism. What he aspired to in his encounter with Tibetan Buddhists will be evaluated by looking at his dual approach to them as a pilgrim student and a contemplative monk.

Chapter 3 will demonstrate that through contemplative dialogue and inter-monastic exchanges, Merton created a new paradigm for interreligious dialogue. For this purpose, I will first present Merton's motives for interreligious dialogue with monastics. As a monk himself, he easily appreciated and identified with certain Buddhist monastic practices. He could see that monasticism was profoundly embedded in Asian religions. Their various forms of monasticism are a treasured "traditional religious *way*" that can cultivate a "contemplative, enlightened, or spiritually transformed [experience]."[14] Merton believed that inter-monastic dialogue could contribute to mutual enrichment as well as challenge for both monastic traditions. It could, in fact, contribute to the renewal of Catholic monasticism and the discovery of a monastic and contemplative dimension in all religions. Second, I will explore how Merton's inter-monastic exchanges through contemplative dialogue proceeded from finding the *self*, to discovering *friendship* with other monastics, to a bonding of the *spiritual family*. He expected that an inter-monastic contemplative communion could foster a transcultural consciousness for contemplatives that went beyond religious and cultural boundaries. Merton believed that

14. AJ, 310 (emphasis in original).

spiritual communion between monastics could point the way to universal communion with all contemplatives. But what did he mean by spiritual communion? Does Buddhism have the concept of communion? I will explore this and other themes more explicitly. Furthermore, I will attempt to answer two questions regarding Merton's monastic interreligious dialogue: Is inter-monastic dialogue an esoteric activity for the spiritual elite alone? and Was Merton's monastic encounter with Asian monasticism too idealistic and/or romantic?

Chapter 4 will explore Merton's legacy within the context of current monastic interreligious dialogue in order to determine how his contribution can evolve beyond the models he proposed. First, I will present the history of inter/intra-monastic dialogue from Aide à l'Implantation Monastique (hereafter AIM) to DIMMID, its value, and the prospects for its future development. Second, I will explore the Monastic Hospitality program and the Spiritual Exchange program, which were indirectly inspired by Merton. During his Asian journey, he emphasized the significance of *living* and *sharing* the experience of monastic life and appealed to his fellow monastics to devote themselves to serious engagement with the spiritual riches of Asian monasticism. The Gethsemani Encounters, Merton's direct legacy, will also be examined. These Encounters have focused on contemplative dialogue in a spirit of openness, spiritual friendship, communion, and concrete collaboration. They were not limited to communion between monastics but were open to communion with all contemplatives. Programs like those mentioned here are still needed to encourage Eastern Buddhists and Christians to become involved in dialogue and to provide opportunities for them to do so.

Finally, I will propose that Merton's legacy can be developed in an Asian context through an intra-monastic exchange and contemplative dialogue between different Asian monastics. To achieve this, I will explore the value and possibility of intra-monastic dialogue in relationship to intra-religious dialogue and inter-monastic dialogue. Intra-monastic dialogue includes Merton's contemplative dialogue as well as dialogue between monastics within the same culture and region but also involving different religions. This type of dialogue also includes interior dialogue for the individual monk and nun, as well as communal dialogue within a specific community of the same faith. Beginning at the level of the individual monastic or monastic community will be helpful for inter-monastic dialogue in the Asian monastic context since many Asian monastic communities still need to recognize and accept the value of dialogue. Intra-monastic dialogue is not separate from inter-monastic dialogue since it can pave the way to interreligious dialogue between different religions in a similar cultural and ethnic group.

Finally, in order to show the possibility for developing Merton's legacy of intra-monastic dialogue in the Asian context, I will point to three South Korean models: 1) St. Joseph's Monastery, for exploring the adaptation of monastic life in its own cultural context; 2) "Samsohoe" (三笑, three smiles), for providing an example of intra-monastic encounter in the same nation; and 3) monastic experience programs in Buddhist and Christian monasteries, for developing contemplative dialogue between monastics and lay contemplatives. These examples will show that Korean monasteries are in a unique position to initiate such dialogue with various Buddhist centers throughout the country and beyond.

I will conclude with three suggestions for the development of inter/intra-monastic dialogue in the South Korean context: 1) the development of spiritual solidarity between Buddhist and Christian monastics; 2) the development of Korean-style Christian monasticism through monastic exchange programs; and 3) the development of the concept of "*Jeong*" (정, 情—feeling, affection) among Korean people for monastic hospitality programs.

CHAPTER 1

Merton's Own Inner Experience and Interreligious Dialogue

Thomas Merton wrote more than sixty books and many articles and poems on topics ranging from contemplation and monasticism to social movements and interreligious dialogue. His autobiography, *The Seven Storey Mountain*, has sold millions of copies and has been translated into twenty languages. His other writings continue to have an impact on such fields as theology of spirituality, social justice, racism, feminism, literature, and interreligious dialogue. In particular, his spiritual writings and journals chronicle his ongoing spiritual growth, which provides a model for self-transcendence and self-transformation.[1]

In comparing his early writings and later writings, it can be observed that he acquired different views of God, humanity, the world, and other religions throughout the course of his life. In his early writings, Merton tended to describe contemplation with a certain naiveté, with a sense of superiority as a contemplative monk who followed a traditional view of contemplation. In his

---

1. Merton noted, "My conversion is still going on. . . . Its progress leads it over a succession of peaks and valleys, but normally the ascent is continuous in the sense that each new valley is higher than the last one." See Thomas Merton, "The White Pebble," in *Thomas Merton: Selected Essays*, ed. Patrick F. O'Connell (Maryknoll, NY: Orbis Books, 2013), 9.

later writings, he modified his early view of contemplation and suggested that the different forms of contemplation did not depend on one's identity but on the diversity of God's gifts and the different capacity of each person for contemplative experience. In developing toward spiritual maturity, he had various inner-mystical experiences during his life. For example, he experienced what he called the "Glory of Christ" in an ancient basilica in Rome (1933) and "Heaven" in the Church of St. Francis in Havana (1940), an "Epiphany of God" among ordinary people at the corner of Fourth and Walnut in Louisville (1958), and the "Void of God" through his exposure to another religious symbol at Polonnaruwa in Sri Lanka (1968).

The following questions emerge from the dynamic relationship among inner-mystical experience, transformation of consciousness, contemplation, and interreligious dialogue in Merton's life journey: 1) To what degree did Merton integrate his inner experience and interreligious dialogue in his own personal development and self-transcendence? 2) What influence did he receive from his inner-mystical experience, specifically from his interpretation of Zen experience, for his new view of contemplation? 3) What did he discover that was useful for bringing the nondual experience of Buddhism into dialogue with the theistic mystical experience of Christianity?

My responses to these questions lead to the hypothesis I wish to develop in this chapter, namely, that Merton's inner-mystical experience facilitated his self-transformation, his union with God, his new view of contemplation, and his dialogue with Asian traditions, especially Buddhism.

In his spiritual journey toward union with God, Merton experienced three main transformations of consciousness: 1) from that of a nonbeliever to a Roman Catholic with an awareness of God's presence in the church; 2) from a traditional view of contemplation to a modern view of contemplation with an awareness of God's presence in people; and 3) from a solely Western Christian consciousness to a universal religious consciousness with an awareness of God's immanence in the created order. In this process, Merton's inner-mystical experiences aided his conversion to Catholicism, his overcoming of various psychological and spiritual frustrations, his integration of contemplation and action, his becoming open to others, and his discovery of a new path for Buddhist-Christian dialogue. In discovering the value of inner-mystical experience as a universal path, his dialogic way of regarding Buddhism moved from a Christian theological perspective to an experiential and existential perspective. His belief in the common ground of religious experience stimulated him to learn more about different religious expressions at a deep transcendental level. He used various concepts taken from Buddhist spirituality to express and interpret his own inner experience. He realized that Buddhists and Christians could be mutually enriched by exchanging their different ways of expressing inner experience. In his experiential dialogue with Buddhists, he neither rejected a Christ-centered soteriology nor accepted a syncretism. Rather, he realized that the Spirit of God transcended religious systems. Finally, his progress to the final integration (the transcultural state) through his inner experience contributed to the development of a fruitful ongoing dialogue between Buddhists and Christians at a deep spiritual and universal level.

In this chapter, I seek to demonstrate that inner experience leading to spiritual transformation was deeply connected to Merton's understanding of and engagement in interreligious dialogue. I will do so, first, by examining his most significant and memorable inner-mystical experiences and his ensuing self-transformation, while also taking into account the apparently less significant but important minor conversions that were part of his daily life and that also fostered, and made possible, his decisive inner-mystical experience. Second, for a hermeneutical exploration of the evolution of his view of contemplation, I will compare Merton's early and later writings with the terms he used to speak of his inner-mystical experience. Furthermore, in the light of his new consciousness and self-transformation, I will analyze his inner-mystical experiences, particularly the Louisville Epiphany and the Polonnaruwa Enlightenment Experience, in order to discern the ways such experiences are interpreted in the Christian and Buddhist traditions and the dynamic interaction that is possible when these two traditions are placed side by side. Demonstrating the ways in which Merton's inner-mystical experiences affected his spiritual maturity and his openness to others will help us to come to a deeper understanding of his pioneering works in Buddhist-Christian dialogue and inter-monastic exchange, the topics of the next two chapters.

Merton's Own Inner Experience and Self-Transformation

In his writings, beginning with *The Seven Storey Mountain*, Merton recounted the story of his life prior to his conversion to theism and then to Catholicism, which he understood as a continual movement of the human spirit responding to God and following wherever the Spirit led, as well as the progress of his ongoing personal self-transformation. As he noted, "It is evident that the story of my life up to the day of my baptism is hardly the adequate story of my 'conversion.' My conversion is still going on. Conversion is something that is prolonged over a whole lifetime."[2] In this journey toward conversion, Merton had to change his naive vision of God, of humanity, and of the world as he became more aware and more informed.

Merton's ongoing journey toward self-transformation reveals how he became a contemplative monk, attained a nondualistic perspective, and developed an openness to the world and to other religions. As Walter Principe suggests, the stages of Merton's self-transformation have to be analyzed in the context of his whole life as well as from various perspectives—historical, theological, psychological, mystical, anthropological, sociological, and non-

2. Ibid., 9.

Christian.[3] Indeed, throughout his whole life, Merton had to deal with many periods of depression and frustration. His deep inner-mystical experiences, which he attributed to the grace of God, and his engagement in various social movements contributed to his spiritual and human maturity. We will therefore examine the stages of Merton's transformation of consciousness through his religious experiences and try to identify markers in the degree of spiritual integration and wholeness he achieved during different periods of his life's journey.

Premonastic: 1915–1941

During the premonastic period of his life, Merton's latent conversion and contemplative vocation were influenced by 1) psychological factors and family background, 2) the impact of people he met and books he read, and 3) mystical experiences. A fuller explication of each of these factors follows.

First, the heartbreak and depression Merton experienced in his childhood and his rebellious temperament during his school years inevitably induced him eventually to seek a stable home for an "authentic identity and communion."[4] Following his mother's death from cancer when he was six years old, he looked back on his early years as a "desperate, despairing childhood."[5] His father,

---

3. See Walther Principe, "Toward Defining Spirituality," *Studies in Religion* 12, no. 2 (1983): 127–141. Dom Aldhelm Cameron-Brown claims that for Merton, contemplative life was not merely a matter of progress in prayer, but a matter of transformation of the whole person. See Aldhelm Cameron-Brown, "Thomas Merton and the Contemplative Tradition," *The Merton Journal* 4, no. 2 (Advent 1997): 3–12.

4. Raab, *Openness and Fidelity*, 57.

5. Thomas Merton, *Learning to Love: Exploring Solitude and Freedom*, ed. Christine M. Bochen (San Francisco, CA: HarperSanFrancisco, 1997), 11 (hereafter LL). Merton said that when his mother died, "a tremendous weight of sadness and depression settled on me. It was not the grief of a child . . . [but] the heavy perplexity and gloom of adult grief, and was therefore all more of a

an irregular presence during his adolescence due to his struggling career as an artist, died of brain cancer when Merton was sixteen.[6] After his father's death, he described how desperate he felt:

> I sat there in the dark, unhappy room . . . with all the innumerable elements of my isolation crowding in upon me from every side: without a home, without a family, without a country, without a father, apparently without any friends, without any interior peace or confidence or light or understanding of my own— without God, too, without God, without heaven, without grace, without anything.[7]

His parents' early deaths spawned a feeling of psychological, emotional, and religious emptiness. From a Jungian perspective, his mother's death may have caused him to lose the specific function of the female *anima,* which serves "as a mediatrix between the ego, the center of consciousness, and the Self, the center of the unconscious mind."[8] In addition, his father's death may have formed the shadow archetype in his unconsciousness that led him to seek solitude and reject the world.[9]

---

burden because it was, to that extent, unnatural." See Thomas Merton, *The Seven Storey Mountain* (New York, NY: Harcourt Brace, 1998, Fiftieth Anniversary Edition), 16 (hereafter SSM).

6. Reflecting on his childhood, Merton wrote, "It is almost impossible to make much sense out of the continual rearrangement of our lives and our plans from month to month in my childhood. . . . Sometimes Father and I were living together, sometimes I was with strangers and only saw him from time to time. People came into our lives and went out of our lives. We had now one set of friends, now another. Things were always changing." See SSM, 20–21.

7. Ibid., 79.

8. Robert Waldron, *The Wounded Heart of Thomas Merton* (New York/Mahwah, NJ: Paulist Press, 2011), 10. See also Anne E. Carr, *A Search for Wisdom and Spirit: Thomas Merton's Theology of the Self* (Notre Dame, IN: University of Notre Dame Press, 1988), 128.

9. See Waldron, *The Wounded Heart of Thomas Merton*, 17–20; Anne Hunsaker Hawkins, *Archetypes of Conversion: The Autobiographies of Augustine, Bunyan, and Merton* (Lewisburg, PA: Bucknell University Press, 1985), 130–138.

After his father's death, Merton's desperate and lonely child-hood created ongoing problems throughout his adolescence and young adulthood. He fell into despair and became "an intellectual rebel" and dissolute person.[10] He was "spiritually dead," and there was no room for God or religion.[11] For example, in 1931, when Merton was sixteen years old, he stood in the chapel at Oakum School and, during the recitation of the Apostles' Creed, kept his lips shut tight with full deliberation and set purpose. He professed his own creed, which was "I believe in nothing."[12] Merton scholar William Shannon describes Merton at the time: "Like all too many of his contemporaries, he was adrift on a sea of aimlessness, amo-rality, and lack of faith."[13]

Merton experienced loneliness during his school years. He wrote that when his schoolmates taunted him with obscenities, "I knew for the first time in my life the pangs of desolation and emptiness and abandonment."[14] This feeling of alienation ac-companied him when he entered Gethsemani Abbey in 1941. On November 24, 1941, he wrote, "The sense of exile bleeds inside me like a hemorrhage—it is always the same wound, whether it is a sense of sin, or of loneliness, or of one's own insufficiency, or a spiritual dryness."[15] However, his loneliness would begin filtering through his solitude in the new loneliness of Gethsemani. The ma-ture Merton noted, "My moments of depression and despair turn out to be renewals, new beginnings."[16] Monica Furlong, author of *Merton: A Biography*, contends that "in his nineteenth year at Cambridge in England, Merton suffered an excruciating sense of

10. SSM, 84.

11. Ibid., 175, 94.

12. Ibid., 108.

13. William H. Shannon, *Silent Lamp: The Thomas Merton Story* (New York, NY: Crossroad, 1992), 54.

14. SSM, 54.

15. Thomas Merton, *Run to the Mountain: The Story of a Vocation* (San Francisco, CA: HarperSanFrancisco, 1995), 452 (hereafter RM).

16. Thomas Merton, *A Thomas Merton Reader* (Garden City, NY: Image Books, 1974), 16 (hereafter TMR).

guilt and a conviction that a lifetime's expiation was demanded of him, and this certainly played an important part in taking him into the Trappists."[17] Later, Merton was able to write that "learning to lose ourselves in the understanding of [our] weakness and deficiency can help us to become true contemplatives."[18]

Second, Merton's positive experiences with persons and books played an important role in his conversion and new consciousness. Although he grew up without a mother's love from the age of six and without any religious education, he had the opportunity to live with a religious family, a Roman Catholic couple, the Privats. Merton was deeply inspired by their faith, which he lacked. He remembered that "I had never met people to whom belief was a matter of such moment. . . . And I thank God from the bottom of my heart that they were concerned, and so deeply and vitally concerned, at my lack of faith."[19] He stayed with them for two years as part of the "religious phase" of his childhood.[20]

At Columbia University, Merton met many persons who influenced his conversion and vocation, such as Professor Mark Van Doren, who encouraged his intellectual vocation and impressed him with his dignity and moral integrity.[21] A Hindu monk, Mahanambrata Bramachari, introduced Merton to the Christian mystical tradition and encouraged him to read *Confessions* by St. Augustine and *The Imitation of Christ* by Thomas à Kempis.[22] Professor Dan Walsh played a role in directing Merton's vocation to the priesthood and Trappist monastic life, as well as toward a more spiritual, mystical, and experiential way of thought, rather

---

17. Monica Furlong, *Merton: A Biography* (New York, NY: Harper & Row, 1980), xiv–xv.

18. Thomas Merton, *Seeds of Contemplation* (Norfolk, CT: New Directions, 1949), 108 (hereafter SC); Thomas Merton, *New Seeds of Contemplation* (New York, NY: New Directions, 2007, 1st ed. 1962), 191 (hereafter NSC).

19. SSM, 64.

20. Ibid., 71.

21. See ibid., 153–155, 196, 261, 397–398.

22. See ibid., 216–217.

than the speculative way of Thomism.[23] His friends Robert Lax, Edward Rice, and Robert Gibney were also positive influences in his life.[24] Lax, especially, offered Merton unconditional love and trust and challenged him to be a saint, a writer, and a peacemaker.[25]

Books were also instrumental in Merton's spiritual development. First of all, he discovered a whole new concept of God by reading Étienne Gilson's *The Spirit of Medieval Philosophy*. He realized that the Christian understanding of God was neither superstitious nor unscientific, but rather was intelligent and reasonable.[26] His intellectual mind was stimulated, and he was led to a rational appreciation of Catholic theology. Yet, he still did not feel drawn to a personal response to God. However, his heart was touched, and his spiritual eyes opened by Aldous Huxley's ideas on the Oriental sources of asceticism and mysticism.[27] Huxley's book *Ends and Means* fired Merton's enthusiasm for mysticism, and he began to ransack the library for writings on Oriental mysticism and asceticism. Although his reading of Asian texts was not fully developed at that time, the ideas he accumulated prompted a

23. See ibid., 240–242, 290, 339.

24. Merton's three friends Robert Lax, Edward Rice, and Robert Gibney from Columbia days encouraged one another in their personal journey throughout their entire lives. The close friendship influenced Merton's relationship with others, which was difficult to develop in his childhood. See SSM, 260–261; Raymond Bailey, *Thomas Merton on Mysticism* (Garden City, NY: Image Books, 1976), 35.

25. See John Dear, *Thomas Merton, Peacemaker: Meditations on Merton, Peacemaking, and the Spiritual Life* (Maryknoll, NY: Orbis Books, 2015), 108–113.

26. Shannon argues that "it was Merton's discovery of the reasonableness of Catholic belief in God that put him on the way toward his Christian conversion. The grace of Gilson's book was an important stage along the interior journey, on the 'holy way.'" See Shannon, *Silent Lamp*, 87. Waldron says that the effect of Gilson's book on Merton can be compared to the fascination he experienced on seeing ancient and luminous mosaics in Rome. See Waldron, *The Wounded Heart of Thomas Merton*, 33–34.

27. Merton reflected on Huxley's book, "Asceticism! The very thought of such a thing was a complete revolution to my mind." See SSM, 203.

desire for mystical experience and a sense that the Asian traditions could help him to realize that desire. Merton wrote his master's thesis on William Blake, who crystallized faith and love in Merton's soul. Merton noted, "I think my love for William Blake had something in it of God's grace. . . . [T]hrough Blake I would one day come, in a round-about way, to the only true Church, and to the One Living God, through His Son, Jesus Christ."[28] Blake's synthesis of mystical graces and aesthetic sensitivity influenced him to transcend rationality and intuit mystery. Like Blake, Merton was a poet, a prophet, and a mystic.[29]

Third, Merton's mystical experiences inspired him to be open to new horizons. In his premonastic period, he had several mystical experiences that took divergent forms. His first mystical experience occurred in the old Basilica of Sts. Comas and Damian in Rome in 1933, more than a year after his father's death.[30] While pondering on a Byzantine mosaic of the crucifixion, he was fascinated by its mystery and its tremendous seriousness and simplicity. He wrote, "[I] was suddenly awed and surprised to find that this was something I recognized and understood. Something I had been looking for."[31] After this dramatic experience, he began "to find out something of Who this Person was that men called

28. Ibid., 94, 97.

29. Sr. Mary Julian Baird wrote that "Merton followed Blake in adopting Blake's prophetic role in writing poetry so that at least one-third of all Merton's poetry is a crying in the wilderness to a doomed world." See Mary Julian Baird, "Blake, Hopkins and Thomas Merton," *Catholic World* 183 (April 1956): 48.

30. Paul Wilkes claims that in 1925 before Merton's spiritual experience in Rome, the first stirrings of transcendence came to him at the medieval monastery of St. Michel de Cuxa in France. However, it seems that the impact of St. Michel de Cuxa may have been more emotional than spiritual. See Paul Wilkes, "Merton in These Places Early Days in Europe—Final Days in the East," in *Toward an Integrated Humanity: Thomas Merton's Journey*, ed. Basil Pennington (Kalamazoo, MI: Cistercian Publications, 1988), 262–263; cf. SSM, 6–7.

31. Thomas Merton, *The Labyrinth* [unpublished manuscript] (Louisville, KY: Thomas Merton Studies Center, Bellarmine University), 178, 181.

Christ," and to read the Gospels, and to pray to God.[32] In Rome, he also had a vision of his father. He intuited that "[t]he sense of [my father's] presence was as vivid and as real and as startling as if he had touched my arm or spoken to me. . . . I was overwhelmed with a sudden and profound insight into the misery and corruption of my own soul."[33] Later in his life, Merton considered this vision to be a deep spiritual experience: "The one thing that seems to me morally certain is that this was really a grace, and a great grace."[34] Michael Mott, Merton's official biographer, comments that through this graced moment Merton apparently learned the way of prayer, which brought him to "an acute sense of self-consciousness and self-disgust."[35]

According to Shannon, the Byzantine mosaics of Christ allowed Merton "to see obscurely . . . what 'he [was] looking for,' and the vision of his father [seemed] to be showing him what he was *not* looking for: it [sought] to expose the misery toward which his pride and self-centeredness were leading him."[36] Merton saw his own misery and pride and his "soul desired escape and liberation and freedom from all this with an intensity and an urgency unlike anything ever known before."[37]

Despite this insightful experience, a young Merton perceived that his conversion was still a long way off. When he remembered this mystical experience later, he regretted that he did not follow it during Clare College, Cambridge: "If I had only followed it through, my life might have been very different and much less

32. SSM, 120.

33. Ibid., 123.

34. Ibid., 124.

35. Michael Mott, *The Seven Mountains of Thomas Merton* (Boston, MA: Houghton Mifflin, 1984), 69.

36. Shannon, *Silent Lamp*, 70 (emphasis in original).

37. SSM, 123. Pennington points out that the mystical experience in Rome opened "his soul to a flood of repentance [and] a desire of a new kind of freedom." See Basil Pennington, *Thomas Merton, Brother Monk: The Quest for True Freedom* (San Francisco, CA: Harper & Row, 1987), 57.

miserable for the years that were to come."[38] Indeed, both experiences did not survive for long, and in the following year at Clare College, he reached the nadir of his life spiritually, morally, and academically. He degenerated into a kind of morbid hedonism, fathered an unplanned child out of wedlock, and left Cambridge.

The next mystical experience occurred in 1938, in New York, during the time Merton embraced the Roman Catholic tradition. He claimed that he heard a mystical voice that invited him to attend Mass in a Catholic Church. He remembered that "[f]inally the urge became so strong that I could not resist it. . . . I will not easily forget how I felt that day. First, there was this sweet, strong, gentle, clean urge in me which said: 'Go to Mass! Go to Mass!' "[39] In describing the experience, he said that he heard a voice which he could not account for. However, it was new and strange, creating an interior conviction that propelled him to act. He therefore canceled a weekend in the country to attend a Mass at Corpus Christi Church. Afterward, the fruit of this experience was a graced consolation of joy and peace. Merton then began to enjoy a new perspective on life and on the way he had been living.

Later, while Merton was reading the biography of Gerard Manley Hopkins SJ, he was further graced. He recalled, "All of a sudden, something began to stir within me, something began to push me, to prompt me. It was a movement that spoke like a voice. 'What are you waiting for?' it said. 'Why are you sitting here?'. . . . 'You know what you ought to do?' "[40] When he could no longer bear the inner voice, he went to Corpus Christi Church and said to Father George B. Ford, "Father, I want to become a Catholic."[41] After receiving preparation, Merton was baptized on November 16, 1938.

During the period between his baptism and his entrance into the monastery, Merton had a remarkable religious experience. It

38. SSM, 124.
39. Ibid., 225, 226.
40. Ibid., 236.
41. Ibid., 237.

occurred at Mass in the Church of St. Francis in Havana, Cuba, in 1940 when he made a pilgrimage to the shrine of Our Lady of Charity in Cobre. He described it as follows:

> The Creed. But that cry, "*Creo en Diós!*" It was loud, and bright, and sudden and glad and triumphant. . . . Then, as sudden as the shout and as definite, and a thousand times more bright, there formed in my mind an awareness, an understanding, a realization of what had just taken place on the altar, at the Consecration: a realization of God made present by the words of Consecration in a way that made Him belong to me. . . . It was the light of faith deepened and reduced to an extreme and sudden obviousness. It was as if I had been suddenly illuminated by being blinded by the manifestation of God's presence.[42]

In *The Secular Journal*, Merton again sought to describe what he had experienced: ". . . the unshakable certainty, the clear and immediate knowledge that heaven was right in front of me, struck me like a thunderbolt and went through me like a flash of lightning and seemed to lift me clean up off the earth."[43] As deduced from these two descriptions from *The Seven Storey Mountain* and *The Secular Journal*, Mott claims that "Merton tries to explain both the ordinary and the extraordinary aspects of this 'movement of God's grace.'"[44] In *The Seven Storey Mountain*, Merton reflected on his radical affirmation of the Catholic spiritual tradition; in *The Secular Journal*, he expressed the moment of the experience as "a thunderbolt" and "a flash of lightning," interpreting it as "a sudden illumination" that offered him certainty. The language of religious experience, which reaches beyond human language, offered him a way to describe the various mystical experiences

42. Ibid., 311.

43. Thomas Merton, *The Secular Journal of Thomas Merton* (New York, NY: Farrar, Straus & Cudahy, 1959), 76–77.

44. Mott, *The Seven Mountains of Thomas Merton*, 151.

that were to come later in his life.[45] Through these experiences, he encountered the presence of God in the Church and made two vows, to become a priest and to celebrate his first Mass in honor of the Mother of God.

Before entering the Abbey of Gethsemani, another religious experience led him to discern his monastic vocation. Following his journey to Cuba, he applied to enter the Franciscan Order, but his application was rejected because of his past life. Later, Friendship House in Harlem, New York, gave him an opportunity to experience ministry to the poor. Gethsemani Abbey, a contemplative monastery in Kentucky also attracted him. Back at St. Bonaventure University, while he was trying to discern whether to choose Friendship House or the Abbey of Gethsemani, he heard a bell ringing: "Suddenly . . . in my imagination, I started to hear the great bell of Gethsemani ringing in the night. . . . The impression made me breathless. . . . The bell seemed to be telling me where I belonged."[46] This experience led him to decide to enter the Trappist monastery without hesitations and doubt. Finally, on December 10, 1941, Thomas Merton entered into the Abbey of Gethsemani to dedicate his whole life to God in the silence and solitude of monastic life.

On the basis of his description of his life prior to entering the Trappist community at Gethsemani, we can conclude that Merton's mystical experiences played a crucial role in his conversion to Catholicism and his conviction that God was calling him to the contemplative life.

Early Monastic Life: 1941 to the Mid-1950s

Comparing his early writings and later writings, we can observe that Merton's monastic life can be divided into his early monastic life (1941 to the mid-1950s) and his later monastic life (1958 to

---

45. See ibid.
46. SSM, 400.

1968). In the 1940s, his formation as a Cistercian monk and priest was based on the traditional teaching and practices of contemplative cenobitic (strict communal) life. However, the transformation of consciousness that occurred during the 1950s created a longing for union with God in and through solitude in him.

It should be emphasized, however, that the ordinary monastic routine of prayer, meditation, fasting, solitude, silence, and self-examination created the foundation for the development of a more mature spiritual life. Initially, he sought an intimate relationship with God through traditional monastic practices and the common life. His daily discipline in the monastic cloister cultivated a contemplative awareness of God. During this period, he reveled in the monastic life, which he believed could provide the perfect way to attain supernatural divine grace. He noted, "If happiness were merely a matter of natural gifts, I would never have entered a Trappist monastery when I came to the age of a man."[47] The young monk also sensed that monastic life was superior to a life lived outside the cloister. He was convinced that the monk could achieve a deeper spiritual life than was possible for the laity. He also had a triumphalist view of Roman Catholicism, as can clearly be seen in the pages of *The Seven Storey Mountain* (1948). Shannon points out in a Note to the Reader that "confident in his belief that he belonged to the 'one true' church, he all too often speaks disparagingly about other Christian churches—mirroring the church's complacent triumphalism himself."[48] In the years during which Merton wrote his autobiography, he was in some ways the *typical*

---

47. Ibid., 4. During this period he was infatuated with the monastic life. See, for example, the way he spoke about his experience of Mass at Gethsemani: "It is a mystery to me. The silence, the solemnity, the dignity of these Masses and of the church, and the overpowering atmosphere of prayers so fervent that they were almost tangible choked me with love and reverence that robbed me of the power to breathe. . . . After communion I thought my heart was going to explode." See ibid., 354, 355.

48. Ibid., xxi.

convert, filled with wondrous happiness and still under the glowing ardor of his conversion experience.[49]

After the *honeymoon period*, which lasted to the later 1940s, Merton's idealism was tempered by his recognition of its limitations and his preoccupation with the distinction between natural and supernatural grace.[50] Two conflicts in particular generated much frustration, depression, and unhappiness for him: 1) between being a writer and being a contemplative (the secular world versus the cloister) and 2) between being a Cistercian monk of strict observance and a Carthusian monk (community life versus the solitary life). Paradoxically, his struggles with these problems facilitated a new vision of contemplative spirituality. His contemplative experience would eventually help him to become aware of a spiritual consciousness that surpassed these binary choices.

Merton struggled with being a writer while being a contemplative until the early 1950s. The success of his book *The Seven Storey Mountain* confused him: how could one reconcile being a successful writer with withdrawal from the secular world? His dilemma was anchored in the dualistic point of view that set the secular world over against the monastic cloister. He noted, "I brought all the instincts of a writer with me into the monastery. . . . [T]here was this shadow, this double, this writer who had followed me into the cloister."[51] His conflict was radically described: "Maybe in the end he [a writer] will kill me, he will drink my blood. . . . There are the days when there seems to be

49. Merton noted, "He [God] knew that there would be joy in heaven among the angels of His house for the conversion of some of us, and He knew that He would bring us all here to Gethsemani together, one day, for His own purpose, for the praise of His love." See SSM, 458–459.

50. For example, in the later years of the 1940s, Merton described his depression on recalling that "tomorrow it will be eight years since I came to Gethsemani. I somehow feel less clean than I did then when I thought I was throwing my civil identity away." See Thomas Merton, *Entering the Silence: Becoming a Monk & Writer* (San Francisco, CA: HarperSanFrancisco, 1995), 376 (hereafter ES).

51. SSM, 428, 448.

nothing left of my vocation—my contemplative vocation—but a few ashes."[52] This thought was perhaps influenced by the writings of Thomistic scholastics such as Jacques Maritain and Réginald Garrigou-Lagrange, who considered pure contemplation as superior to artistic intuition.[53] Merton was faced with what he saw as a threefold dilemma: did he hope to be a writer; did he want to achieve a mystical relationship with God; or did he simply wish to adhere to his newfound Cistercian vocation, which did not easily include writing given that it is a life of manual labor?

In order to overcome this impasse, he first attempted to transfer responsibility to his superiors.[54] His strict interpretation of the vow of obedience, however, could not completely resolve the dilemma. His ongoing struggle led him to realize that the purpose of his life was not to be a contemplative or a writer with artistic intuition, but union with God, and that contemplation could not be separated from human activities. In *The Sign of Jonas* (1953), he wrote that "the important thing is not to live for contemplation, but to live for God."[55] He added that "my lamentations about my writing job have been foolish."[56] In fact, writing helped him to access real silence, solitude, and prayer; at times he even felt the presence of God during his writing.[57] When he came to this

52. Ibid., 449.

53. See Thomas Merton, *Spiritual Master: The Essential Writings*, ed. Lawrence Cunningham (New York/Mahwah, NJ: Paulist Press, 1992), 251, 294; IE, 32.

54. See Thomas Merton, *The Sign of Jonas* (New York, NY: Harcourt, Brace, 1953), 27 (hereafter SJ).

55. Ibid., 30.

56. Ibid., 207.

57. Merton noted that "the writing is one thing that gives me access to some real silence and solitude. Also I find that it helps me to pray, because when I pause at my work I find that the mirror inside me is surprisingly clean and deep and serene and God shines there and is immediately found, without hunting, as if He had come close to me while I was writing." See SJ. Victor Kramer points out that "*The Sign of Jonas* is, perhaps, most importantly Merton's journal of his acceptance of a dual vocation. It is the record of someone gradually coming

realization, Merton's world, which had been enclosed by the four walls of the cloister, gradually opened up. By the late 1950s, his dualistic way of thinking about the cloister and the secular world, monastics and laity, contemplation and action, had been overcome.

Second, from the late 1940s to the mid-1950s, Merton struggled with the form of his monastic vocation. Due to his earnest desire for greater solitude, he wished to become a Carthusian or a Camaldolese. He noted, "I am more convinced than ever of the necessity of a truly solitary, truly contemplative life."[58] He tried to transfer to the Camaldolese Order, but his request for a transfer was refused by the decision of the Abbot General, Dom Gabriel Sortais. Merton had to remain a Trappist at Gethsemani. He stopped looking for a "perfect monastery" but continued his efforts to achieve "perfect solitude."[59] Merton's views regarding more solitude shifted from day to day. During the late 1950s, he integrated his thoughts on solitude into his mystical experience, and this was reflected in his writings in the 1960s. For instance, in his book *Disputed Questions* he noted, "True solitude is not mere separateness. It tends only to *unity*. The true solitary does not renounce anything that is basic and human about his relationship to other men. He is deeply united to them—all the more deeply because he is no longer entranced by marginal concerns."[60]

Merton's famous Louisville Epiphany in 1958, in which he briefly felt a strong spiritual connection with all of the ordinary

---

to the realization that not only had he not been in control of his life as he moved through Gethsemani, but ironically he would never be in control of such a deep mystery. His job as a writer was to accept what God asked him to do." See Victor Kramer, "Literary Patterns in *The Sign of Jonas*: Tension Between Monk and Man of Letters," in *Toward an Integrated Humanity*, 22.

58. Thomas Merton, *The School of Charity: The Letters of Thomas Merton on Religious Renewal and Spiritual Direction*, ed. Patrick Hart (New York, NY: Farrar, Straus, Giroux, 1990), 63 (hereafter SCL).

59. SJ, 10.

60. Thomas Merton, *Disputed Questions* (New York, NY: New American Library, 1960), 186 (emphasis in original) (hereafter DQ).

strangers around him on the street corner, played a significant role in his coming to this new outlook and his new understanding of solitude and of the secular world beyond the walls of the cloister.[61] This mystical experience deeply penetrated his heart, and he became a different person with a new vocation to the world of humanity.[62]

Following this experience, his spirituality matured in the 1960s. As he noted, "I am perhaps at a turning point in my spiritual life: perhaps slowly coming to a point of maturation and the resolution of doubts—and the forgetting of fears."[63] Moreover, his view of his monastic vocation had also been transformed. As he put it, "I have never had any doubt whatever of my monastic vocation. . . . I am in some sense everywhere. My monastery is not a home."[64] His new view of monastic life nourished his longing for a more barren environment, in deep solitude, and made his spiritual orientation even more firm in the final years of his life.

In summary, during the period of his spiritual adolescence in the 1940s, Merton relied heavily on the traditional view of Christian contemplative life, intellectually and practically, and then in the 1950s, he spent a period in "the belly of the whale," which he

61. Through his religious experience, Merton realized that in true solitude there must coexist "non-presence and attendance, non-participation and engagement, hiddenness and hospitality, disappearance and arrival." See Jim Forest, *Living with Wisdom: A Life of Thomas Merton* (Maryknoll, NY: Orbis Books, 2008), 135.

62. See Thomas Merton, *Conjectures of a Guilty Bystander* (Garden City, NY: Image Books, 2014, 1st ed. 1966), 153–154 (hereafter CGB). Merton's Louisville Epiphany will be dealt with in more detail later in this chapter.

63. Thomas Merton, *Turning Toward the World: The Pivotal Years,* ed. Victor A. Kramer (San Francisco, CA: HarperSanFrancisco, 1997), 172 (hereafter TTW).

64. Thomas Merton, *Introductions East & West: The Foreign Prefaces of Thomas Merton*, ed. Robert E. Daggy (Oakville, ON: Mosaic Press, 1981), 45 (hereafter IEW).

described in his book *The Sign of Jonas*.[65] Paradoxically, his struggle to overcome a dualistic attitude and his desire for more solitude fostered his self-acceptance and self-transformation. His religious experience helped him to realize an integrated contemplation and action and opened his mind and heart to the secular world and to humanity. At the end of this period, he achieved a deeper solitude that allowed him to realize his true self and to unite with God.

Later Monastic Life: 1959–1968

Merton's life blossomed in his later period of the 1960s. He felt freer to attempt to integrate contemplation and action in novel ways. The contemplative monk became a peacemaker for the world and a pioneer in inter-monastic and interreligious dialogue with various religions, especially Buddhism. In October of 1960, he conceded that "I have always been a Platonist," and then he actively began to reveal his critical social views with assurance.[66] All the years of contemplative prayer and personal struggle in the monastery had filled him with love and compassion in this later phase. He confessed that "as a contemplative, I do not need to lock myself into solitude . . . rather this poor world has a right to a place in my solitude. . . . I also have to think in terms of a contemplative grasp of the political, intellectual, artistic and social movement in this world."[67]

Thus, Merton drew closer to other people and to *their world*, as he wrote about and confronted the problems facing modern society. This spectrum included alienation, violence, racism, nuclear war, injustice, and the difficulties faced by those who pursued peace through nonviolence. Merton wrote, "I feel myself involved

65. SJ, 10.

66. TTW, 59.

67. Thomas Merton, *The Hidden Ground of Love: The Letters of Thomas Merton on Religious Experience and Social Concerns*, ed. William H. Shannon (New York, NY: Farrar, Straus, Giroux, 1985), 482 (hereafter HGL).

in the same problems and I need to work out the problems of the world with other men because they are also my problems."[68] He worked especially hard to promote peace in the world because he lived through a period in twentieth-century history when war and violence were the order of the day.

Merton's involvement in peacemaking was the fruit of his integration of contemplation and action. Even though he was radically engaged in social justice movements, his desire for solitude and silence in order to achieve mystical union with God was ongoing. In 1965 his ardent longing for solitude was realized when he was given permission to spend time in a hermitage about a twenty-minute walk from the monastery. When he was allowed by the abbot to live there full-time, he described this moment as a transformative experience:

> The five days I have had in real solitude have been a *revelation*. Whatever questions I may have had about it are answered. Over and over again I see that this life is what I have always hoped it would be and always sought. A life of peace, silence, purpose, meaning. It is not always easy but calls for a *blessed and salutary effort*. Everything about it is rewarding.[69]

He described real solitude, which was being with God in his own new hermitage, as "a blessed and salutary effort." Shannon proposes that this event was a symbol of his deep inner change and the starting point of his transcultural consciousness: "The year 1965 marked a decisive change in Merton's life. . . . [He] finally became a 'full-time' hermit living in the woods. . . . But this change of place symbolized a deep inner change. . . . [He became] truly catholic in the sense of all-embracive and . . .

---

68. Thomas Merton, "The Monk Today," in *Contemplation in a World of Action* (Garden City, NY: Doubleday, 1973), 245.

69. Thomas Merton, *Dancing in the Water of Life: Seeking Peace in the Hermitage*, ed. Robert E. Daggy (San Francisco, CA: HarperSanFrancisco, 1998), 283 (emphasis added) (hereafter DWL).

transcultural."[70] Ironically, Shannon connects Merton's solitary life as a hermit with his being a "true catholic" aware of the "transcultural state" of the world. Merton's new consciousness had evolved to the point where he became aware of the interdependence of everything in universal reality beyond his own religious and cultural boundaries. In the hermitage, he realized that the self, which was united with God, was connected to everything, and in union with God, one could see all whom one encountered through the eyes of God.[71] He moved further away from the secular world and his monastic community, and at the same time, he moved toward the world with compassion and openness. In the mid-1960s, his consciousness was expanded to "cosmic proportions" with the notion of the cosmic Christ.[72] Thus, he became a living witness with those whose prophetic voices to the world were spoken out of solitude.

During this period, Merton engaged in ecumenical and interreligious dialogue. His religious experience facilitated his openness for dialogue with other religions. He was influenced in his spiritual development by Christian mysticism and by a wide knowledge of Eastern religions, particularly those of Zen Buddhism and Taoism. These opened him up to a new view of contemplation that invigorated and inspired him. From an ecumenical perspective, Merton was also in close contact with Protestant traditions, seeking spiritual union with them through the Holy Spirit rather than hoping for institutional or sacramental union.[73]

It was during this period—in 1966—that Merton fell in love with a student nurse. Since he was a celibate vowed monk, this episode raises all sorts of questions from an ethical and monastic perspective. Some psychologists and feminists suggest that his

70. Shannon, *Silent Lamp*, 4–5.

71. Cf. ZBA, 24, 57.

72. Bailey, *Thomas Merton on Mysticism*, 190; Pennington, *Thomas Merton, Brother Monk*, 102; CWA, 206.

73. See HGL, 377–378.

affair was a "life-enhancing event" and was a positive factor in Merton's becoming "a *whole* man, capable of loving *and* being loved."[74] Caught, as he was, between the most exhilarating instinctive emotions (id) and a guilty conscience (super-ego), Merton's ego was confused. As a monk who professed to love God exclusively, he knew he should not be involved in a romantic relationship with a woman, but at the same time, he was absurdly happy. He confessed, "I have got to dare to love, and to bear the anxiety of self-questioning that love arouses in me."[75] He added, "I just don't know what to do with my life, finding myself too much loved, and loving so much, when according to all standards it is all wrong, absurd, [and] insane."[76] In this conflicted situation he wrote, "I have to lead this absurd existence. In some mysterious way I am condemned to it. Not as to something wonderful and mysterious, but as though to a vice."[77] Although they decided to end the relationship, this passionate affair made Merton sense an enormous emotional energy that he had never been conscious of before.[78] This deep loving experience may also have contributed to his spiritual maturity. He described the power of the direct experience of love and its value: "When people are truly in love . . . [t]hey are made over into new beings. They are transformed by the power of their love. Love is the revelation of our deepest personal meaning, value, and identity."[79] Robert Waldron, author of *The Wounded Heart of Thomas Merton*, points out that in a relationship such as this, "Spiritual growth surely occurs [since]

74. Waldron, *The Wounded Heart of Thomas Merton*, 158, 159 (emphasis in original).

75. LL, 44.

76. Ibid., 50.

77. Ibid., 341.

78. See Waldron, *The Wounded Heart of Thomas Merton*, 159–169; Bailey, *Thomas Merton on Mysticism*, 36.

79. Thomas Merton, *Love and Living*, ed. Naomi Burton Stone and Patrick Hart (San Diego, CA: Harcourt Brace Jovanovich, 1985), 34–35 (hereafter L&L).

love has been described as the willingness to extend oneself in the service of one's own or another's spiritual growth: the act of loving is an act of self-transcendence."[80] Even Basil Pennington, a Trappist monk, argues that:

> I do not think there was ever any question or danger of this romance going beyond the reality of a passing romance that did not exclude a true friendship. Merton felt free and secure enough to open himself to this beautiful experience precisely because he was so solidly grounded in his commitment as a monk.[81]

In fact, his capacity for ordinary responsible love as a human being might have been made possible by his experience of falling in love with this young woman, although he did not live much longer after it.

Final Two Months in Asia: 1968

Merton's final two months in Asia were an especially significant time for integrating the experience of contemplation with a faith that was not limited to one religious or cultural tradition. He saw his journey not merely as a trip for knowledge and discovery, but also as a pilgrimage that would enable him to become "a better and more enlightened monk."[82] He wanted to have a direct experience of Asian wisdom and traditions in order to attain greater spiritual maturity.

Merton's ardent wish to visit Asia began in the late 1960s, but the Abbot of Gethsemani, Dom James Fox, forbade the trip. However, a new Abbot, Dom Flavian Burns, permitted him to go, and Merton left San Francisco on October 15, 1968. On behalf of Aide à l'Implantation Monastique, an international and inter-monastic

---

80. Waldron, *The Wounded Heart of Thomas Merton*, 172.
81. Pennington, *Thomas Merton, Brother Monk*, 122.
82. AJ, 313.

network, his friend Father Jean Leclercq, OSB had invited him to give a major address at the Congress of Asian monastic leaders in Bangkok, Thailand.[83]

Before the Congress, Merton went to Calcutta, India, where he spoke at a meeting of world religious leaders at the Temple of Understanding and at the Conference for Religious of India. In these meetings, Merton spoke of the importance of the monastic experience for East-West dialogue, and suggested that contemplative dialogue could be achieved through spiritual communion among monastics who were seeking self-transcendence and enlightenment. In India, he met the Fourteenth Dalai Lama, Tenzin Gyatso, on three occasions, as well as several rinpoches, who practiced a special type of contemplation called *dzogchen*. Merton also encountered Cambodian monks of the Theravada Buddhist tradition and representatives of Muslim Sufism.[84]

The transcultural and transreligious state of contemplation was confirmed in his Polonnaruwa Enlightenment Experience, which might be seen as a still deeper surrender to the creative action of love and grace in his heart. In Polonnaruwa, an ancient city in Ceylon (now Sri Lanka), Merton experienced a culminating moment of enlightenment before the enormous stone figures of Buddha. He was overwhelmed by the aesthetic experience of these towering Buddhist statues and described an experience of transformed

83. The Congress is often referred to as an interreligious conference. Although the Thai Buddhist Patriarch was invited to address the participants, the Congress was, in fact, organized by AIM, an organization of the Benedictine confederation that is now known as Alliance inter Monastères/Alliance for International Monasticism, to help Christian monastic men and women in Asia, most of whom were European or "Europeanized" Asians, better understand and relate to the Asian religious and cultural setting in which they were now living.

84. *Dzogchen* means "the simplest and most beneficial way to rediscover instantly for oneself the transcendental awareness that is within, whose all-inclusive qualities are either presently active or lying latent in all human beings." See Thomas Merton, *The Other Side of the Mountain: The End of the Journey*, ed. Patrick Hart (San Francisco, CA: HarperSanFrancisco, 1998), 332 (hereafter OSM).

consciousness of emptiness and fullness. After this experience, Merton noted in his journal that he was uncertain about the future, but realized that "the journey [had] only begun."[85]

On December 8, 1968, Merton arrived in Bangkok, and two days later he gave his presentation, which was titled "Marxism and Monastic Perspectives." In his lecture, he compared monasticism with Marxism, asserting that monasticism was concerned with changing the world through a transformation of consciousness and not, as with Marxism, through changing social structures.[86] He concluded with a call for a new openness to Asian culture and religion and suggested that dialogue with Asian traditions could provide spiritual as well as cultural enrichment for Christians.[87] Unfortunately, after this lecture, Merton was accidentally electrocuted by an electric fan in his room at the retreat house. His body was flown back to the United States and was buried at Gethsemani.

During his two months in Asia, Merton's meetings with Tibetan masters, lamas, and other monastics, and his religious experience at Polonnaruwa made him more conscious of Asian traditions and Asian religious experiences, which brought him to a deeper level of integration.

A New View of Contemplation

An analysis of Merton's early and later writings will help to clarify the terminology he used for contemplative experience and to come to a better understanding of how he went about synthesiz-

---

85. AJ, 238. Merton's Polonnaruwa experience will be explored in more detail below.

86. Merton noted, "The difference between the monk and the Marxist is fundamental insofar as the Marxist view of change is oriented to the change of substructures, economic substructures, and the monk is seeking to change man's consciousness." See ibid., 330.

87. Merton concluded, "I believe that by openness to Buddhism, to Hinduism, and to these great Asian traditions, we stand a wonderful chance of learning more about the potentiality of our own traditions." See ibid., 343.

ing the various ways of understanding contemplation and making it comprehensible to modern men and women. This examination will also show how Merton's new view of contemplation is related to Eastern contemplative traditions and will shed light on what he means when he speaks of "contemplative dialogue" between Christian monastics and contemplatives of other religious traditions, which will be treated in greater detail in chapter 3.

Clarification of Merton's Terminology regarding Contemplative Experience

To describe the experience of contemplation, Merton used such terms as spiritual experience, religious experience, mystical experience, transcendental experience, inner experience, enlightened experience, and awakening experience. His understanding of contemplation changed over the course of his life, and specifically the terms he used to explain contemplation changed dramatically following his encounter with non-Christian religions. The terminology Merton used in his early writings on contemplation were rooted in the literature of traditional Christian mysticism, but later he began to use contemporary and non-Christian language to describe the Christian mystical experience.[88]

In order to explain the two terms "contemplation" and "mysticism," Merton attempted to examine the terms in context of the Christian spiritual tradition. He commented, "For the Greek Fathers—'Mystical Theology' and 'Contemplation' are two ways of saying the same thing. . . . Both terms mean the hidden knowledge of God by experience, the 'passive' illumination of the soul by the divine light 'in darkness.' "[89] Although both terms refer to a direct experience of God, he argued that mystical theology became the study of professional mystics, such as St. John of

88. See Carr, *A Search for Wisdom and Spirit*, 93.

89. Thomas Merton, *The Cistercian Fathers and Their Monastic Theology: Initiation into the Monastic Tradition 8* (Collegeville, MN: Liturgical Press, 2016), 238 (hereafter CFMT).

the Cross and St. Teresa of Avila, and even their writings, such as *Ascent of Mount Carmel* and *The Way of Perfection*, became guidebooks of techniques for ascending the degrees of the spiritual life. In the eighteenth century, according to Merton, mystical theology became the study of extraordinary mystics and exceptional cases, and the idea of contemplation was then "obscured and forgotten, and 'mysticism' becomes something rare and suspicious, from which the average man must flee and which even saints will not necessarily experience."[90] This was seemingly the reason he preferred the term "contemplation" to "mysticism" in his later writings, thus avoiding giving the impression that he was speaking of something esoteric or extraordinary.[91] He noted, "Contemplation is not trance or ecstasy. . . . It is not enthusiasm, the sense of being 'seized' by an elemental force and swept into liberation by mystical frenzy."[92] Beyond the distinction of the two terms, however, Merton pointed out that in modern times, both "mysticism" and "contemplation" were being used to refer to "a renewal of the traditional emphasis on the more 'ordinary' forms of contemplation."[93] He insisted that the contemplative experience

90. Ibid., 238–239.

91. See William H. Shannon, "Mysticism," in *The Thomas Merton Encyclopedia*, ed. William H. Shannon, Christine M. Bochen, and Patrick F. O'Connell (Maryknoll, NY: Orbis Books, 2002), 314. The negative connotations of "mysticism," which were reminiscent of pagan mystery cults and the primitive and esoteric rites, may have led Merton to avoid using the term. See Bailey, *Thomas Merton on Mysticism*, 20. The later Merton used the terms "contemplative," "mystical," "aware," "enlightened," or "spiritually transformed" interchangeably. For example, see AJ, 310.

92. NSC, 10–11.

93. CFMT, 239. Carr points out that "Merton's recovery of the contemplative tradition for ordinary readers brought new meaning and spiritual depth to the authoritative faith. . . . For he wrote vividly about the possibility of the *experience* of God in faith, the possibility of a spiritual adventure that was the *experience* of union with God." See Carr, *A Search for Wisdom and Spirit*, 11 (emphasis in original).

of participating in the mystery of God-who-is-love was open to all Christians.

Merton's encounter with Buddhism revealed the richness of the Zen experience to him. He began to use Buddhist terms to express his own inner experience. Pennington argues that "Eastern thought served [Merton] better in his efforts to express that inner unity of all that is that our mystics have tried so hard to express."[94] Theologian Anne E. Carr claims that "Merton translates the goal of simplicity and wisdom witnessed in the contemplative traditions of East and West into contemporary language."[95] Merton discovered that his contemporaries had an almost natural affinity for the different ways Buddhists spoke of inner experiences. In his later writings, he frequently used such Buddhist terms as "*anatta*" (no-self), "*sunyata*" (emptiness), and "*satori*" (enlightened experience) to explain the meaning of contemplation.[96]

For Merton, the use of Buddhist terms did not mean a "facile syncretism" that saw all mystical experience as essentially the same thing and claimed that all religions could "meet at the top."[97] Yet, these Buddhist terms, inadequate as they might be, could be used to give expression to religious experience. Indeed, the direct experience of God (or *Atman* or *Sunyata*) could not be captured in the net of human thoughts and images. He keenly perceived the limitation and inadequacy of human language to articulate religious experience. However, Merton believed that borrowing various interpretations and terms from different traditions could facilitate mutual enrichment. Bonnie Thurston, an authority on Merton and Buddhism, argues that even though Merton's contemplative experience was rooted in his own Christian context, he found proper terms and ways to articulate it through Buddhist

94. Pennington, *Thomas Merton, Brother Monk*, 131.
95. Carr, *A Search for Wisdom and Spirit*, 93.
96. See IE, 7–11; NSC, 1–13; ZBA, 35–37.
97. AJ, 316; ZBA, 43.

explanations of religious experience.[98] Shannon claims that Merton was "drawn especially to Zen as offering insights most congenial to the Christian mystical experience."[99] Merton discovered a confluence of religious experience between Western contemplatives and enlightened Eastern masters. He envisioned the possibility of true mysticism among Zen masters and believed that their experience, expressed in ways that went beyond the categories of Western mysticism, could be a source of enrichment for Christian spirituality.[100] This discovery of the value of inner experience, and of the appropriateness of interchanging terminology from both traditions to describe it, facilitated Merton's interreligious dialogue with Eastern traditions, especially Buddhism.

From a Traditional to a Synthetic and Modern View of Contemplation

Merton's new vision of contemplation involved a transition from an intellectual perspective to one that was existential and experiential. The transition is evident when one compares his early and later writings on the spirituality of contemplation. For example, in his early booklet *What is Contemplation?* (1950), Merton depicted contemplation as an intuition of "a supernatural love and knowledge of God . . . infused by Him into the summit of the soul" and claimed that "the great majority of Christians will never become pure contemplatives on earth."[101] This definition was very close to the traditional Christian view of contemplation.[102]

---

98. See Bonnie B. Thurston, "Thomas Merton: Pioneer of Buddhist-Christian Dialogue," *The Catholic World* 233 (May/June 1989): 127.

99. Shannon, "Mysticism," 315.

100. See MZM, 37.

101. Thomas Merton, *What is Contemplation?* (Springfield, IL: Templegate Publishers, 1978, 1st ed. 1948), 36, 30–31.

102. For example, St. John of the Cross defines contemplation as "an infused and loving knowledge of God, which enlightens the soul and at the same time enkindles it with love, until it is raised up step by step, even unto God its Creator."

In this book he dealt with the nature of contemplation for the first time and suggested practical guidelines for contemplative prayer based on Scripture, St. Thomas Aquinas, and St. John of the Cross. He distinguished between infused or pure contemplation and acquired contemplation. Only the former was considered to be true contemplation, and it was equivalent to mystical union with God, the highest goal of the Christian life.

Merton's book *The Ascent to Truth* (1951) was the fruit of his obvious interest in traditional contemplation. His intention was to provide links between the scholastic theology of St. Thomas Aquinas, the mystical insight of St. John of the Cross, and the dogmatic essentials of mystical theology, which were based on the intellectual heritage of the church, Scripture, liturgy, and revelation. For him, traditional Christian mysticism was rational and intellectual.[103] In his writings and thought after the mid-1950s, Merton's systematic approach to contemplation undergoes a transformation. For example, in *The Sign of Jonas* (1953) he wrote:

> I found in writing *The Ascent to Truth* that technical language, though it is universal and certain and accepted by theologians, does not reach the average man and does not convey what is most personal and most vital in *religious experience*. Since my focus is not on dogmas as such, but only on their repercussions in the life of a soul in which they begin to find a concrete realization, I may be pardoned for using my own words to talk about *my own soul*.[104]

This statement indicates his movement from a dogmatic perspective to that of personal religious experience.

See St. John of the Cross, *Dark Night of the Soul*, trans. E. Allison Peers (Garden City, NY: Image Books, 1959), 82.

103. See Thomas Merton, *The Ascent to Truth* (New York, NY: Harcourt, Brace, 1951), 14 (hereafter AT).

104. SJ, 8–9 (emphasis added).

Another example can be found in *No Man Is an Island* (1955), in which he made clear that he would approach matters of faith by sharing his own experience of the contemplative life and his reflections on that experience.[105] He wrote, "Contemplation is an experience of divine things. . . . We enter thus into a great mystery which cannot be explained, but only experienced."[106] He realized the value of experience in contemplation and did not ignore the classical Catholic contemplative tradition. Rather, he rediscovered and developed the value of the tradition and synthesized it with his own contemplative experience.[107] His study of Zen also influenced his new approach to contemplation and to Asian traditions.

105. Merton noted, "I only desire in this book to share with the reader my own reflections on certain aspects of the spiritual life." See Thomas Merton, *No Man Is an Island* (New York, NY: Harcourt, 1955), ix (hereafter NMI). He already confirmed this position in *Seeds of Contemplation* (1949), saying that he was "talking about spiritual things from the point of view of experience rather than in the concise terms of dogmatic theology or metaphysics." See SC, 7. His approach to contemplation from the viewpoint of experience did not emerge abruptly. *Seeds of Contemplation* shows that he had already attempted to approach contemplation from an experiential perspective in the late 1940s. From the mid-1950s, his movement away from a systematic approach to one that is experiential is increasingly evident.

106. NMI, 23, 46.

107. According to Merton, "Tradition is living and active. . . . Tradition, which is always old, is at the same time ever new because it is always reviving— born again in each generation, to be lived and applied in a new and particular way." Ibid., 150–151; however, he cautioned against a traditionalism that "was emptied of its truly living traditional content." See AJ, 313–314. According to Shannon, "Though firm as ever in his desire to remain faithful to the faith-formulations of the past, Merton is inching his way toward an understanding of Catholic tradition that will more and more submit that tradition to the test of actual experience. Another way of putting this is to say that Merton is beginning more and more to trust his own experience. . . . His understanding of his Catholic faith will more and more begin to take on a dynamic and dialogic character in which age-old formulas must be tested in the crucible of experience." See Shannon, *Silent Lamp*, 165.

His writings in the late 1950s and the 1960s, such as *The Inner Experience, New Seeds of Contemplation, The Climate of Monastic Prayer,* and *Contemplation in a World of Action,* reflected these three influences directly or indirectly: the Christian contemplative tradition, Zen Buddhism, and his own contemplative experience. The following examination of such writings will explore these influences in more detail.

First, the word, "experience" in the title of the book *The Inner Experience* (1959) seems to signal a bridge between a theological approach and an experiential approach to contemplation.[108] In this book, Merton modified the view of contemplation he had expressed in his earlier writings, a view that was in accord with traditional Catholic writing on the subject.[109] *What is Contemplation?* was written from an undeveloped and immature perspective of the contemplative life, and *The Ascent of Truth* also had limitations, since it took little if any account of the fact that true contemplation goes beyond words and concepts.[110] In *The Inner Experience,* he intended to go beyond a systematic approach that gives predominant emphasis to logic and rationality. He realized that a contemplative was not interested in God in the abstract, but

108. In 1959, Merton wrote *The Inner Experience* to revise the views on contemplation that he had expressed in his previous book, *What is Contemplation?* In 1968, when *The Inner Experience* was republished, he added some things to the 1959 text and made minor corrections. Shannon claims that the 1959 text was a "bridge" between the early and later Merton. For the first time, Merton forged "a link with Eastern religious thought." See IE, xiv.

109. During the writing of the book, on July 12, 1959, Merton stated in his journal, "This week I have been rewriting 'What Is Contemplation?'. . . . How poor were all my oversimplified ideas." See Thomas Merton, *A Search for Solitude: Pursuing the Monk's True Life,* ed. Lawrence Cunningham (San Francisco, CA: HarperSanFrancisco, 1996), 303 (hereafter SS). He also confessed that "a lot of Zen people read *The Ascent to Truth* . . . it is my wordiest and in some ways emptiest too." See DWL, 116.

110. See Thomas Merton, *The Road to Joy: The Letters of Thomas Merton to New and Old Friends,* ed. Robert E. Daggy (New York, NY: Farrar, Strauss, Giroux, 1989), 233 (hereafter RJ).

in the experience of God revealing himself in the intimate embrace of Love. In contrast to his approach in the previous two books, he now saw that "contemplative experience . . . is not arrived at through any step-by-step process. It is something you either 'see' or don't see. It just bursts upon you, and is there."[111] He attempted to avoid the traditional distinction between "acquired and infused contemplation," because "the legitimacy of this division has been hotly contested by theologians."[112] Rather, he described contemplation based on "a distinction made by the Greek Fathers: that between natural contemplation (*theoria physike*) and theology (*theologia*), or the contemplation of God."[113] Moreover, he admired the "active contemplatives" who had penetrated the secular world to bear witness to God's love.[114]

The Inner Experience can be seen as a confluence of Merton's deep knowledge of the traditional concepts of contemplation found in the church fathers, the Scriptures, the Rhenish and Spanish mystics, modern psychology, and existential philosophy, as well as his exposure to and experience of non-Christian traditions, such as Zen Buddhism and Taoism. In particular, he appreciated that Eastern contemplative traditions had a great deal to contribute to the Western contemplative tradition. He noted, "As we grow in knowledge and appreciation of oriental religion we will come to realize the depth and richness of its varied forms

---

111. IE, 81.

112. Ibid., 66.

113. Ibid., 67. According to Merton, natural contemplation (*theoria physike*) is "the intuition of divine things in and through the reflection of God in nature and in the symbols of revelation," and pure contemplation (*theologia*) is "a direct quasi-experiential contact with God beyond all thought, that is to say, without the medium of concepts." See ibid., 67–68.

114. For instance, Merton noted, "The most significant development of the contemplative life 'in the world' is the growth of small groups of men and women. . . . [T]hey *are* Christ. And where they are present, Christ is present. . . . This of course is a strictly contemplative view of the Christian life." See ibid., 142, 144 (emphasis in original).

of contemplation."[115] Beyond religious boundaries, his view of contemplation had expanded from a focus on the inner self to an awakening to universal Reality through the inner experience. Moreover, *The Inner Experience* revealed that his early romantic fantasies of contemplation had been mellowed by his discovery of the universality of contemplative experience.

His new existential and experiential approach blossomed in his book *New Seeds of Contemplation* (1962), which was a revised version of *Seeds of Contemplation* (1949). In this book he constructed his own definition of contemplation as one that originated from a far richer contemplative experience:

> Contemplation is the highest expression of . . . intellectual and spiritual life. It is that life . . . fully awake, fully active, fully aware that it is alive. . . . It is a vivid realization of the fact that life and being in us proceed from an invisible, transcendent and infinitely abundant Source. Contemplation is . . . [an] awareness of the reality of that Source. . . . Contemplation is a sudden gift of awareness, an awakening to the Real within all that is real. A vivid awareness of infinite Being at the roots of our own limited being.[116]

Merton's use of the terms "abundant Source," "Real," and "Being" instead of "God" reveals his new understanding of the universality of contemplation, and his frequent use of the terms "awareness," "awakening," "void," "nothingness," "emptiness," and "enlightenment" in the same book indicates his involvement with Zen Buddhism. In the last chapter of the book, "The General Dance," he connected Christian contemplation with Zen enlightenment: "We hear an old frog land in a quiet pond with a solitary splash—at such times the awakening, the turning inside out of all values, 'the

---

115. Ibid., 32. Properly, Merton understood and appreciated Asian thought that could lead him to a deeper and wiser understanding of his own magnificent mystical tradition. See TMR, 303.

116. NSC, 1–3.

newness,' . . . the emptiness . . . provide a glimpse of the cosmic dance."[117] The new understanding of contemplation that Merton put forth in *New Seeds of Contemplation* was attained through his experience of self-emptying in Christ and through his encounter with the Eastern traditions of his day.

Merton's new approach to contemplation was further developed in *The Climate of Monastic Prayer*, written between 1963 and 1965. The book provided monks and all Christians with a practical method of arriving at an experience of contemplation in a more integrated and incarnational framework. He did not discriminate between the contemplative and the active lives in true contemplative prayer. Rather, he suggested that when a contemplative person prays deeply with purity of spirit, contemplation and action are "fused into one entity by the love of God and of our brother in Christ."[118] He wrote, "We do not reason about dogmas of faith, or 'the mysteries.' We seek rather to gain a direct existential grasp, a personal experience of the deepest truths of life and faith, *finding ourselves in God's truth*."[119] The book also explored the traditional Christian spirituality of the Desert Fathers, Pseudo-Dionysius, Meister Eckhart, and St. John of the Cross in *modern* language.[120]

117. Ibid., 297.

118. Thomas Merton, *The Climate of Monastic Prayer* (Washington, DC: Consortium Press, 1973, 1ˢᵗ ed. 1969), 153 (hereafter CMP). This book was also published under the title *Contemplative Prayer* in 1969.

119. Ibid., 92 (emphasis in original).

120. For example, Merton had different ways of explaining a *dark night* in the spirituality of St. John of the Cross. In his early book *The Ascent to Truth*, he stressed an "asceticism" and a "blackout of desire." He wrote that "the key word in each of his [St. John of the Cross's] rules for entering into the ascetic night is the word 'desire.'" See AT, 52–54. In *The Climate of Monastic Prayer*, Merton explained the *dark night* with "enlightenment" and a "perfect light." He noted, "God brings . . . people into darkness . . . in order to fill them with a higher and purer light. . . . The darkening is therefore at the same time an enlightenment. The reason that the light of faith is darkness to the soul is, says St. John, that this is in reality an *excessive light*." This change demonstrates what he said in an introduction to this book: "We will appeal to ancient texts on

Merton modernized the concept of contemplation to make it clear that it was for all Christians. As he noted on the last page of the book, "Without contemplation and interior prayer the Church cannot fulfill her mission to transform and save mankind."[121]

In his article "Final Integration: Toward a 'Monastic Therapy,'" written in 1965, Merton defined the final integration of contemplation as a state of transcultural maturity at a universalizing level.[122] In and through contemplation he saw that it would be possible to establish a spiritual family of human beings who were not separated by religious and cultural boundaries. His last writings reflected his increasing attraction to dialogue with Eastern contemplatives, and during his journey to Asia he suggested that "contemplative dialogue" and "intermonastic communion" were the way to bond the world's "spiritual family."[123] Merton invited all people to universal communion through true love, a love at the core of everyone's inner being that could be awakened by contemplation. He believed that in this "very love itself and nowhere else" contemplatives could find themselves, the world, and Reality, and could connect with one another.[124] He saw that contemplation was not a "question of either-or but of all-in-one," not a "matter of exclusivism and 'purity,' but of wholeness, wholeheartedness, unity . . . which finds the same ground of love in everything."[125] He realized that when one attained the maturity of full contemplative awareness in one's own religious and cultural context, a truly universal consciousness would also emerge in that person in the form of openness to others and spiritual freedom.

---

occasion, but our development of the theme will be essentially modern." See CMP, 62–63 (emphasis in original), 34.

121. Ibid., 154.

122. The phrase "final integration" was not specifically a Buddhist-inspired notion but came from a Persian psychoanalyst, Dr. Reza Arasteh, who was interested in Sufism, Zen, and other Eastern traditions. See CWA, 200–212.

123. AJ, 316; MZM, x.

124. CWA, 153.

125. Ibid.

In summary, through dynamic interaction between his own contemplative experience and his encounter with Zen Buddhism, Merton's traditional view of contemplation in Christianity was reconstructed to a Buddhist-Christian view of contemplation. He discovered that the final integration of contemplation was a state of transcultural or transreligious maturity at a universalizing level that could be attained in one's own specific religious context. This realization became a key point of Merton's interreligious dialogue, a topic to be developed in the following section.

Relationship between Inner Experience and Interreligious Dialogue

Merton's own inner experiences, in particular the Louisville Epiphany and the Polonnaruwa Enlightenment Experience, exemplify his understanding of the relationship between inner experience and interreligious dialogue. An examination of these two experiences will help explicate the importance of spiritual maturity and the value of the inner experience for Buddhist-Christian dialogue and inter-monastic dialogue.

Nondualistic Perspective and Openness: The Louisville Experience

Merton's Louisville Epiphany at the corner of Fourth and Walnut illustrated that religious experience could bring about a nondualistic outlook as well as openness to others. Until the early 1950s, Merton felt torn between being a writer and being a contemplative, and at the same time, he possessed a privileged view of the monastic vocation vis-à-vis the laity and the secular world. Yet his dualistic view of himself as both monk and writer and his privileged stance gradually evolved in the mid-1950s. The religious experience of his Louisville Epiphany in 1958 offered him a new awareness of himself and a new paradigm for contemplation and interreligious dialogue.

Merton realized what he had attained from the experience and he could describe it in detail. He became aware that he loved all the people passing by on the street in Louisville. He experienced a mystical unity with them. He noted:

> In Louisville . . . I was suddenly overwhelmed with the reali-
> zation that I loved all those people. . . . I am still a member
> of the human race. . . . It was like waking from a dream of
> separateness, of spurious self-isolation in a special world, the
> world of renunciation and supposed holiness . . . the concep-
> tion of 'separation from the world' . . . [was] a complete illu-
> sion: the illusion that by making vows we become a different
> species of being, pseudo-angels, 'spiritual men,' men of interior
> life, what have you . . . 'thank God that I *am* like other men,
> that I am only a man among others.'. . . It is because I am one
> with them that I owe it to them to be alone, and when I am alone
> they are not 'they' but my own self. There are no strangers![126]

Through the Louisville experience, he became aware that he was connected with all human beings. He awakened from "a dream of separateness" and realized himself as "a member of the human race." All people were his equals. This religious experience en-nobled him to be gratefully aware of his humanity. It also played a significant role in the renewal of his vocation to God and God's people. The world was no longer regarded as an *object*. He ac-knowledged that he had "a sort of stereotype of the world-denying contemplative," and it was his "own fault."[127] He realized that the contemplative life was communion with God, and with God's people, in love. Contemplative life, he said, "is not a matter of *either* God *or* man, but of finding God by loving man and dis-covering the true meaning of man in our love for God. Neither is

---

126. CGB, 153–155 (emphasis in original).
127. CWA, 141.

possible without the other."[128] This insight would likely affect his integration of contemplation and action. In this integrated view, he opened his mind and heart toward others and the world, and began to feel obliged to love people as they were loved by God.

This shift in consciousness obviously was not a question of black or white. Before the experience at Louisville, Merton already had an inkling of nondualism between the love of God and the love of God's people (cf. Matt 22:34-40; 25:31-46). From the teaching of the Bible as well as from the light of reason, he knew that the love of God could not be separated from the love of neighbor. In *No Man is an Island* (1955), he appreciated the fact that all people retained the "image of God" and could be one in the mystical body of Christ through their love for one another.[129] However, this was an abstraction. Through a profound movement at the experiential level in Louisville, Merton came to a radically new awareness of his own and others' identity, in both his mind and heart. He discerned that in Louisville, "the touch of [God's] hand makes me a different person."[130] He reflected, "What matters is . . . the love that brings him back to all the others in one Christ. This love is not our love but the Divine Bridegroom's. . . . God is seen and reveals Himself as *man*, that is, in us, and there is no other hope of finding wisdom than in God-manhood: our own manhood transformed in God!"[131] The self-transformational experience in Louisville led him to his "second conversion."[132]

---

128. Thomas Merton, *Faith and Violence: Christian Teaching and Christian Practice* (Notre Dame, IN: University of Notre Dame Press, 1968), 262 (emphasis in original) (hereafter FV).

129. See NMI, xv, 245, 252.

130. Thomas Merton, *The Intimate Merton: His Life from His Journals*, ed. Patrick Hart and Jonathan Montaldo (San Francisco, CA: HarperSanFrancisco, 1999), 125 (hereafter IM).

131. Ibid., 125–126 (emphasis in original).

132. Robert Inchausti, *Thomas Merton's American Prophecy* (Albany, NY: State University of New York Press, 1998), 71.

Merton's subsequent radical social engagement and his involvement in interreligious dialogue became an outgrowth of his Louisville Epiphany. For instance, on November 10, 1958, Merton wrote a remarkable letter to Pope John XXIII in which he stated his realization that he, as a contemplative monk, could offer abundant apostolic opportunities without any need "to lock [himself] into solitude and lose all contact with the rest of the world."[133] Regarding his openness to other religions subsequent to his Louisville Epiphany, Merton began to incorporate Buddhist terminology in order to explain his new understanding of contemplation in *The Inner Experience*, which was largely written in 1959, and in his letters to D.T. Suzuki, which began in March 1959. Early in his monastic life, Merton's sense of Western superiority prevented him from forming any deep friendships with Eastern contemplatives. After Louisville, things changed. For example, on May 28, 1966, meeting with Thich Nhat Hanh, a Buddhist monk, Merton said, "Nhat Hanh is *my brother.*"[134] His changed attitude toward other people as well as toward Eastern religions following his Louisville Epiphany leads one to conclude that this religious experience was a significant factor in bringing about his openness to others, his sense of solidarity with the world, and his interest in interreligious dialogue that so marked the next decade of his life.

Cross-Cultural Religious Experience: The Polonnaruwa Experience

As a Christian contemplative monk, Merton employed Christian categories and terminology to express and interpret his religious experience. However, he turned to Buddhism to elucidate his experience at Polonnaruwa in Sri Lanka. On December 2, 1968, Merton was deeply moved by the mammoth Buddhist figures at

133. HGL, 482.
134. Thomas Merton, *Passion for Peace: The Social Essays*, ed. William H. Shannon (New York, NY: Crossroad, 1997), 261 (emphasis added) (hereafter PP).

Polonnaruwa and experienced some dramatic form of spiritual enlightenment. He described this most important experience of his entire Asian trip as follows: "I was suddenly, almost forcibly, jerked clean out of the habitual, half tired vision of things, and an inner clearness, clarity, as if exploding from the rocks themselves, became evident and obvious."[135] The spiritual enlightenment he gained through this mystical experience offered him a new awareness of what is ineffable. Although Merton himself could not fully capture the experience in words, what he wrote makes it clear that what occurred was absolutely extraordinary:

> Polonnaruwa was such an experience that . . . I was knocked over with a rush of relief and thankfulness at the *obvious* clarity of the figures, the clarity and fluidity of shape and line, the design of the monumental bodies composed into the landscape, figure, rock and tree. . . . Looking at these figures . . . there is no puzzle, no problem, and really no "mystery." All problems are resolved and everything is clear, simply because what matters is clear. The rock, all matter, all life, is charged with dharmakaya . . . everything is emptiness, everything is compassion. I don't know when in my life I have ever had such a sense of beauty and spiritual validity running together in one aesthetic illumination. Surely, with . . . Polonnaruwa my Asian pilgrimage has come clear and purified itself. I mean, I know and have seen what I was obscurely looking for. I don't know what else remains but I have now seen and have pierced through the

135. AJ, 233–235. Walter Conn claims that "this description of the Polonnaruwa experience has significant similarities with Merton's understanding of the Zen breakthrough experience of satori." See Walter Conn, *The Desiring Self: Rooting Pastoral Counseling and Spiritual Direction in Self-Transcendence* (New York/Mahwah, NJ: Paulist Press, 1998), 129. John Dadosky also argues that through the Polonnaruwa experience, Merton "is mediated by way of the giant Buddha images to an immediacy that is presumably Zen-like in character. He cannot describe it in Western vocabulary." See John D. Dadosky, "Merton as Method for Inter-Religious Engagement: Examples from Buddhism," *The Merton Annual* 21 (2008): 41.

surface and have got beyond the shadow and the disguise. . . .
It is we, Asians included, who need to discover it. The whole
thing is very much a Zen garden, a span of bareness and openness and evidence, and the great figures, motionless, yet with
the lines in full movement, waves of vesture and bodily form,
a beautiful and holy vision.[136]

Following this aesthetic illumination, Merton expressed mystical
experience in terms of such common qualities as quiet, isolation,
simplicity, freshness, no "mystery," openness, and wholeness. The
expressions "emptiness and fullness" and "love and compassion"
encapsulated aspects of the spiritual journey in both Mahayana
Buddhism and Christianity.[137] Merton's experience of the divine
presence as he stood before the statue of Buddha imbued him with
a sense of spiritual freedom and compassionate love. His description, "everything is emptiness (*sunyata*), everything is compassion

---

136. AJ, 230–236 (emphasis in original).

137. Buddhism has several lineages that are linked with a certain country or
the teachings of certain masters. The first main lineage is Theravada Buddhism,
which follows the oldest record of the Buddha's teachings; monastics in this
lineage train in the attainment of enlightenment and an ethic of non-harming. The
lineage spread to Southeast Asia, particularly to Sri Lanka, Myanmar, Cambodia,
Laos, and Thailand. The second main lineage, Mahayana Buddhism, follows the
path of the *bodhisattva*, which focuses on seeking complete enlightenment for
the benefit of all sentient beings. It is widespread in Inner Asia and East Asia.
In Inner Asia, Mahayana represents Tibetan Buddhism, which concentrates on
the *Vajrayana* stage, that is, "cutting off ordinary perception and, acting from
the pure perspective of a Buddha, embodying all the virtues." In East Asian
Mahayana, the Chinese developed *Tiantai* (The Lotus School), which focuses
on self-discipline as well as on compassion for others, but omits the *Vajrayana*
stage, and also developed *Huayan* (Flower Garland), which teaches that everything is the Buddha and is based on the *Avatamsaka Sutra* (Flower Ornament
Scripture). The *Tiantai* divided into Zen Buddhism and Pure Land Buddhism,
which are the popular forms of Buddhism in East Asia (China, Korea, and Japan)
and Vietnam today. In Vietnam, Theravada and Chinese Mahayana Buddhism
coexist as a form of various syntheses. See Roger Corless, "An Overview of
Buddhism," in *Merton & Buddhism*, 3–12.

(*karuna*)," is perhaps his way of suggesting that the experience of the mystery of God can be spoken of within a Buddhist as well as a Christian framework. It resonates with "the [Christian] dialectic of the All and the Nothing, *todo y nada*" in the spirituality of St. John of the Cross and the Buddhist understanding of *sunyata* as the primary element of enlightenment.[138] Merton encountered the divine presence in all things, including other religions, through the experience of *kenosis*, and he unearthed the fullness of love and compassion as the ground of all being. This powerful *satori*-like experience represented for him the possibility of "crossing over religious experience" between Buddhism and Christianity.[139]

His interpretation of the experience was a culmination and validation of his dialogue with Buddhists in the 1960s. Joseph Raab, a Merton scholar, points out that "Merton's dialogue with Zen Buddhism became an obvious choice to focus on given Merton's own level of interest in that tradition and the influence of that tradition helping to facilitate his religious experience in Polonnaruwa."[140] Donald Grayston, a former president of the International Thomas Merton Society, claims that Merton "arrived at the first level of *bodhisattvahood*. . . . Whatever the deepest meaning of the experience, it is clear that the Polonnaruwa illumination represents

---

138. MZM, 212; cf. Raab, *Openness and Fidelity*, 89. Merton claimed that psychologically, Buddhist *sunyata* (emptiness) exactly corresponded with the dark night of St. John of the Cross. See MZM, 242.

139. The theologian John Dunne argues that "passing over" or "crossing over" to other religious experiences is possible as well as enriched and deepened by the experience and "coming back" with new insight to one's own religion. See John S. Dunne, *The Way of All the Earth: Experiments in Truth and Religion* (New York, NY: Macmillan, 1972), ix–x; Lawrence Cunningham claims that Merton was "crossing over" to the realm of Asian religions. See Lawrence Cunningham, "Crossing Over in the Later Writings of Thomas Merton," in *Toward an Integrated Humanity*, 197–198.

140. Raab, *Openness and Fidelity*, 8.

the peak experience of Merton's journey."[141] However, Shannon argues that the Polonnaruwa experience of a sudden and climactic enlightenment should not be interpreted as if it had no relation to his previous life.[142] Merton used similar language when speaking of unexpected experiences that had occurred previously. For example, one of the expressions Merton used to describe his experience at Polonnaruwa—"I have seen what I was obscurely looking for"—was also used by him to describe what he felt in Rome as he stood before a Byzantine fresco in 1933, what he felt when he was allowed to make occasional use of St. Anne's hermitage in 1953, and what he felt when he took up residence in his new hermitage in 1965.[143]

Merton also spoke, however, of what occurred at Polonnaruwa as an experience of enlightenment: "I was suddenly, almost forcibly, jerked clean out of the habitual" and "everything is emptiness and everything is compassion."[144] Raab points out that "at Polonnaruwa Merton had reached the pinnacle of self-emptying in 'dzogchen,' that he had finally gotten lost in that 'great realization' where the totality of the experience of love, freedom and awe became perfectly clear and distinct."[145] In fact, in his conversation with Chatral Rinpoche seventeen days before this experience, Merton confessed that he had still not attained enlightenment. The experience at Polonnaruwa was a "realization, an actualization, of

---

141. Donald Grayston, "In the Footsteps of Thomas Merton: Asia," *The Merton Seasonal* 33 (Winter 2008): 26 (emphasis in original). Merton's long-time friend Edward Rice claims that Master Thomas was an "Incarnate Buddha." See Edward Rice, *The Man in the Sycamore Tree: The Good Times and Hard Life of Thomas Merton* (New York, NY: Doubleday & Company, 1970), 139.

142. See Shannon, *Silent Lamp*, 276–278.

143. See ibid., 68–70.

144. AJ, 233, 235.

145. Raab, *Openness and Fidelity*, 92. Furlong argues that in Polonnaruwa, Merton "had released the love and joy in his heart that he had been seeking all his life, that he had come home, and the home was God." See Furlong, *Merton: A Biography*, xix.

what he had been seeking in all his encounters with other religions, namely, an experience of the ineffable essence of the religion."[146]

Even though the Polonnaruwa awakening was not a unique moment of sudden enlightenment in his life, this *satori*-like experience was an extremely powerful kenotic transformation and the fulfillment of self-transcendence, which he had never experienced before. Since he died shortly after this experience, we cannot be certain in what directions he would have gone or how he would have subsequently interpreted this experience. However, there can be little doubt that for him Polonnaruwa was an experience of enlightenment, and this experience influenced his interreligious encounter at a deep spiritual level beyond his own particular religious context.

Merton's Contributions to Contemplative Experience

Thomas Merton's contemplative experiences brought about a transformation of his consciousness, a new view of contemplation, and an openness to others. At the same time, his openness to and dialogue with other religions, especially Buddhism, led him to attain deep inner experiences through this immersion and to come to a deeper appreciation of contemplation in Christianity. In this dynamic process, Merton's inner-mystical experiences on contemplative life can be evaluated under three headings: 1) the importance of religious experience in the transformation of human consciousness, 2) the development of a new view of contemplation, and 3) the value of the inner experience for Buddhist-Christian dialogue.

The Role of Religious Experience in the Transformation of Human Consciousness

Merton's life and work exemplify the significant role of religious experience in the transformation of human consciousness. His

---

146. Robert H. King, *Thomas Merton and Thich Nhat Hanh: Engaged Spirituality in an Age of Globalization* (New York, NY: Continuum, 2001), 119.

various inner-mystical experiences facilitated a new consciousness morally, psychologically, religiously, spiritually, and universal in scope. For example, in Havana his vision of "heaven" in the Church of St. Francis could be described as an experience of the transcendent God of the Old Testament that made possible a new *religious* consciousness for Merton. In Louisville, his vision of God in ordinary people on the street could be interpreted as an immersion in the immanence of God that facilitated his moral and psychological healing and his new *human* consciousness.[147] In Polonnaruwa, his enlightenment experience before the statue of the Buddha could perhaps be described as the experience of the universality of the Holy Spirit that facilitated his *universal* consciousness. Merton's ongoing transformation of consciousness through these experiences illustrates two significant functions of such transformative experiences: 1) they facilitate a new consciousness through union with the divine consciousness and 2) they transform social consciousness through a new personal consciousness.

First, Merton shows that inner-mystical experience could facilitate an awareness of a new consciousness through union with the divine consciousness. According to Shannon, there was a double movement: Merton entered through an inner experience and transcended himself to arrive at divine consciousness. He recognized and accepted his inner-mystical experience as a blessing, yet he became increasingly aware of the tension between the blessing of the experience and the inevitable burdens this divine gift placed on him. He finally was able to integrate this tension, which led to a transformed consciousness.[148] Merton proposed that this state was not "consciousness of" but "*pure consciousness*, in which the subject as such 'disappears.' "[149] He called the

---

147. In Havana, Merton noted, "Heaven is right here in front of me: Heaven, Heaven!" In Louisville, he saw that "the gate of heaven is everywhere." He was not concerned about "heaven" in Polonnaruwa, but realized that "everything is emptiness and everything is compassion." See SSM, 312; CGB, 156; AJ, 235.

148. See Shannon, *Silent Lamp*, 15.

149. ZBA, 24 (emphasis in original).

resulting experience of pure consciousness the *transcendent self*, meaning that the self is no longer conscious of itself as a subject, but rather experiences itself as a "no-self" that perfectly identifies with the divine consciousness.[150] In the transcendent experience, individuals really undergo self-transformation and are aware of themselves "as a self-to-be-dissolved in self-giving, in love, in 'letting-go,' in ecstasy, in God."[151] Thus, Merton understood that one could be united with God or Reality at the deepest center of consciousness and could attain a new mode of being in the world and a new relationship to the world.[152]

Second, Merton discovered the importance of the transformation of *individual* consciousness, which was the basic and universal path for the transformation of *social* consciousness. Near the end of his life, he stressed the transformation of individual consciousness since he saw that human and social problems were rooted in individuals.[153] Alexander Lipski, nonetheless, is harshly critical of Merton's approach, claiming that through personal transformation Merton was "seeking a more perfect society either in the past, the European Middle Ages, or in the non-Western

150. See ibid., 71–72.

151. Ibid., 24. However, Buddhism, Hinduism, and Christianity have different ways of expressing the concept of "losing or dissolving one's self." Buddhists describe it as "no-self," which means relinquishing one's self and returning to the void. In Hinduism, *Atman* (the Self), the unified being, is *Brahman* (the Universal Ground of Being) and becomes all by losing one's self. In Christianity, the purpose of losing one's self is to attain the new self through union with God. The individual self does not disappear into God but by denying one's self is reborn in Christ.

152. See David Cooper, "Thomas Merton and the New Theology," in *Toward an Integrated Humanity*, 158.

153. See AJ, 332–333. Merton believed that transformation of human consciousness was an urgent quest for those who groaned at the ills of the modern world and craved spiritual transformation, perhaps because they sensed that "the problem [was] no longer merely political or economic . . . [but] a spiritual problem of a society." See FV, 174.

world, Asia. . . . [But] Merton conveniently ignored the fact that a truly contemplative civilization had never existed even in Asia."[154] However, Lipski may overlook the fact that contemplation is not merely a "civilization" in the Western sense, but an inner transformation through union with God or Reality, and that there were deep contemplative traditions in Asia from which Merton suggested Christians could learn. He also does not seem to understand that for Merton, social engagement, as an extension of one's inner experience, did not mean setting up "a more perfect society," but rather developing a social consciousness and "a true universal consciousness in the modern world."[155]

On the other hand, Merton proposed in the 1960s that a new personal consciousness founded on religious experience could establish new horizons of openness, love, compassion, freedom, and holiness for the world. In addition, through his dialogue with Buddhism, Merton came to the realization that the transformation of human consciousness was the universal ground and common goal of the human journey in both Eastern and Western religious traditions.[156] Thus, he claimed that the final integration of the spiritual journey not only involved psychological consciousness but demanded a "total inner transformation" and "universal consciousness" through self-emptying and self-transcendence.[157]

154. Alexander Lipski, *Thomas Merton in Asia: His Quest for Utopia* (Kalamazoo, MI: Cistercian Publications, 1983), 1, 11.

155. AJ, 317.

156. As Merton put it, "Christianity and Buddhism look primarily to a transformation of man's consciousness." See ibid., 332–333. The Dalai Lama also agreed that the development of a new consciousness through spiritual practice could influence a transformation of social consciousness that would lead to genuine world peace. See The Dalai Lama, "His Holiness, the Dalai Lama," in *Merton by Those Who Knew Him Best*, ed. Paul Wilkes (San Francisco, CA: Harper & Row, 1984), 146–147.

157. AJ, 340, 317; CWA, 203–206.

Merton's Contributions in a New View of Contemplation

An analysis of the early and later writings of Merton on the topic of contemplation discloses that his exposure to Eastern religious traditions affected his understanding of contemplation and provided him with the wherewithal to offer a more modern understanding of contemplation. Reflecting on his own direct experiences, he tried to determine precisely what union with God or Reality meant and how one could achieve this union through contemplation. Merton's altered view of contemplation can be described in two ways: 1) he discovered a new direction for contemplation and 2) he modernized the traditional view of contemplation.

First, Merton clarified the stages of contemplation: its starting point is finding the true self, its goal is union with God or an awakening to Reality, and its fruit is openness and sharing of compassionate love with others. Merton began his search for God not from outside the self but *inside* the self. He stated, "Our real journey in life is interior: it is a matter of growth, deepening and of an ever greater surrender to the creative action of love and grace in our hearts."[158] He claimed that if contemplative life was conceived merely in classical categories such as "a life of withdrawal, tranquility, retirement, silence," and rigid ascetical disciplines for the monk only, it would be "finished" for his contemporaries.[159] However, if contemplative life developed out of a process of "new self-discovery," proceeded with real discipline, and was at the same time theologically sound, the contemplative life could be renewed for *all* people.[160]

The meaning of the inner self became a fundamental and central issue for Merton. Since he believed that God was present in the depths and the ground of all human beings and that the seeds of contemplation were planted in the inner self, for Merton, the

158. AJ, 296.
159. CWA, 224.
160. See ibid., 224–226.

deepest self was not the "I" or "ego" of everyday consciousness but the inner and hidden self, the deepest reality of the human person in which he or she was truly sustained by a most fundamental union with God as the Ground of being.[161] The realization of this union with God through delving into one's inner world was the goal of contemplation. Thus, an awakened person's life was revealed by openness and compassionate love for others, the fruits of contemplation. Merton's new path of contemplation was similar to that of the Mahayana Buddhist tradition, especially the way of the *bodhisattva*, who lived in freedom and compassionate love for the salvation of all people after attaining enlightenment through finding the true self. The similarity of the contemplative path between Buddhist and Christian traditions will be dealt with in more detail in the following chapter.

The second contribution of Merton's new concept of contemplation was that he extended it to the whole human world. The mature Merton confessed, "how mistaken I was to make contemplation only *part* of a man's life. For a contemplative man's whole life is contemplation."[162] He realized that in the contemplative life, union with God in Christ was not only for monastics in the

161. Merton's understanding of "the hidden self" and "the ground of being" echoes his understanding of *Atman* (the Self) and *Brahman* (the Universal Ground of Being) in Hinduism. In 1967, in his letter to Amiya Chakravarty, a Hindu scholar, Merton described his understanding of *Atman* and *Brahman* as synonyms for "Being," "the Pneuma," or "Silence," and "the hidden ground of Love" that is present to and in the self. Moreover, in 1965, in his letter to Philip Griggs, a Hindu scholar, Merton wrote that "man is divine *not by nature but by grace*, that is to say that his union with God is not an ontological union in one nature but a personal union in love and in the Holy Spirit . . . in Christ. For a Catholic, this applies to Hindu saints as well as any other." However, he questioned "whether the Vedantic [one of the six orthodox schools of Hinduism] position is really conveyed in its fullness by treating *Atman* as a concept of *Nature*." See HGL, 115, 339–340. From the perspective of self-transcendence, he considered a self-realization of *Atman* in the same line with the Void in Buddhism, life in Christ in Christianity, and *fana* (annihilation) and *baqa* (reintegration) in Sufism. See AJ, 310.

162. SS, 303 (emphasis in original).

cloister but for anyone. In fact, until the middle of the twentieth century, contemplation was rarely discussed in relation to ordinary Christians, and mystical theology was considered to be something esoteric or extraordinary. He saw that "the term 'contemplative life,' already in some ways suspect theologically today, [was] used more and more negatively as the 'non-active' life . . . [and was] being used defensively as an excuse to keep monks in the monastery."[163] According to Merton, however, contemplation was an *experience* of oneness and of transcendent unity, which was open to anyone, since "the direct and pure experience of reality in its ultimate root is man's deepest need."[164] Indeed, many contemplatives outside the cloister were longing for some experience of God or Reality and for attaining a new consciousness as a living and personal reality in their life. Merton opined, however, that "the seeds of contemplation and sanctity, planted in [human being's] souls, merely lie dormant. They do not germinate. They do not grow," unless one enters into prayer.[165] Thus, Merton invited all people to enter into contemplative prayer to search for their inner selves and, hopefully, to find God or Reality through the experience of self-transcendence.

The Value of the Inner Experience for Buddhist-Christian Dialogue

Buddhist nontheist religious experience differs from the supernatural category of Christianity, and its expressions or interpretations are distinct from theist religious experience.[166] Merton dealt

---

163. SCL, 342.

164. IEW, 65.

165. IE, 48.

166. Yaroslav Komarovski, a Buddhist scholar, argues that Buddhist mystical experience must be interpreted from within the context of a Buddhist worldview, using the category of "(un)mediated mystical experience," rather than the categories of theistic and non-theistic—to which one might respond that mysti-

with the issue between the nondualistic experience of Buddhism and the theistic mystical experience of Christianity in his writings.[167] Although he was still grappling with the problem between "the strongly personalistic tone of Christian mysticism" and the Buddhist impersonal language of a Zen experience, he discovered that religious experience was useful for Buddhist-Christian dialogue

---

cal experience transcends all categories. See Yaroslav Komarovski, "Buddhist Contributions to the Question of (Un)mediated Mystical Experience," *Sophia* 51 (2012): 87–88. Michael Stoeber discovers the similarity between Buddhist and Christian meditation by going beyond religious categories and exploring the progress and dynamics of mystical contemplative meditation in the Christian mystical tradition (e.g., in the prayer of Recollection by Evelyn Underhill and contemplative prayer by St. Teresa of Avila) and Buddhist *Samatha Vipassana* (calming insight). He claims that "in both Christian Recollection and Buddhist Insight meditation participants become familiar with their thoughts and feelings and their processes and patterns, and are able to free themselves from habitual attachments to them." See Michael Stoeber, "Exploring Progresses and Dynamics of Mystical Contemplative Meditation: Some Christian-Buddhist Parallels in Relation to Transpersonal Theory," *European Journal for Philosophy of Religion* 7, no. 2 (Summer 2015): 41–42. In his encyclopedic article "The Comparative Study of Mysticism," Stoeber observes that beyond Western hegemony, which tends to see Asian mystical traditions through the lens of Christian anthropology and theology, there is "an intimate relationship between [Buddhist] non-dual and [Christian] theistic experiences in some mysticism across various religions, where a personal and creatively dynamic mystical idea is only realized through a radically static immersion in or oneness with Reality." See Michael Stoeber, "The Comparative Study of Mysticism," in *The Oxford Research Encyclopedia of Religion* (September 2015), http://religion.oxfordre.com/view/10.1093/acrefore/9780199340378.001.0001/acrefore-9780199340378-e-93.

167. For instance, in a letter to Erich Fromm on February 7, 1966, he wrote, "We had some discussion on the question of a non-theistic religious experience. The point I was trying to convey was that religious experience in the Jewish, Christian, Zen Buddhist or in a general mystical human way, is an experience which may not be different as a human experience in the case of a theist or a non-believer." See unpublished in the archives of the Thomas Merton Center, Bellarmine University; cited in William H. Shannon, *Thomas Merton's Paradise Journey: Writings on Contemplation* (Cincinnati, OH: St. Anthony Messenger Press, 2000), 234.

because of *the differences*.[168] Zen experience was not something beyond human nature, even though it went beyond human reason. Through the discovery of "a Zen core" of experience in the great religions, he reoriented his dialogic method from an intellectual approach to the experiential approach of Buddhism and learned from Buddhism different expressions of inner experience.[169]

In the 1960s, Merton immersed himself in the study of the Eastern religious experience. He discovered that the inner experience manifested in Buddhism could contribute to spiritual renewal and enrichment for Christians and could also become a bridge for Buddhist-Christian dialogue. If we consider the current pattern of Buddhist-Christian dialogue, we can see that Merton's existential and experiential approach played a prophetic role.[170] His role will be discussed in more detail in the following chapter. At this point, his discovery of the value of the inner experience for Buddhist-Christian dialogue can be evaluated by examining: 1) the significance of experiential dialogue with Buddhists and 2) the mutual enrichment and challenges of exchanging ways of understanding and expressing religious experience.

Recognizing the importance of the inner experience in Buddhist-Christian dialogue, Merton moved from the mind to the heart in his dialogue with Buddhists and Buddhism. Before the mid-1950s, he considered all forms of Eastern mysticism, including Buddhism, as techniques and natural religions, which he tried to understand intellectually. Later, he acknowledged that he was mistaken in taking this approach: "I was tempted to cut out my own

---

168. ZBA, 135.

169. Addison H. Hart argues that Merton discovered that "every religion has a Zen core." See Addison H. Hart, *The Ox-herder and The Good Shepherd: Finding Christ on the Buddha's Path* (Grand Rapids, MI: Eerdmans, 2013), 62.

170. See Michael Barnes, "Theological Trends: The Buddhist-Christian Dialogue," *Way* 30, no. 1 (January 1990): 56–61; Peter C. Phan, "Multiple Religious Belonging: Opportunities and Challenges for Theology and Church," *Theological Studies* 64 (2003): 496–497, 509–513.

'final remarks' in the dialogue because they [Buddhists] are so confusing. Not that they are 'wrong' . . . because any attempt to handle Zen in theological language is bound to miss the point."[171] He modified his previous comparative theological approach and evolved toward an experiential and existential approach to Buddhism. He noted, "[Zen] is a 'way' and an 'experience,' a 'life,' but the way is paradoxically 'not a way.' "[172] After his discovery of the value of inner experience in Buddhism, Merton began to regard Buddhism more in terms of "acts emerging out of a certain quality of consciousness and of awareness" in order "to share in the values and the experience which they embody."[173] He saw that the Zen enlightenment experience could lead to transformation of consciousness and that it could include the experience of union with Reality or Being. Like the Zen experience, "the heart of Catholicism, too, is a *living experience* of unity in Christ which far transcends conceptual formulations."[174] He appreciated that both religions began from a transcendent experience beyond a sensate experience at the primary level of consciousness, and that they have similar practical methods for it. These discoveries helped him to discover the importance of a dialogic path at a deep spiritual experiential level in Buddhist-Christian dialogue.

Second, through an understanding of the different ways of expressing the Buddhist inner experience, Merton became aware that a dialogue of religious experience with Buddhists could provide mutual enrichment and challenges. He saw that the religious experience could not be programmed, promoted, or discovered, and that it was ultimately ineffable. Thus, sharing different interpretations of religious experience with contemplatives of other religions could be helpful for enriching the spiritualities of both religions. For example, Merton was enriched by the concept of

171. ZBA, 139.
172. MZM, 12.
173. Ibid., ix.
174. ZBA, 39 (emphasis in original).

enlightenment or *nirvana,* which was not simply a psychological experience but went *beyond experience.* He described *nirvana* as an experience of "Absolute Emptiness" and "Absolute Compassion" that went beyond human emotional experience and had to be understood in terms of "full realization, total awakening, the wide openness of Being itself."[175] He stated, "*My* experiences . . . are more and more woven into the great pattern of the whole experience of man and even something quite beyond all experience."[176] Shannon argues that through sharing religious experience with Asian traditions, Merton "began to understand that the Logos of God is not a Western Word but a divine-human Word speaking in diverse ways and in varied cultures to all women and men of good will."[177] Merton was enriched through experiential dialogue and attempted to interpret Christian contemplative experience in the light of Buddhist enlightenment experience, doing so for the spiritual renewal of Christianity. These efforts became his pioneering work for Buddhist-Christian dialogue.

Conclusion

From the accounts in *The Seven Storey Mountain* to *The Asian Journal,* Thomas Merton's writings allow us to trace his spiritual journey as the record of an ongoing transformation of consciousness through the experience of emptiness and fullness. For example, his experience of emotional and psychological emptiness in childhood was now filled by the love of God, whereas his *kenosis* experience in his monastic life was complemented by the contemplative experience, "the experience of the transcendent and inexpressible God."[178] His experience of emptiness and nothing-

175. Ibid., 86.
176. CGB, 247 (emphasis in original).
177. Shannon, *Silent Lamp,* 272.
178. NSC, 2. Merton noted, "This dynamic of emptying and of transcendence accurately defines the transformation of the Christian consciousness in

ness not only led him to self-transcendence but also generated for him a bridge between Buddhism and Christianity. On a profound spiritual level, Merton discovered the possibility of contemplative dialogue with all contemplatives who sought the transformation of human consciousness through the experience of enlightenment within their respective spiritual traditions.

Merton's contributions to a broader and deeper understanding of inner-mystical experience could be summarized as follows. First, he showed that the mystical experience could contribute to the spiritual healing of one afflicted by psychological wounds and moral sins. Merton himself bore the burden of the psychological wounds he received in his childhood and adolescence as well as the sins he committed. His struggles with his past life continued until the mid-1950s. Through mystical experience, however, especially his Louisville Epiphany, his wounds from the past were healed and his consciousness was transformed and reoriented. He knew he was loved by God and called to return that love.

Second, Merton showed that a deep contemplative experience of being born again in Christ could facilitate the attainment of a new identity for both lay people and religious. As his interior journey progressed, his inner awareness of his union with Reality led him to a spiritual rebirth. He wrote, "This deep consciousness to which we are initiated by spiritual rebirth is an awareness that we are not merely our everyday selves but we are also one with One Who is beyond all human and individual self-limitation."[179] For Merton, this contemplative awareness was ultimately a discovery of the true self in God, a sudden awareness of the fact that one's whole being was filled with Reality. This awakening of the true self was not the awakening of rational consciousness, but a

---

Christ. It is a kenotic transformation, an emptying of all the contents of the ego-consciousness to become a void in which the light of God or the glory of God, the full radiation of the infinite reality of His Being and Love are manifested." See ZBA, 75.

179. L&L, 198.

deep spiritual consciousness that was an "insatiable . . . diamond of spiritual awareness" that took a person beyond the level of one's individual ego.[180] In this new consciousness, the self of the awakened person is transformed "with a new set of activities and a new lot of religious practices," since one's new self is "divinized in Christ" and lives in spiritual freedom and love with openness to others.[181] Merton concluded that the direct experience of God could lead one to see that God is everywhere and that everything is connected. An experiential awareness of the immanence of God and the interdependence of all things call contemplatives to take full responsibility for the world in which they live.

Third, Merton contributed to a fuller understanding of religious experience by his rediscovery of the value of his own Catholic contemplative tradition and his contribution to a more modern and integrated understanding of it through dialogue with the Buddhist traditions. The Desert Fathers and Mothers and the great mystics of the Christian tradition were not speculative theologians but theologians of contemplative experience. Merton went beyond the Western tendency of approaching the Eastern traditions intellectually. By emphasizing an experiential approach to them, he came to understand that the transformation of consciousness through transcendent experience was the common ground and goal of both the Eastern and Western contemplative traditions. His experiential dialogue with Buddhist traditions helped him to develop a synthetic and more modern understanding of contemplation and to open a new path for interreligious dialogue and inter-monastic exchange.

---

180. Thomas Merton, *The New Man* (New York, NY: Farrar, Straus & Cudahy, 1961), 208 (hereafter NM); William H. Shannon, "Thomas Merton and the Discovery of the Real Self," in *The Message of Thomas Merton*, ed. Patrick Hart (Kalamazoo, MI: Cistercian Publications, 1981), 196.

181. L&L, 200; Thomas Merton, *Life and Holiness* (New York, NY: Herder and Herder, 1963), 60 (hereafter LH); cf., NM, 48.

Merton's universal view of religious experience thus generated a radical shift in the Western understanding of contemplation, which was influenced by Hellenic and Cartesian philosophy and had been affected by those modern philosophers who proclaimed the "death of God."[182] In his article "New Consciousness," he suggested that one of the reasons individuals turned to Asian traditions was because they had inherited the distorted understanding of them propagated by the strong anti-metaphysical prejudice of modern Western philosophy.[183] In the new climate following Vatican II, he discovered the value of *the experience of Asian religions* for a new spiritual consciousness and a new way of interreligious dialogue, one that recognized the importance of Christian contemplation. Against the background of Merton's understanding of contemplation and his inner experience, the following chapter will explore Merton's pioneering contributions to Buddhist-Christian dialogue.

182. ZBA, 23.
183. See ibid., 18–19, 25, 29–32.

CHAPTER 2

Merton's Pioneering Work with Buddhist-Christian Dialogue

The climate among religions today has gradually evolved from that of isolation to one of mutual relation through friendlier dialogue and cooperation. For example, when Pope Francis spoke to a gathering of Buddhist and Christian religious leaders on June 24, 2015, he said, "[This] is a visit of fraternity, of dialogue, and of friendship, and this is good. This is healthy. And in these moments, which are wounded by war and hatred, these small gestures are seeds of peace and fraternity."[1] His Holiness Dalai Lama in a similar manner also emphasizes the "necessity of friendship as a basis for genuine dialogue, one that reaches a profound level of mutual recognition of each other's traditions, their equal authenticity, and their intrinsic complementarity."[2] Persons engaged in interreligious dialogue are opening their minds

---

1. "Pope Francis, Catholics, Meet with Buddhists at Vatican" (June 25, 2015), https://www.lionsroar.com/pope-francis-catholics-meet-with-buddhists-at-vatican.

2. Cited in Wayne Teasdale, "The Ocean of Wisdom as Human and Spiritual Presence," in *Understanding the Dalai Lama*, ed. Rajiv Mehrotra (New York, NY: Hay House, 2008), 106.

and hearts to each other's religion and considering ways to build a world community out of our divided societies.

Despite doctrinal differences, dialogue between Buddhists and Christians has occurred frequently. We may classify the main areas in Buddhist-Christian dialogue under three headings: 1) the dialogue of *religious experience*, 2) the dialogue of *theology*, and 3) the dialogue of *action*. As we shall see, in dialogue with Buddhism these issues are interconnected. For example, experience has shown that without dialogue between praxis and spirituality, Christians cannot really understand Buddhist theology. Moreover, without being grounded in dialogue as related to spirituality and social practice, there can be no real progress toward communion.

In this regard, Thomas Merton is one of the pioneers of Buddhist-Christian dialogue. He strove for an integrated dialogic path based on actual experience and for contemplative dialogue that facilitates openness to others and leads to friendship and self-transformation. Today, Merton's knowledge of Buddhism can be questioned, but his contemplative experience and paths of dialogue still provide a model for Buddhist-Christian dialogue. Merton's journey toward his inner self through his continuous spiritual development, his openness to learning from others, and his transcendent experiences, offer a personal and spiritual model that enhances interreligious dialogue. DIMMID and other scholars are presently attempting to improve upon his insights regarding Zen and to give greater attention to his encounter with Tibetan Buddhism.

This chapter will explore how Merton paved new avenues for Buddhist-Christian dialogue. To this end, his encounter with Buddhists and Buddhism during his lifetime will be examined. This section will help to understand how his attitude toward Buddhists changed from seeing them initially as pagans to regarding them as teachers, friends, and brothers. Second, the chapter will present Merton's understanding of Buddhism intellectually, experientially, spiritually, and practically to demonstrate that his knowledge of Zen and Tibetan Buddhism was advanced for his time. Finally, the chapter will examine Merton's three areas for promoting

Buddhist-Christian dialogue. It will evaluate his contribution to the project and also speak to the limitations of his undertaking.

Merton's Encounter with Buddhists and Buddhism in His Life's Journey

Merton's life exemplifies a process of development: the methods and the goals of Buddhist-Christian dialogue. In a dramatic way, he experienced a personal transformation from exclusivism to openness, from triumphalism to respect, and from simply talking to a deeper listening that preceded the Catholic Church's more positive view of Eastern religions as signified by the Second Vatican Council (1962–1965). The documents of Vatican II provided added incentive for the kind of monastic and contemplative dialogue with Eastern traditions that Merton envisioned.[3]

Merton encountered Eastern traditions, including Zen, in the process of exploring his own understanding of contemplation. These traditions had a significant influence on his view of the relationship between contemplation and openness to others. In order to grasp Merton's understanding of the relationship between contemplation and dialogue in Buddhist-Christian relations, it is beneficial to explore how his familiarity with Buddhism developed. Bonnie Thurston divides Merton's acquaintance with Buddhism into three periods: premonastic (1937–1941), monastic (1941–1968), and Asian (1968).[4] Evidence of Merton's interest in Zen prior to his entrance into the monastery is very limited, as is also true of the first fifteen years or so of his monastic life. However, in *The Inner Experience*, written in 1959, Merton presented the fruit of a deep interest in Zen that began in the mid-1950s.

---

3. See Thurston, "Thomas Merton: Pioneer of Buddhist-Christian Dialogue," 128.

4. See Bonnie B. Thurston, "Unfolding of a New World: Thomas Merton & Buddhism," in *Merton & Buddhism*, 15–22.

William Shannon claims that *The Inner Experience* is the first time in Merton's writings that he linked his notion of Christian contemplation to Eastern religious thought.[5] Therefore, another way of showing Merton's increasing interest in Buddhism is by dividing it into three periods: The Exploratory Period (1937 to the mid–1950s), The Transformational Period (1959 to 1968), and The Intensive and Enlightened Period (1968).

The Exploratory Period: 1937 to the mid-1950s

The exploratory period commenced when Merton read Aldous Huxley's book *Ends and Means* in 1937. This book stimulated Merton's attraction not only to mysticism in general but to an apophatic mysticism that would later enable him to relate it to Buddhist teachings about the void and emptiness.[6] However, when he initially encountered Asian thought, he looked at Buddhism through the lens of Christian soteriology and considered the practice of Zen to be primarily a useful practical tool. He noted, "The emphasis on technique, on bodily control, on interior discipline in both Oriental and Orthodox mysticism makes me realize how supremely indifferent we are to techniques. I have never had any method of contemplation."[7] He also believed that Buddhism led to nihilism or heresy because of what he considered to be its life-denying emphasis on self-emptying.

---

5. See IE, xiv.

6. The most important effect of Huxley's book on Merton was to make him "start ransacking the university library for books on Oriental mysticism." See SSM, 204. Fabrice Blée argues that "under the influence of Aldous Huxley, Merton was deeply moved by the thought that employing mystical techniques could bring about peace, tolerance, and charity, ideals dear to his heart. However, his study of the East at this point in his life was superficial and scattered, and ultimately without much fruit." See Fabrice Blée, *The Third Desert: The Story of Monastic Interreligious Dialogue*, trans. William Skudlarek and Mary Grady (Collegeville, MN: Liturgical Press, 2011), 40.

7. ES, 402; cf. SSM, 205.

In 1949, however, Merton's view of Buddhism gradually became more positive and he became absorbed in the practice of Zen. For instance, on June 4 he was impressed by the talk Archbishop Paul Yu-Pin of Nanking gave to the monastic community at Gethsemani. Merton wrote that the archbishop spoke about "China and the contemplative life and Buddhist monasticism—and about the reproach that Buddhists fling at us, that is, we are all very fine at building hospitals but we have no contemplatives."[8] On November 24, Merton's interest in contemplation can be seen in his correspondence with a Hindu in Simla about Patanjali's yoga in which he asked him to send some books. He also wrote about a Hawaiian chemist, a former Zen postulant, who spoke to the monastic community about Zen Buddhism.[9]

In the mid-1950s, Merton's reading of Suzuki's works deepened his interest in Zen. He referred to Zen as an important instrument of his "apostolate" and began to see similarities between the spirituality of the Desert Fathers and Zen Buddhists.[10] These similarities included a search for the true self, an orientation toward self-transcendence, the use of *koans* and sayings, and the acceptance of suffering in the self-emptying process. After his Louisville Epiphany in 1958, when he was overwhelmed by the realization that he loved all people and that people could not be alienated from one another, he further opened his mind and heart to other religions, including Buddhism. Thus, we can say that Merton's interest in Zen and Buddhism did not emerge abruptly

8. SJ, 197.

9. See ibid., 243.

10. See SS, 48, 57, 232, 272–273. Shannon clams that "[Merton's] studies in the mystical tradition of the West—the Egyptian fathers, St. Basil, Pseudo-Dionysius, St. Bernard and other Cistercian writers, Eckhart, St. John of the Cross, and so many others—gave him the elements of a way of viewing life and reality that finally prepared him to return to Eastern thought with an openness and an appreciation such as he could not have had earlier. He became an articulate and highly respected interpreter of Eastern thought to the Western world." See Shannon, *Silent Lamp*, 279.

in the mid-1950s; it had been slowly developing during the twenty years following his reading of Huxley's book.

The Transformational Period: 1959–1968

After writing his book *The Inner Experience* (1959), and prior to his journey to Asia, Merton's attitude toward Buddhists was completely transformed. He no longer regarded them pejoratively, but positively as friends and brothers. He studied Zen and Mahayana Buddhism so assiduously that this period can be aptly called his Transformation through Zen (1959–1968). Following the publication of his book *The Wisdom of the Desert* in 1959, Merton began an earnest dialogue with Buddhists and Buddhism, especially with D. T. Suzuki, who at that time was the major interpreter of Zen for the Western world. Merton stated that "[the] uniqueness of Dr. Suzuki's work lies in the directness with which an Asian thinker has been able to communicate his own experience of a profound and ancient tradition in a Western language."[11] He deepened his understanding of Zen through reading Suzuki's books, corresponding with him, and meeting with him in New York in 1964.[12] Merton also met or corresponded with Dr. John C. H. Wu, Fr. Heinrich Dumoulin, SJ, Masao Abe, Marco Pallis, and Thich Nhat Hanh, among others, and he wrote many books and articles related to the Asian traditions.[13] His correspondence with

11. ZBA, 63. Thurston argues that "during the monastic years Merton's study focused on the Mahayana tradition of Zen, perhaps because it was most readily available to him in an English translation. There is no question but that Suzuki was formative in his understanding of Zen." See Thurston, "Unfolding of a New World," 17.

12. Merton's correspondence with Suzuki began in 1959 and continued until Suzuki's death in 1966.

13. These included *The Way of Chuang Tzu* (1965), *Mystics and Zen Masters* (1967), *Zen and the Birds of Appetite* (1968), "Christian Culture Needs Oriental Wisdom" (1962), "Zen: Sense and Sensibility" (1963), "The Zen Revival" (1964), and "The Zen Insight of Shen Hui" (1965).

Buddhists and Buddhist scholars helped him modify his earlier ideas about Zen. He now stated that "it is quite false to imagine that Zen is a sort of individualistic, subjective parity. . . . It is not a subtle form of spiritual self-gratification. . . . Nor is it by any means a simple withdrawal from the outer world of matter to an inner world of spirit."[14] Under the influence of dialogue with Buddhists, Merton's enriched understanding of Zen contributed to his spiritual transformation, especially in the area of the integration of contemplation and action through nondualistic thought in Buddhism. His interest in social justice and in other Asian religions emerged from this expanding worldview.[15]

Through friendship with Buddhists, Merton saw the possibility of interreligious dialogue between Zen and Christianity in "a common spiritual climate."[16] He recognized that Zen could help Christians attain spiritual growth and integration, and it could also transform modern Western culture in a profound way.[17] He believed that sharing common spiritual ground in fellowship with Zen practitioners could contribute to a transformation of consciousness for his contemporaries.

In 1965, the Second Vatican Council's Declaration on the Relationship of the Church to Non-Christian Religions (*Nostra Aetate*) also influenced his encounter with Buddhism. He emphasized the Council's statement that "the Catholic Church rejects nothing which is true and holy in [other] religions . . . [that they might] often reflect a ray of that Truth which enlightens all men (no.

---

14. MZM, 13. Merton commented that a Buddhist neither "simply turns away from a world . . . [nor] cultivates meditation in order to enter a trance and eventually a complete negative state of *Nirvana*. But Buddhist 'mindfulness,' far from being contemptuous of life, is extremely solicitious [*sic*] for all life." See ZBA, 93.

15. See Larry A. Fader, "Beyond the Birds of Appetite: Thomas Merton's Encounter with Zen," *Biography* 2, no. 3 (May 1979): 234.

16. ZBA, 138.

17. See ibid., 59.

2).″[18] In the light of that truth, Merton's dialogue with other traditions, especially Buddhism, accelerated through greater respect for those traditions and from a deeper understanding of them.

The Intensive and Enlightened Period: 1968

The Intensive and Enlightened Period began in 1968 when Merton journeyed to Asia, where he looked forward to having "face-to-face, monk-to-monk" encounters with Buddhists.[19] During his time in Asia, his meetings with Theravada and Tibetan Buddhist monks helped to extend his understanding of Buddhism, which had been limited to Mahayana Buddhism prior to his Asian journey. He was especially impressed by the profound spiritual depth of the Tibetan rinpoches and lamas, including the Dalai Lama, whom he encountered in Dharamsala. At Polonnaruwa in Sri Lanka, a predominantly Theravada context, Merton experienced a kind of spiritual enlightenment before the statue of the Buddha. Thus, these two months in Asia could be called the Intensive and Enlightened Period.

Although he read some books about Tibetan Buddhism before his journey, it had not been possible for him to encounter Tibetan Buddhists since they had not yet migrated to America in any substantial way. In the course of his Asian pilgrimage, however, he had the opportunity to meet various Tibetans, lamas, and rinpoches who had gone into exile in India following the destruction of Tibetan civilization by their Chinese conquerors in the late 1950s.

The first Tibetan guru he met was Chögyam Trungpa Rinpoche, the youngest *tulku* (reborn master of Tibetan Buddhism) with whom Merton spoke. On October 19, 1968, the very day Merton arrived in India, they met at the Central Hotel in Calcutta. Merton wrote in his journal that "Chögyam Trungpa is a completely marvelous person. Young, natural, without front or artifice, deep awake wise . . . [and] a genuine spiritual master. . . . His own

18. MZM, ix.
19. Thurston, "Unfolding of a New World," 18.

meditations and talks, from what I have seen, are extraordinary."[20] Trungpa was also impressed by Merton's open heart and deep spirituality, and felt like "an old friend, a genuine friend."[21] Trungpa and Merton talked about "spiritual materialism," which is "spiritual practice or life used to promote and confirm personal status, reputation, and identity."[22] Their meeting showed that the way beyond spiritual egotism in the contemplative life involved "befriending one's own state of being without the intention of changing or improving it . . . [since] two such authentic human beings should recognize each other immediately as genuine friends."[23] In their bonding, Trungpa gave Merton a copy of the *Sadhana* text, which had provided inspiration to Trungpa himself in his search for the best teaching to overcome spiritual materialism.[24] Through meeting with Trungpa, Merton reconfirmed the value of friendship and a common spiritual concern in Buddhist-Christian dialogue.

A few days later, Merton met with the Nyingma lama, Chokling Rinpoche, a *dzogchen* master and founder of a Tibetan monastery in Bir near Dharamsala.[25] They questioned each other about

20. AJ, 30–31.

21. Chögyam Trungpa, *The Collected Works of Chögyam Trungpa III*, ed. Carolyn Rose Gimian (Boston, MA: Shambhala, 2003), 477.

22. Simmer-Brown, "The Liberty that Nobody Can Touch," 58.

23. Steven R. Shippee, "Trungpa's Barbarians and Merton's Titan: Resuming a Dialogue on Spiritual Egotism," *Buddhist-Christian Studies* 32 (2012): 120–121.

24. According to Simmer-Brown, "[t]he *sadhana* introduces the practitioner to the antidote to spiritual materialism, a genuine spirituality that awakens the naked and luminous mind." See Simmer-Brown, "The Liberty that Nobody Can Touch," 60. A month later, Merton and Trungpa briefly met again at the Canadian High Commissioner's home in Calcutta. In his address on "Marxism and Monastic Perspectives" at the meeting in Bangkok, Merton referred to him as "a good friend of mine—a very interesting person indeed." See AJ, 337–338.

25. Before meeting with Chokling, Merton met Khamtrul Rinpoche, who was known as a *dzogchen* master. In the meeting, Khamtrul was interested in Merton's investigation of meditation and spoke "about the need for a guru and direct experience rather than book knowledge; about the union of study and meditation." See AJ, 89.

enlightenment and reincarnation. Chokling spoke of the need of finding a master and meeting with some of the tulkus in India. When Chokling asked him "a koanlike question about the origin of the mind," he seemed pleased with Merton's non-answer.[26] Judith Simmer-Brown, a specialist in Merton and Tibetan Buddhism, comments that "Chokling Rinpoche's testing and interrogation of Merton was excellent preparation for his later meeting with [Chatral] Rinpoche."[27] Chokling introduced Merton to *phowa* transmission through "an esoteric practice associated with realization of the ultimate nature at death."[28] Merton learned about a new way of enlightenment through the practice of conscious dying from the Tibetan Rinpoche.

On November 4, Merton had his first meeting with His Holiness the Dalai Lama in Dharamsala. The conversation was congenial and progressed in an atmosphere of mutual respect. He described the Dalai Lama as "a very solid, energetic, generous and warm person . . . a very consecutive thinker."[29] Their conversation was about philosophy and religion, especially the way of meditation. Merton was impressed with the Dalai Lama's clear explanation regarding *dzogchen* meditation. The Dalai Lama advised him to get a good basis in the *Madhyamika* "middle way" school.[30] Merton also talked about his personal concerns about Tibetan mysticism. The Dalai Lama described his concerns about partial and distorted Western views of Tibetan mysticism. The first meeting showed that dialogue on contemplative life was a familiar theme of Buddhist-Christian dialogue.

---

26. Ibid., 97.

27. Simmer-Brown, "The Liberty that Nobody Can Touch," 66.

28. Ibid., 83. *Phowa*, one of Tibetan Buddhist meditation practices, can be described as transference of consciousness at the time of death. About a month later Merton passed away, and Chokling Rinpoche's son Dzigar Kongtrul Rinpoche comments, "Maybe [Chokling] Rinpoche saw what was coming and gave the transmission to help [Merton]." See ibid.

29. AJ, 101, 113.

30. See ibid., 101–102, 115–116.

On November 6, Merton had his second meeting with the Dalai Lama. They discussed epistemology, *samadhi*, various theories of Tibetan Buddhism, and Western Thomistic knowledge, and their conversation returned to the question of *samadhi* and meditation. Merton emphasized that meditation was important for monastics since it could facilitate spiritual freedom and the transformation of consciousness. The Dalai Lama not only showed him the Tibetan meditation posture but also explained using the mind itself to achieve a stage of *samadhi* in "the sense of controlled concentration."[31] In his letter to friends, Merton described what he learned from the Dalai Lama:

> The Tibetans have a very acute, subtle, and scientific knowledge of "the mind" and are still experimenting with meditation. . . . [T]he highest mysticism is in some ways quite "simple"—but always and everywhere the Dalai Lama kept insisting on the fact that one could not attain anything in the spiritual life without total dedication, continued effort, experienced guidance, real discipline, and the combination of wisdom and method.[32]

Merton enjoyed learning about Tibetan meditation and mysticism. Through their lively conversation, he realized that the Dalai Lama's ideas of the interior life were built "on very solid foundations and on a real awareness of practical problems."[33] He was impressed with the Dalai Lama's integrated view between

---

31. Ibid., 112. Talbott remembers the Dalai Lama's instructions at that meeting that "he gave us very, very clear, sound meditation instructions that would be completely familiar to Vipassana practitioners. He was leading up to teachings on emptiness and compassion and then went on to a gentle explanation of tantra as a field of Mahayana Buddhism." See Helen Tworkov, "The Jesus Lama: Thomas Merton in the Himalayas, An Interview with Harold Talbott," in *Tricycle: The Buddhist Review* 4, no. 1 (Summer 1992): 19.

32. AJ, 322.

33. Ibid., 113.

detachment from worldly life and participation in the problems of the world, and also with his humility.

Merton considered that his third meeting with the Dalai Lama, on November 8, was in some ways the best. The Dalai Lama asked many questions regarding Western monastic life. And Merton asked the Dalai Lama about Marxism and monasticism, which was a topic of his upcoming address for the Congress in Bangkok. Then they discussed the last topic of their meeting—mind. Merton noted, "We got into a rather technical discussion of mind, whether as consciousness, prajna or Dhyana, and the relation of prajna to sunyata."[34] Their dialogue at a deep spiritual level produced a very warm and cordial conversation, and they became very close friends. In great respect and fondness, Merton realized there was a real spiritual bond between them.

Subsequent encounters with other rinpoches deepened Merton's appreciation of Tibetan spirituality. On November 16, Merton met with Chatral Rinpoche, one of the great living masters of *dzogchen*, at his hermitage. There was an instant mutual recognition without barriers between them. Merton was deeply impressed by him: "the greatest rimpoche [*sic*] I have met so far and a very impressive person."[35] Chatral also instantly recognized Merton's profound spiritual level and said, "Let's see who can get enlightened first."[36] Chatral called Merton a "rangjung sangay" (naturally arisen Buddha) and predicted that they perhaps would attain complete enlightenment in their next lives, or even in this life.[37] They mostly talked about the idea of *dzogchen* and shared Christian doctrine regarding the risen Christ, their current stage on the way to perfect enlightenment, and four preliminary practices of *ngondro* (foundation ritual practices). Chatral's complete simplicity and freedom offered Merton a vivid example of the spiritual

34. Ibid., 125.
35. Ibid., 143.
36. Thurston, "Footnotes to the Asian Journey of Thomas Merton," 230.
37. AJ, 144.

depth of Tibetan Buddhism through intensive practice, *dzogchen*. Merton wished to see more of Chatral, the best of the *Nyingmapa* lamas, and asked the Rinpoche to become his teacher. There was no doubt that Merton was greatly moved by Tibetan Buddhists. He concluded:

> I can say that so far my contacts with Asian monks have been very fruitful and rewarding. We seem to understand one another very well indeed. . . . I find that the Tibetans above all are very alive and also generally well-trained. . . . [T]hey are also specialists in meditation and contemplation. . . . I do not say they are all saints, but certainly they are men of unusual quality and depth, very warm and wonderful people.[38]

During his time in Asia, Merton became all the more convinced of the indispensable need for monastic interreligious dialogue between Eastern and Western religions. He realized that inter-monastic dialogue, based on contemplation, would lead to "the growth of a truly universal consciousness . . . of transcendent freedom and vision."[39] However, his untimely death cut short his first intensive experiential dialogue with Eastern monks.

Merton's Understanding of Zen and Tibetan Buddhism

Merton attained a richer horizon regarding Christian teachings through his encounter of the Zen understanding of the self.[40] Despite the doctrinal differences between Zen and Christianity,

38. Ibid., 324.
39. Ibid., 317.
40. For example, when David Steindl-Rast questioned Merton about his relationship between the new understanding of Christian teaching and his exposure to Buddhism, Merton replied, "I think I couldn't understand Christian teaching the way I do if it weren't in the light of Buddhism." See Robert Aitken and David Steindl-Rast, *The Ground We Share: Everyday Practice, Buddhist and Christian* (Boston: Shambhala, 1996), 47.

he realized that the two traditions share a "psychic 'limitless-ness' in common, [and] they tend to describe it in much the same language."[41] Thus, this section will explore what Merton discovered as an enrichment in understanding of Christian teachings from Zen.

For Merton, the core of Zen went beyond religious systems, and this plays a significant role in his new understanding of the ways he could move forward in Buddhist-Christian dialogue. We will further compare Christian ways for arriving at contemplative awareness with Buddhist ways for coming to enlightenment. Attention will be paid to the meaning of finding the true self. Finally, Merton's understanding of Tibetan Buddhism will be focused on the practice of *dzogchen*, as taught by the Nyingma school of Tibetan meditation.

Zen as a Transreligious and Transformed Consciousness

The word *"Zen"* derives from the Sanskrit term *dhyana* and translates as "meditation" or "contemplation." Basically, according to Chalmers, there are two ways of defining Zen: First, from a historical and cultural perspective, Zen is a Buddhist school of meditation that developed in China (the sixth century), Korea (the seventh century), and Japan (the eighth century). The second definition of Zen is that it is a "meta-religion" that essentially goes beyond any particular religious structure or tradition.[42] Merton's study of Zen led him to adopt the second definition. He denied that Zen was merely a method of meditation or a countercultural lifestyle that belonged exclusively to a certain school of Buddhism. The aim of Zen is ultimate liberation to a pure void beyond dualistic division. Such liberation comes about not through teaching but through awakening of the inner self. Hence, he defined Zen as "the ontological *awareness of pure being beyond subject and object*, an

---

41. ZBA, 8.

42. See Chalmers MacCormick, "The Zen Catholicism of Thomas Merton," *Journal of Ecumenical Studies* 9, no. 4 (Fall 1972): 803.

immediate grasp of being in its 'suchness' and 'thusness.' . . . For want of a better term, we may call it 'purely spiritual.' "[43]

Zen does not deny human life and the world; it is the very awareness of life. According to Merton, Hui Neng, the great Sixth Patriarch of *Ch'an* (禪) Buddhism, taught that "the Zen discipline consisted in seeking to realize . . . wholeness and unity of *prajna* [wisdom] and *dhyana* [meditation] in all one's acts. . . . Zen could not be found merely by turning away from life to become absorbed in meditation. Zen is the very awareness of life living itself in us."[44] This Zen approach to life led Merton to the realization that Zen was essentially contemplative and that it could offer Christians spiritual enrichment "in the way of inner purification and freedom from systems and concepts."[45] Moreover, since Zen neither affirms nor denies the existence of a Supreme Being—"it simply *is*"—he saw that it could be fused into many theistic religions or no religion at all as a view of reality or a way of being in the world.[46] He noted that "[Zen] can shine through this or that system, religious or irreligious, just as light can shine through glass that is blue, or green, or red, or yellow."[47] This understanding of the nature of Zen led Merton not only to a deep affinity for Buddhism but to the discovery of the possibility of Buddhist-Christian dialogue at a deeper spiritual level.

The Japanese term "Zen" comes from Chinese *Ch'an*, a fusion of Mahayana Buddhism with Taoism and Confucianism that is native to China.[48] Merton saw that Zen (*Ch'an*), a common element

43. MZM, 14 (emphasis in original).

44. Thomas Merton, "The Zen Revival," *Continuum* 1 (Winter 1964): 531 (hereafter ZR). Merton noted, Zen is "nondoctrinal, concrete, direct, existential, and seeks above all to come to grips with life itself, not with ideas about life." See ZBA, 32.

45. HGL, 443.

46. ZR, 527 (emphasis in original). See also ZBA, 4; MZM, 13–14.

47. ZBA, 4.

48. See Hsueh-Li Cheng, "Confucianism and Zen (Ch'an) Philosophy of Education," *Journal of Chinese Philosophy* 12 (1985): 197–215.

of Taoism, Confucianism, and Buddhism, could enrich Christian spirituality. His view was influenced by Aelred Graham's book, *Zen Catholicism*. In a letter to Graham, Merton wrote, "I liked the book so much . . . [Zen] is actually a life-saver for many people, here at the exhausted end of an era in which thinking has been dominated by Cartesianism, Kant and so on."[49] Both Merton and Graham saw that Zen was not in conflict with the Catholic faith, and they encouraged Christians to explore Zen for their spiritual growth.[50]

Merton knew, of course, that there were irreducible differences between Christianity and Zen; that comparing them would be like "trying to compare mathematics and tennis."[51] However, he saw that beyond the intellectual level, a Zen enlightenment experience was compatible with a Christian contemplative experience. He stated, "Zen is . . . not revelation but consciousness, [and it is] awareness of the ontological ground of our own being here and now. . . . Zen is perfectly compatible with . . . Christian mysticism."[52] His understanding of Zen enlightenment was integral to his new view of contemplation, which was defined as "a sudden gift of awareness, an awakening to the Real within all that is real . . . beyond knowledge and method."[53] The following section will explore in more detail what Merton discovered as the Zen core in Christian contemplative life.

The No-Self in Zen and the True Self in Christianity

Merton's understanding of *anatta* (the no-self in Zen) contributed to his spiritual journey and allowed him to discover his true self through detachment from the ego or false self. He observed

49. SCL, 167.
50. See ZBA, 58.
51. Ibid., 33.
52. Ibid., 47.
53. NSC, 1–3.

that "we are plagued today with the heritage of that Cartesian self-awareness, which assumed that *the empirical ego* is *the starting point* of an infallible intellectual process to truth and spirit."[54] In opposition to Descartes, he claimed that the central goal of the monastic spiritual tradition is the transcendence of our empirical ego. He noted that "[our] superficial 'I' [or ego] is not our real self. . . . Nothing could be more alien to contemplation than the *cogito ergo sum* of Descartes."[55] Going beyond Cartesian self-awareness, he saw that "[the] whole question of 'ego-self' and 'person' [true self is] a matter of crucial importance for the dialogue between Eastern and Western religion."[56]

Merton's encounters with Zen led him to conclude further that our inner or true self is not "a part of our being . . . [and] cannot be held and studied as [an] object, because it is not 'a thing.' "[57] Moreover, he wrote that "only when there is no self left as a 'place' in which God acts . . . do we at last recover our 'true self' (which is in Zen terms 'no-self')."[58] The true is the Void.[59] How, then, does Merton reconcile finding the true self in God with the "no-self" in Zen, which has no subject-object relationship?

In response to this question, Merton attempted to overcome the split between subject and object in the discovery of the inner self. While Zen seeks an immediate disappearance of a subject-object duality through an experience of enlightenment, Christianity sees "an infinite metaphysical gulf between the being of God and the being of the soul, between the 'I' of the Almighty and our own inner 'I.' "[60] Despite the metaphysical gap between God and self,

54. MZM, 26 (emphasis added).

55. NSC, 7–8.

56. ZBA, 77.

57. IE, 6–7.

58. ZBA, 10.

59. See ibid., 74.

60. IE, 12. Zen Buddhism teaches that the subject-object relationship with one's self will become one and then disappear when Enlightenment is achieved. William Johnston comments that "what he [Merton] stated well and with rough

Merton claimed that "there is always a possibility that what an Eastern mystic describes as Self is what the Western mystic will describe as God, because we shall see presently that the mystical union between the soul and God renders them in some sense 'undivided' in spiritual experience."[61] He acknowledged that transcending the dualism of subject and object was possible in Christ, since "in the Incarnation . . . [Christ] has become not only one of us but even our very selves."[62] Through detachment from one's ego and losing one's self by imitating Christ's *kenosis*, one's self can be born again in Christ and live in his freedom and love.[63] The awakened person can come to the realization that there is no separation between the subject and the object, and that everything is one: "It is no longer I who live, but it is Christ who lives in me (Gal. 2:20)."[64]

That is, by going beyond the subject-object dichotomy in Christianity, Merton discovered a connection between the true

---

clarity is that Zen goes beyond all categories and all duality. . . . In certain areas of apophatic experience the subject-object relationship disappears, and this is . . . simply another way of experiencing God." See William Johnston, *Christian Zen* (New York, NY: Harper & Row, 1971), 23.

61. IE, 13.

62. SS, 381. Merton wrote that "the 'true Self' . . . is manifested in the basic unification of consciousness in which subject and object are one. Hence the highest good is 'the self's fusion with the highest reality.' " See ZBA, 69.

63. See LH, 60. James Finley points out that one's struggle in finding a true self is a blessing that arises when one becomes a new being through the contemplation of God in Christ, and that is made possible by participating in Christ's contemplation of the Father in the unity of the Holy Spirit. Hence, in Finley's view, through finding the true self, Merton could become Godlike and become God's own action. See James Finley, *Merton's Palace of Nowhere: A Search for God through Awareness of the True Self* (Notre Dame, IN: Ave Maria Press, 1978), 107–120.

64. See ZBA, 5, 75, 117. Merton noted that "by a paradox beyond all human expression, God and the [inner self] seem to have but one single 'I.' They are (by divine grace) as though one single person. They breathe and live and act as one." See IE, 18.

self and the no-self, which could be disclosed by transcending the ego-self through the transcendent mystical experience; the true self is fused with the highest reality or disappears into the Nothingness of God. Through understanding of the no-self in Buddhism, he realized that the notion of the no-self may become a bridge for connecting Christianity and Buddhism via the process of self-emptying or *kenosis*. He believed that Buddhist-Christian dialogue must "be sought in the area of the true self-transcendence and enlightenment. It is to be sought in the transformation of consciousness in its ultimate ground, as well as in its highest and most authentic devotional love."[65] Thus, he saw that the way of self-emptying or self-transformation through self-forgetfulness or self-losing could become the basic principle for Buddhist-Christian dialogue.

Purity of Heart and the Apophatic Mystical Way and Sunyata (Emptiness or Void)

Through John Cassian's understanding of purity of heart as the intermediate end of the contemplative life, Merton strove to describe *sunyata* as the emptiness of Zen. Yet he acknowledged that although Cassian's purity of heart roughly corresponded to Suzuki's term "emptiness," there was "a significant difference" between the two concepts.[66] The ultimate end of the Christian monk's contemplative striving is not purity of heart, but the kingdom of God, and the latter has no place in the realm of Zen. He therefore regretted choosing Cassian's purity of heart in order to express emptiness in his dialogue with Suzuki. While purity of heart contained "Platonic implications" and a "transcendent fulfillment of personality," emptiness in Buddhism completely denied every dualistic view and personality.[67] He confessed that he was

65. AJ, 316.
66. ZBA, 131.
67. Ibid., 9, 117–118.

not prepared to discuss this complex question and suggested that the relationship between the Christian "purity of heart" and the "emptiness" of Zen should be further studied.[68]

Merton also brought the apophatic mystical traditions of Christianity into dialogue with the cryptic and enigmatic expression of emptiness in Zen. More concretely, he brought the perspectives of Meister Eckhart and St. John of the Cross to bear upon the concept of emptiness in Christian spirituality and Zen.

Merton appreciated that "[an] expression of Zen in Christian experience [was] given by Meister Eckhart."[69] Eckhart, the thirteenth-century mystical theologian, noted that all concepts of God must be abandoned at the deepest level of contemplation: "The soul must exist in a *free nothingness*. That we should forsake God is altogether what God intends, for as long as the soul has God, knows God, and is aware of God, [it] is far from God."[70]

68. See ibid., 131. Recently, Bruno Barnhart developed "purity of heart" as a natural meeting place between Christian and Asian traditions. He defined purity of heart as "a characterization of the 'new self' of the baptized Christian, under the aspect of interiority." He argued that "baptismal rebirth and illumination is the primordial Christian contemplative experience, as an experience of nonduality, of the 'nondual self.' . . . The human person, in the new infusion of the divine Spirit, is newly centered in the heart." See Bruno Barnhart, "Christian Self-Understanding in the Light of the East," in *Purity of Heart and Contemplation: A Monastic Dialogue between Christian and Asian Traditions*, ed. Bruno Barnhart and Joseph Wong (New York, NY: Continuum, 2001), 302–303.

69. ZBA, 9.

70. Meister Eckhart, *Selected Writings*, trans. Oliver Davies (London, UK: Penguin Books, 1994), 244 (emphasis added). Suzuki believed that when Eckhart described God's "breaking-through" in nondualistic terms, he drew nearest to Zen Emptiness (*Sambodhi*). See ZBA, 114. However, David Tracy argues that there is not an exact match between Eckhart's "nothingness" and the "absolute nothingness" of Zen thought since "Eckhart's dialectic . . . demands a move which Buddhism does not; the self-manifestation of the Godhead in the distinct *bullitio* as the Trinity and the *ebullitio* of the creature. To be more exact, a Buddhist dialectic of dynamic sunyata may have a similar self-manifestation character insofar as dynamic sunyata manifests itself *as* wisdom and *as* compas-

Eckhart's mystical intuition of God's nothingness and emptiness led Suzuki to consider him to be the Christian mystic most akin to Zen. Suzuki offered, "As I interpret Eckhart, God is at once the place where He works and the work itself. The place is zero or 'Emptiness as Being,' whereas the work which is carried on in the zero-place is infinity or 'Emptiness as Becoming.' "[71] Merton agreed with Suzuki that the empty ground of divine nothingness in Eckhart's mystical intuition coincided with *Prajna* (intuitive wisdom of Zen). As Eckhart noted, "God's ground and the soul's ground are one ground," Merton and Suzuki saw that the light of *Prajna* "penetrates the ground nature of consciousness."[72] Suzuki frequently quoted the sentence of Eckhart: "The eye wherein I see God is the same eye wherein God sees me," which, according to Merton, was "an exact expression of what Zen means by *Prajna*."[73] Merton suggested that *Prajna* was "a kind of spiritual insight into the truth of Emptiness [*Sunyata*]" and "the mature grasp of the primordial emptiness in which all things are one."[74]

---

sion to the enlightened one. But this is still unlike Eckhart's explicit revision of neo-Platonic 'emanation' language into the more radically dialectical language of *bullitio* and *ebullitio*." See David Tracy, *Dialogue with the Other: The Inter-Religious Dialogue* (Louvain, Belgium: Peeters, 1990), 88–90.

71. ZBA, 110.

72. Meister Eckhart, *The Essential Sermons, Commentaries, Treaties, and Defense*, trans. Edmund Colledge and Bernard McGinn (New York/Mahwah, NJ: Paulist Press, 1981), 192; Daisetz T. Suzuki, *Essays in Zen Buddhism*, Third Series (London, UK: Rider and Company, 1970), 34; ZR, 535. According to Hans Urs von Balthasar, Eckhart's statement leads to a pantheism. See Hans Urs von Balthasar, *The Glory of the Lord: A Theological Aesthetics*, vol. 5 (San Francisco, CA: Ignatius Press, 1982), 45.

73. ZBA, 57. According to Merton, "*Prajna* is not *self*-realization, but realization pure and simple, beyond subject and object," and it consists "in abiding *nowhere in particular*." It is " 'in us,' or better, we are 'in it.' " See ZR, 535 (emphasis in original).

74. ZBA, 112, 68. According to Suzuki, six *Paramita* in Mahayana Buddhism start from *Dana*, "giving," and the last is *Prajna*. He wrote, "The Buddhist life starts with 'giving' and ends in *Prajna*. . . . The giving is possible only

Through dialogue with Suzuki, Merton concluded that Eckhart's "emptiness of [the divine] Ground" could be compatible with *Prajna* in the void of *sunyata*.[75]

Merton also proposed that the meaning of emptiness in Zen could be compared with the negative way (*via negativa*) or apophatic theology of John of the Cross. He suggested that "St. John of the Cross compares man to a window through which the light of God is shining. If the windowpane is clean of every stain, it is completely transparent, we do not see it at all: it is 'empty' and nothing is seen but the light."[76] Merton intuited that the basic notion of emptiness could be a way of integrating Zen and Christianity since "both religions [have] the [concept] of emptiness in which one has attained [an] egoless 'primary state of being.' "[77] However, he saw that Zen does not concern itself with the Christian conceptualization of God and thus "cannot be properly judged as a mere doctrine," even though "one is entitled to discover sophisticated analogies between the Zen experience of the Void (*Sunyata*) and the experience of God in the 'unknowing' of apophatic Christian mysticism."[78]

For Merton, the experience of *sunyata* in Zen corresponds to the experience of the *nothingness* and *fullness* of God that comes through losing one's self in Christ. He saw that the unknown holi-

---

when there is Emptiness, and Emptiness is attainable only when the giving is unconditionally carried out—which is *die eigentlichste Armut* of Eckhart." See ZBA, 111–112.

75. MZM, 244. According to Matthew Fox, Merton's dialogue with Suzuki influenced the evolution in his thinking about Eckhart. For example, in the mid-1950s, "Merton's main treatment of Eckhart was to caution against his so-called heresies." However, with the help of Suzuki, his appreciation of Eckhart evolved, and Eckhart became his "lifeboat." See Matthew Fox, *A Way to God: Thomas Merton's Creation Spirituality Journey* (Novato, CA: New World Library, 2016), 41–42.

76. ZBA, 119.

77. Fader, "Beyond the Birds of Appetite," 245.

78. ZBA, 35.

ness of God and the known compassion of Christ Jesus could both be included in the concept of *sunyata*, emptiness and fullness, in Zen.[79] Merton noted that "all transcendent experience is for the Christian a participation in 'the mind of Christ.' . . . It is a kenotic transformation . . . to become a *void*."[80] This *kenosis* in Christ is nothingness, but at the same time, it is fullness in God's love. The contemplative is absorbed into the divine fullness of the presence of God by entering into an "experience of the very Nothingness of God."[81] In his lecture notes on *An Introduction to Christian Mysticism*, Merton wrote, "*Mystical theology* is not just [the] *via negationis*, [an] apophatic theology, dialectical. It is beyond both forms of discursive theology, cataphatic and apophatic. It is the FULFILLMENT OF BOTH."[82] Here Merton's Christology reflected his understanding of God as strongly apophatic, while at the same time as *cataphatic* in Christ. Shannon claims that "if [Merton's] understanding of God was strongly apophatic, it might be said that his Christology was clearly cataphatic: Christ is the revealer and manifestation of the hidden God."[83] Thus Merton's apophatic approach to Buddhist *sunyata* was combined with his *cataphatic* Christology.

79. Merton referred to "the great 'emptiness' of *Sunyata* which is described as emptiness only because, being completely without any limit of particularity it is also perfect fullness." See ZBA, 85. He also noted, "Evidently 'emptiness' is no longer opposed to 'fullness,' but emptiness and fullness are One. Zero equals infinity." See ZR, 535; see more, Andy Lord, *Transforming Renewal: Charismatic Renewal Meets Thomas Merton* (Eugene, OR: Pickwick Publications, 2015), 35–37.

80. ZBA, 75 (emphasis added).

81. James Conner, "The Experience of God and the Experience of Nothingness in Thomas Merton," *The Merton Annual* 1 (1988): 111.

82. Thomas Merton, *An Introduction to Christian Mysticism: Initiation into the Monastic Tradition 3*, ed. Patrick F. O'Connell (Kalamazoo, MI: Cistercian Publications, 2008), 142–143 (emphasis in original).

83. William H. Shannon, "Christology," in *The Thomas Merton Encyclopedia*, 51.

Christian Divinization and Buddhist Nirvana

The enlightenment or self-transcendence of an awakened person is revealed by love, compassion, and openness to those beyond one's own culture or religion. Merton's experience of self-transcendence not only removed the boundary of self-absorption but also helped him to appreciate a transcendent universal perspective. With regard to his own seeking of union with God, his relationship to others, and his quest to find his true self, Merton stated, "This inner 'I,' who is always alone, is always universal: for in this inmost 'I' my own solitude meets the solitude of every other man and the solitude of God. . . . This 'I' is Christ Himself, living in us; and we, in Him, living in the Father."[84] He described this dynamic process as the divinization (*theosis*) of the human being, which was a concept in Eastern Christianity. He defined divinization as "the ultimate in man's self-realization, for when it is perfected, man not only discovers his true self, but finds himself to be mystically one with the God by whom he has been elevated and transformed."[85] Through divinization, he began to experience more integrally the reality of his true self already living in Christ beyond interior and exterior personal boundaries. For instance, Merton felt that his Louisville Epiphany of love for all awakened him from "a dream of separateness" in that his actions were now oriented toward working for the world with charity and compassion.[86]

Merton discovered that Christian charity toward others as a fruit of divinization was similar to Buddhist *karuna* (compassion) in *nirvana*. He noted that:

> Christian charity seeks to realize oneness with the other "in Christ." Buddhist compassion seeks to heal the brokenness of division and illusion and to find wholeness not in an abstract

84. DQ, 207.
85. NM, 48.
86. CGB, 153–154.

> metaphysical "one" or even a pantheist immanentism but in *Nirvana*—the void which is Absolute Reality and Absolute Love. In either case the highest illumination of love is *an explosion of the power of Love's evidence* in which all the psychological limits of an "experiencing" subject are dissolved, and what remains is the transcendent clarity of love itself, realized in the ego-less subject in a mystery beyond comprehension.[87]

Although Buddhists do not seek to realize oneness with the transcendent Other, Merton saw a common ground between Christian charity through divinization and Buddhist compassion through *nirvana* in the perfect oneness of the power of love, in the ego-less subject, and in the openness of Being itself. In Christianity, salvation can be found in losing oneself in Christ and the true self's openness to the other. According to Merton, *nirvana* is not merely an experience of love; it is beyond experience; it is "the wide openness of Being itself, the realization that Pure Being is Infinite Giving, or that Absolute Emptiness is Absolute Compassion."[88] In addition, "*Nirvana* is found in the midst of the world around us, truth is not *somewhere else*."[89] Likewise—in Christian terms—the reign of God is among us (cf. Luke 17:21) and has already begun in the here-and-now. Love and *karuna* for others and the world are the fruit of an awakening that goes beyond religious and cultural boundaries. Through love and *karuna*, awakened Buddhists and Christians can cooperate in addressing current social problems.

Merton saw that sharing compassionate love with others was the fundamental value and the fruit of self-transcendence in both traditions. He discovered that his vocation was similar to that of the *bodhisattva* of Zen—one who has attained enlightenment but postpones *nirvana* in order to help others to attain enlightenment

---

87. ZBA, 86–87 (emphasis added).
88. Ibid., 86.
89. Ibid., 87 (emphasis in original).

with great compassion, love and sympathy.[90] Merton realized that "truly *Prajna* [transcendental wisdom] and *Karuna* [compassion] are one (as the Buddhist says), or *Caritas* (love) is indeed the highest knowledge," as Christians claim.[91] Merton discovered that interreligious dialogue had to be based on spiritual formation that sought true self-transcendence and the transformation of consciousness. This transcendent self becomes the compassionate self, and that self is expressed as openness and compassionate love for others beyond religious and cultural boundaries.

Dzogchen *in Tibetan Buddhism*

During his Asian pilgrimage in 1968, Merton's understanding and appreciation of Buddhism was further developed by his encounters with Tibetan lamas and several respected teachers or rinpoches.[92] He was fascinated by their extraordinarily practical methods and deep spirituality. For example, on November 2, 1968, he noted that the Tibetan Buddhists "have a really large number of people who have attained to extraordinary heights in meditation and contemplation. . . . I do feel very much at home with the Tibetans."[93] The same day, Sonam Kazi, a lay teacher of the *Nyingma* school of Tibetan meditation, suggested that Merton could follow the path of *dzogchen* meditation in order to arrive at realiza-

90. See ibid., 38.

91. Ibid., 62. Suzuki also said that "the most important thing is Love!" See ibid.

92. Merton's first acquaintance with Tibetan tradition was through Marco Pallis, a student of Tibetan Buddhism. In 1963, Merton read Pallis's book *Peaks and Lamas* and corresponded with him until 1968. See Thomas Merton, *Thomas Merton, a Life in Letters: The Essential Collection*, ed. William H. Shannon and Christine M. Bochen (New York, NY: HarperOne, 2008), 366–369. Merton also read the sources on Tibetan Buddhism: "the realization songs of the saint Milarepa, Giuseppe Tucci's work on Tibetan sacred art, and Desjardins' introduction." See Simmer-Brown, "The Liberty That Nobody Can Touch," 52.

93. AJ, 82.

tion or great perfection. Merton replied to Kazi that "what you're calling *dzogchen*—that's what I want."[94] Merton very quickly became interested in this advanced state of meditation, *dzogchen*.[95]

Dzogchen meditation was a topic he discussed with the Dalai Lama. The Dalai Lama looked at Merton and said, "What do you want?" Merton replied, "I want to study *dzogchen*."[96] The Dalai Lama responded, "It's true that *dzogchen* is the highest yana (vehicle for Buddhist study), but if you want to study *dzogchen*, I propose a series of meetings in which I will teach you the preliminary practices at the end of which I should hope that you will be ready to go on to *dzogchen*."[97] He also talked extensively about *dzogchen* with Chatral Rinpoche at his hermitage above Ghoom in the Darjeeling Himalayan hill region of West Bengal. Merton said to him, "I came to Asia to study Zen in Japan and now I have changed my itinerary and I'm going to study *dzogchen* in India with the Tibetans."[98] Although this plan was not realized because of his sudden death in 1968, it reflected Merton's interest in *dzogchen*, a "special type of Tibetan contemplation."[99]

Since Merton did not further explain the reasons behind his interest in *dzogchen*, we cannot be certain why he was interested in it and what he hoped to discover through it. However, the fact that he expressed a desire to delve more deeply into Tibetan Buddhist practices of meditation under the tutelage of a famous and reclusive rinpoche has led to some speculation about what those reasons might be. The attraction of *dzogchen* may have coincided

94. Cited in Tworkov, "The Jesus Lama," 18. Merton also said to Talbott that "*Dzogchen* is where it's at and that's what I'm going to do." See ibid., 19.

95. Talbott points out that Merton's attraction to *dzogchen* can compare to Picasso's encounter with art. See ibid., 23.

96. Cited in ibid., 19.

97. Cited in ibid. Merton noted, "*Dzogchen* was good, [the Dalai Lama] said, provided one had a sufficient grounding in metaphysics—or anyway Madhyamika, which is beyond metaphysics." See AJ, 101–102.

98. Cited in Tworkov, "The Jesus Lama," 18.

99. AJ, 323.

with Merton's longing to learn another advanced Asian spiritual practice other than Zen. He had said that the aim of his Asian trip was to become a better and enlightened monk by learning from an ancient source of monastic experience. This goal closely corresponded to the aim of *dzogchen*. Merton learned that *dzogchen* leads the enlightened mind to "ultimate emptiness [and to] the unity of *sunyata* and *karuna*."[100] He also observed that *dzogchen* was not a process, but the presence of fulfillment, which was already embedded in the nature of the mind from the beginning. Harold Talbott, who arranged Merton's journey in Asia, claims that Merton intuitively understood something about "the nature of the mind and the way to practice to attain full awareness. This is what attracted him to Dzogchen."[101] Through his exposure to *dzogchen*, Merton reached a point where "the Judeo-Christian theistic tradition of the Mother Church in Christendom and *dzogchen* Tibetan Buddhism were not in contradiction."[102]

Through spiritual exchanges with Tibetan Buddhists during his retreat in Darjeeling, near the majestic mountain of Kanchenjunga, Merton saw that there was "another side of the mountain."[103] For him, the mountain was a symbol of that which he had sought on his pilgrimage to Asia. He realized that "God speaks, and God is to be heard, not only on Sinai, not only in my own heart, but in *the voice of the stranger*" on the other side of the mountain.[104] From the Tibetan side, he began to see the mountain in the context of the *Madhyamika* (middle way) dialectic and *Prajna-paramita* (wisdom gone beyond). The middle way cannot be intellectualized, and *Prajna-paramita* refers to "the direct, nonconceptual

100. Ibid., 143.

101. Cited in Thurston, "Footnotes to the Asian Journey of Thomas Merton," 231.

102. Tworkov, "The Jesus Lama," 22.

103. AJ, 152.

104. Thomas Merton, "A Letter to Pablo Antonio Cuadra Concerning Giants," in *Thomas Merton: Selected Essays*, 121 (emphasis in original).

wisdom developed in meditation that 'goes beyond' the limits of conceptuality."[105] Merton's Christian approach encountered the Tibetan one, which gave him a new view of enlightenment in the *Madhyamika* and *Prajna-paramita*. His learning about *dzogchen* meditation as the perfectly awake, limitless and empty awareness, and cultivated this new appreciation. In the wisdom of *Prajna-paramita*, Merton also developed a fuller view of seeing the nature of reality. He noted, "The full beauty of the mountain is not seen until you too consent to the impossible paradox: it is and is not. When nothing more needs to be said, the smoke of ideas clears, the mountain is SEEN."[106] Simmer-Brown comments that "in the clarity of limitless awareness, without conceptuality, the mountain shines beautifully as the inseparability of the observer and the glamour of things as they are (*yatha-bhutam*). She is, inseparably, SEEN."[107] This echoes the famous saying attributed to Ch'ing-yuan Wei-hsin: "After enlightenment, mountains are once again mountains and waters once again are waters."[108] Through his encounter with Tibetan Buddhists, Merton opened "the door of emptiness without sign and wish" and attained a new and profound spiritual view that synthesized elements of Buddhist and Christian monasticism.[109]

Merton's Three Types of Buddhist-Christian Dialogue

Merton's exploration engaged him in three kinds of dialogue: theology, religious experience, and action. These types of Buddhist-Christian dialogue were deeply interconnected with one another as rooted in contemplative experience and the movement from theory to praxis.

105. Simmer-Brown, "The Liberty that Nobody Can Touch," 81.
106. AJ, 156–157 (emphasis in original).
107. Simmer-Brown, "The Liberty that Nobody Can Touch," 82.
108. Alan Watts, *The Way of Zen* (New York: Pantheon, 1957), 126.
109. AJ, 154–155.

The Dialogue of Theology

Theological interreligious dialogue focuses on doctrinal, intellectual, and philosophical issues between the two religions. The Pontifical Council for Interreligious Dialogue defines the dialogue of theological exchange as "where specialists seek to deepen their understanding of their respective religious heritages, and to appreciate each other's spiritual values."[110] Those who engage in theological dialogue believe that finding similarities and differences between dogmatic concepts can promote better understanding between the adherents of the two communities. In order to find a common platform, the no-self and the self, Gautama Buddha and Jesus Christ, *nirvana* and salvation, *sunyata* and Ultimate Reality, evil and suffering, scriptures, and history have been topics of the intellectual dialogue. Other intellectual themes have arisen more recently, such as the question of creation and dual religious belonging.

Among these intellectual themes, Merton's conceptual dialogue with Buddhism was deeply embedded in his spiritual theology. He was "one of the great theologians of the twentieth century, partly for his gift [of communicating] the Christian faith so vividly to others."[111] As a theologian for the people, his primary concern was not "seeking after doctrinal precision so much as exploring the terrain of deep religious experience," looking deeply into the mysteries of God and seeking ways of expressing Christian

---

110. Pontifical Council for Interreligious Dialogue, "Dialogue and Proclamation," 1711.

111. Christopher Pramuk, *Sophia: The Hidden Christ of Thomas Merton* (Collegeville, MN: Liturgical Press, 2009), 24. Pramuk points out that "unlike most of his theological peers, known today almost solely among the elite 'keepers of the mystery' in the academy and church, Merton is still sought out in great numbers by both ordinary seekers in the pews and 'strangers' alike, that is, those outside or alienated from the Catholic Church and its sacramental life. . . . [He is] certainly 'a people's theologian, a theologian of the people of God.' " See ibid.

contemplative experience to his contemporaries.[112] Regarding theological dialogue, he was one of the first contemplative monks to be able to speak of the self and God in terms recognizable to Buddhists. In the mid-1950s, his emerging theological interests in contemplation needed different words, and Zen began to influence his new vision of contemplation. The more he delved into the contemplative life to attain union with God, the more he became interested in Buddhist concepts of religious experience and the Eastern worldview. Indeed, the language of Zen provided him with a way to express his own religious experience beyond the concepts of Greek philosophy and Western thought.

Merton intuited the limitations of Hellenistic concepts when viewed as the exhaustive explanation of Christian religious experience in different cultural contexts.[113] According to Joseph Ratzinger, "The first encounter between Greek thought and biblical faith took place, not in the early Church, but in the course of the biblical path itself."[114] At the beginning of its existence, the early church continued to develop an intercultural encounter with Greek philosophy and biblical faith. Greek philosophy, particularly Platonism and Aristotelianism, provided the creative medium for expressing the church's understanding and experience of God and the world.[115] In the globalized modern world, however, Hellenism is challenged both inside and outside the church. Merton

112. Ibid., 21.

113. For example, Merton noted that ". . . we know how much Greek philosophy and Roman law contributed to the actual formation of Christian culture and even Christian spirituality. . . . It can certainly be said that if a similar use had been made of Oriental philosophy and religious thought from the very start, the development of Christianity in Asia would have been a different story." See Thomas Merton, "Christian Culture Needs Oriental Wisdom," in *Thomas Merton: Selected Essays*, 111–112.

114. Joseph Ratzinger, *Truth and Tolerance: Christian Belief and World Religions* (San Francisco, CA: Ignatius Press, 2004), 91–92.

115. Hellenistic thought patterns were not merely cultural expressions which prescinded a pure religious experience. According to Ratzinger, the Hellenistic

appreciated the rich Asian heritage of wisdom and believed it could contribute to a fuller and more mature Christian religious experience. For example, he discovered that Christians could express the experience of union with God in a way that went beyond the subject-object dualism by incorporating the Buddhist concept of *satori* (enlightenment).[116] He saw that Zen *satori* was "a revolutionary spiritual experience," and one's whole being in *satori* was unexpectedly exploded, thus allowing one to attain one's "original self," or "suchness."[117] Consequently, Merton proposed that Western tendencies toward dualism, expressed in such binaries as body and soul, self and other, world and church, and human and God, could be complemented or even ameliorated by integrating a Buddhist nondualistic paradigm.

However, Merton did not think that Christian doctrine had to be infused with Eastern wisdom. Instead, he saw that the limited framework of Christian culture required engagement with the experiential wisdom and deep spiritual insights of the Eastern religions. He said, "It is quite plausible to assert that the old Hellenistic categories are indeed worn out, and that Platonizing thought, even revivified with shots in the arm from Yoga and Zen, will not quite serve in the modern world."[118] Rather, he claimed that the West ought to focus on community, ordinary life, and integral experience, instead of simply studying the Asian religions and philosophies from a missiological standpoint, that is, as "rival systems."[119] Indeed, Merton attempted to find a correlation between Zen vocabulary and Christian usages, but he never suggested that "it was possible (or even intellectually honest) to

---

influence behind the creedal expressions of biblical faith are by no means accidental to it but must be regarded as a consequence of Providence. See ibid., 85–95.

116. See Bonnie B. Thurston, "Why Merton Looked East," *Living Prayer* (Nov./Dec. 1988): 44.

117. IE, 8–9.

118. ZBA, 30.

119. Merton, "Christian Culture Needs Oriental Wisdom," 112.

simply juxtapose Christian and Buddhist thought as if they were a *priori* similar."[120] Thus, Christians had to begin by listening rather than comparing systems of thought in their approach to Zen. That is to say, he proposed that Buddhist-Christian dialogue should begin by *living the experience* rather than approaching Zen through doctrinal formulations. He appreciated the limitations of comparing dogmatic theology with Eastern religions since "any attempt to handle Zen in theological language [was] bound to miss the point."[121] Buddhists believe that understanding Buddha's teachings and doctrines is not the ultimate goal but only a tool or a guide that must be freed from theory.[122]

The Dialogue of Religious Experience

The Pontifical Council for Interreligious Dialogue emphasizes that the *dialogue of religious experience* is becoming more

---

120. Lawrence Cunningham, *Thomas Merton and the Monastic Vision* (Grand Rapids, MI: W.B. Eerdmans Pub, 1999), 157 (emphasis added).

121. ZBA, 139. Merton stated, "Obviously, the dialogue conducted by theologians and bishops on the level of doctrine and of practical adjustment can never have any serious meaning if, in the background, there persists a deep conviction that the non-Christian religions are all corrupted in their inner heart, and that what they claim as their highest perfection and their ultimate fulfillment is in fact nothing but a diabolical illusion." See MZM, 206.

122. Rita Gross points out that "from beginning to end, in every form of Buddhism, Buddhists declare that concepts, words, and language, while necessary and very useful tools, can only take us so far. . . . Eventually, one must cross over into direct experience, non-conceptual immersion in Reality rather than merely talking, conceptualizing, and arguing about it. And there are no words that convey this simple, direct experience, which is why no one, even a Buddha, can teach it to anyone else." See Rita M. Gross, "Buddhist-Christian Dialogue," in *Monastic Tradition in Eastern Christianity and the Outside World: A Call for Dialogue*, ed. Ines Angeli Murzaku (Leuven, Belgium: Peeters, 2013), 275. Merton also stated, "Zen has always assumed, as one of its basic principles, that the enlightenment of the proficient Zen monk demands a certain freedom with respect to the authority of any literal canonical text." See MZM, 282.

important in the encounter with the great Eastern religions.[123] Christian scholar Benoît Standaert and Buddhist scholar Rita Gross commonly note that Buddhist-Christian dialogue is different from dialogue with other religions. Both scholars consider the dialogue of religious experience to be a priority.[124] Merton foresaw the value of the dialogue of religious experience. He noted that "the great obstacle to mutual understanding between Christianity and Buddhism lies in the Western tendency to focus not on Buddhist *experience*, which is essential, but on the *explanation*, which is accidental."[125] He stressed that genuine Buddhist-Christian dialogue required "the communication and sharing . . . of religious intuitions and truths. . . . A genuinely fruitful dialogue . . . seeks a deeper [spiritual] level."[126] This entailed two components, namely, dialogue centered on mutual religious experiences and a sharing of spiritual practices. However, he knew that in Zen all spiritual practices and all disciplines were not the ultimate goal but tools for facilitating the "discovery

123. See Pontifical Council for Interreligious Dialogue, "Dialogue and Proclamation," 1171. The forms of dialogue identified by the PCID are the dialogue of life, the dialogue of action, the theological dialogue, and the dialogue of religious experience.

124. See Benoît Standaert, *Sharing Sacred Space: Interreligious Dialogue As Spiritual Encounter*, trans. William Skudlarek (Collegeville, MN: Liturgical Press, 2009), 62–65; Gross, "Buddhist-Christian Dialogue," 262. Béthune claims that each one of the multiple forms of dialogue is indispensable, but the "dialogue of religious experience must remain at the horizon of all dialogue" in Buddhist-Christian dialogue. See Pierre-François de Béthune, "Preface," in *The Gethsemani Encounter: A Dialogue on the Spiritual Life by Buddhist and Christian Monastics*, ed. Donald W. Mitchell and James A. Wiseman (New York, NY: Continuum, 1997), xv.

125. ZBA, 37–38, 45 (emphasis in original).

126. MZM, 204. Merton also stressed, "It is important . . . to try to understand the beliefs of other religions. But much more important is the sharing of the experience of divine light." See HGL, 54.

of new dimensions of freedom, illumination and love" through religious experience.[127]

Merton's experiential and spiritual interaction with Buddhists had the twofold aim of achieving his own self-transcendence as well as establishing a profound communion with them. Delving into the inner self was one of the main objectives of Merton's contemplative life. He aimed at discovering his true self by losing his false self in Christ and by attaining self-transformation through contemplative experience. In Buddhism, he saw that the experience of self-awakening was the central goal, and that fully perceiving the nature of the self (or no-self) was the way to define enlightenment. Buddhism and Christianity, according to Merton, both looked primarily to the transformation or liberation of the self. Thus, Merton took the inner self as the starting point for Buddhist-Christian dialogue, and self-transcendence through religious experience as the point of connection between the two traditions. Merton's dialogue with Zen Buddhists on the themes of the true self and self-transcendence led him to a profound spiritual level. For him, achieving self-transcendence was an elusive, mystical, and tedious process; however, without the spiritual evolution of the self on the level of religious experience, dialogue with Buddhists would remain at an immature or surface level.

His focus on dialogue on religious experience led him to the realization that the experience could be "mystical" in all religions since "God is in no way limited in His gifts."[128] Despite the

127. CWA, 160. Merton said, "Zen system include[s] all organizations, all disciplines, and forces . . . to make a breakthrough beyond all disciplines, all organizations, all systems, after which he is able to function in the organization, in the systems, etc. with perfect freedom." See Thomas Merton, "Comments about the Religious Life Today: Transcript of a Recording Made by and Edited by Father Louis Merton for Special General Chapter Sister of Loretto, 1967," *The Merton Annual* 14 (2001): 23. Similarly, for Christians, spiritual disciplines are not means of salvation, but the opening to receive the grace of God. See CWA, 100–101.

128. MZM, 207.

irreducible difference between the religious traditions, Merton discovered that the "inner self" contained the seed of self-transcendence that many religions sought, and it could become the key issue in interreligious dialogue. He noted:

> Transcending the limits that separate subject from object and self from not-self, this development achieves a wholeness which is described in various ways by the different religions; a self-realization of atman, of Void, of life in Christ, of fana and baqa (annihilation and reintegration according to Sufism), etc.[129]

Through experiential dialogue with Buddhists, he discovered that the indispensability of exchanging contemplative experience and spiritual practice was a corollary of the universality of religious experience and self-transcendence. He saw that the experience of self-transcendence could lead to greater open-mindedness toward others expressed as love and compassion. Thus, he believed that monastics or contemplatives needed to be wide open to life and to the experience of other traditions.

The Dialogue of Action

Merton discovered the *principle of socially engaged dialogue*, although he did not directly engage in social movements with Buddhists. He understood that the life of an awakened Buddhist or a divinized Christian was revealed through love, compassion, and openness to others. Buddhism and Christianity could therefore dialogue with each other in actions of love and compassion since the awakened ones in both religions have a responsibility for others. Merton expressed the responsibility of one who is awakened when he wrote, "My solitude is not my own, for I see now how

---

129. AJ, 310; see more, Jacques Goulet, "Merton's Journey toward Ecumenism," *The Merton Annual* 4 (1991): 127.

much it belongs to [others]—and that I have a *responsibility* for it in their regard, not just my own."[130] He began to live for others because of his spiritual experience and his new awareness.

Merton saw that the principles of Buddhist social engagement and of the Christian practice of sharing God's love with others were complementary because they were both anchored in inner transformation. He realized that the practice of compassion, following enlightenment, was one of the central tenets of Mahayana Buddhism. Buddhist social engagement is rooted in the principles of interdependence, nonduality, and nonviolence, as well as in *being peace* through spiritual awakening. Merton pointed out that "the whole idea of compassion, which is central to Mahayana Buddhism, is based on a keen awareness of the interdependence of all . . . living beings, which are all part of one another and all involved in one another."[131] Interdependence means that all things and events are mutually cocreated and coexistent in a web of interrelationships. Hence, for Buddhists, the poor are not *them*, but *us*. Buddhists believe that engagement in social action that flows from the teaching of interdependence and from their nondualistic view can provide humanity with true reconciliation and peace.[132] The suffering of all is interconnected.

Another rationale for Buddhist social engagement is nonviolence. Buddhists believe that the result of all violent actions is more violence, but nonviolence can change the spiraling cycle of violence.[133] The compassionate nonviolence of Buddhism

130. CGB, 155 (emphasis added).

131. AJ, 341–342; see more, Ruben L.F. Habito, "Hearing the Cries of the World: Thomas Merton's Zen Experience," in *Merton & Buddhism*, 97.

132. For instance, Nhat Hanh notes that "I would not look upon anger as something foreign to me that I have to fight. . . . I know that anger is me, and I am anger. Nonduality, not two. I have to deal with my anger with care, with love, with tenderness, with nonviolence." See Thich Nhat Hanh, *Being Peace* (Berkeley, CA: Parallax Press, 2005), 46–47.

133. See Paul O. Ingram, *The Process of Buddhist-Christian Dialogue* (Eugene, OR: Cascade Books, 2009), 90–91.

originates from the *awareness* that all things are interrelated, and is fostered by the practice of self-discipline and meditation.[134] Buddhists do not merely aim to act in an ethical *way* but to become ethical *beings*. Real peace can be actualized in the world by individuals *being peace* and by their achieving *inner peace*. As the Dalai Lama noted, "Everybody loves to talk about calm and peace whether in family, national or international contexts, but without *inner peace*, how can we make peace real?"[135] Nhat Hanh, one of the pioneers of Buddhist social engagement, argues that one must achieve *being peace* through meditation in order to bring about external peace.[136] Through meditational practices, one can cultivate inner peace, selflessness, and mindfulness. The well-being of others is never separate from one's individual well-being in Mahayana Buddhism.

Christian social movements are anchored in the love of God for his creatures, a love revealed through the incarnation and the sacrificial love of his Son, Jesus Christ. Christian social activists engage in the liberation of people and work for a better world. Merton described the relationship between union with God and sharing love with others as contemplation. He saw that Christians can realize the love of God that is within them and share divine love with others through self-emptying and perfect fullness in contemplation. He noted, "The contemplation of the Christian solitary is the awareness of the divine mercy transforming and elevating his own emptiness and turning it into the presence of perfect love, perfect fullness."[137] This insight led him to describe

---

134. Regarding the connection among compassionate nonviolence, meditation and social engagement, Ingram claims that "compassionate non-violence," which is engendered by the practice of meditation, is the "ethical heart of Buddhist social activism." See ibid., 84.

135. The XIV Dalai Lama, *Kindness, Clarity, and Insight*, ed. Jeffrey Hopkins and Elizabeth Napper (Ithaca, NY: Snow Lion, 2006), 75 (emphasis in original).

136. See Nhat Hanh, *Being Peace*, 51.

137. DQ, 192.

living for others as the responsibility of an awakened person. After his Louisville experience of love for all people, his radical involvement with the burning social issues of the 1960s bore witness to a significant inner transformation. He realized that spiritual rebirth could be expressed as compassion. He noted, "Compassion teaches me that my brother and I are one. That if I love my brother, then my love benefits my own life as well."[138] His contemplative awareness led him to the realization that everything was interdependent. Thus, compassionate love knows no religious boundaries.

Merton appreciated that both Buddhism and Christianity sought to bring about a transformation of human consciousness since the root of human problems was consciousness rather than structures. Thus, in order to solve human problems, he stressed the role of awakened persons who could help to develop a new human consciousness. At this point, Merton realized that *awakened* Buddhists and *divinized* Christians could cooperate with one another to transform our current social consciousness through the mutuality of Christian love and Buddhist compassion. As should be obvious, Merton's paradigm of spiritually rooted and socially engaged dialogue is fundamentally different from secular social activism.

Merton's Contributions, Limitations, and Beyond

There are many pioneers in Buddhist-Christian dialogue, among whom one could name Lynn de Silva, Leonard Swidler, John B. Cobb, Aloysius Pieris, and Frederic J. Streng in Christianity, and Kitaro Nishida, D.T. Suzuki, and Masao Abe in Buddhism. Thomas Merton is also considered one of the pioneers in this dialogue. What was his unique contribution to Buddhist-Christian dialogue? Bonnie Thurston claims that it was his existential approach to Buddhism beyond Western duality that enabled him to see that the radical transformation of human experience

138. IEW, 103.

was similar in both traditions.[139] John Dadosky points out that Merton's success as a pioneer is to be found in the experiential and spiritual dimensions as well as in his life and friendship with Buddhists, which provide examples of the "method of mutual self-mediation" for interreligious dialogue.[140] Raab argues that through inter-contemplative dialogue, Merton contributed to opening the "middle path" between "openness" to other religions, especially Buddhism, and "fidelity" to the affirmation of fullness in Christ.[141] Robert H. King, author of *Thomas Merton and Thich Nhat Hanh*, also considered Merton's contemplative dialogical way as a pioneering contribution to Buddhist-Christian dialogue.[142]

Recently, however, scholars such as John Keenan, Roger Corless, and Robert Sharf have raised questions about Merton's knowledge of Buddhism.[143] They argue that Merton's understanding of Buddhism was incomplete since he was still a student of Buddhism at the time of his death, and that this limitation was, at least in part, the result of his overreliance on Suzuki's presentation of Buddhism. Merton's unfamiliarity with Asian languages was perhaps also a factor in his limited knowledge of Buddhism. Merton's limitation will be discussed soon.

139. See Thurston, "Thomas Merton: Pioneer of Buddhist-Christian Dialogue," 126–128.

140. See John D. Dadosky, "Merton as Method for Inter-Religious Engagement," 33–43.

141. See Joseph Q. Raab, "Insights from the Inter-Contemplative Dialogue: Merton's Three Meanings of 'God' and Religious Pluralism," *The Merton Annual* 23 (2010): 90–105.

142. See King, *Thomas Merton and Thich Nhat Hanh*, 11–24.

143. John P. Keenan, "The Limits of Thomas Merton's Understanding of Buddhism," in *Merton & Buddhism*, 118–133; Roger Corless, "In Search of a Context for the Merton-Suzuki Dialogue," *The Merton Annual* 6 (1993): 76–91; Robert H. Sharf, "Whose Zen? Zen Nationalism Revisited," in *Rude Awakenings: Zen, the Kyoto School and the Question of Nationalism*, ed. J. W. Heisig and J. C. Maraldo (Honolulu, HI: University of Hawaii, 1994), 40–51.

This section will explore and supplement Merton's encounter with Buddhism in a more integrated manner and examine his unfinished works and his suggestions for Buddhist-Christian dialogue. It will also evaluate his final involvement with Buddhism, namely, Tibetan Buddhism, from an experiential and existential perspective.

Merton's Pioneering Works for Buddhist-Christian Dialogue

Merton's approach to Buddhism was an *integrated encounter* that specifically focuses on sharing various spiritual practices, experiences, and wisdom as well as social engagement.[144] He also approached Buddhists through heart-to-heart dialogue that led to spiritual friendship with Buddhists.[145] These two dimensions have become models for current Buddhist-Christian dialogue. Thus, Merton's pioneering work in the area of Buddhist-Christian dialogue can be looked at in terms of 1) his integrated approach to Buddhism and 2) his friendship through direct contact and spiritual exchange with Buddhists.

First, when we consider current trends in Buddhist-Christian dialogue, it is clear that Merton created a new dynamic for exchange with Buddhists through an integrated dialogic pattern

---

144. Winston L. King, a scholar of religious studies who focuses on Buddhism, argues that "there should always, or as often as possible, be some component of experiential encounter—shared worship, experience, endeavor, meditation—in Buddhist-Christian dialogue. It cannot substitute for theological effort, but it must be a continual companion and ingredient of it." See Winston King, "Buddhist-Christian Dialogue Reconsidered," *Buddhist-Christian Studies* 2 (1982): 10.

145. Merton's friendship with Buddhists such as Suzuki, the Dalai Lama, and many rinpoches provides "a model for interreligious relating that we can all learn from." See John D. Dadosky, "Merton's Dialogue with Zen: Pioneering or Passé?," *Fu Jen International Religious Studies* 2, no. 1 (Summer 2008): 73. Dadosky also claims that "when one considers Merton's success with interreligious dialogue one must consider that his method . . . was one of friendship." See Dadosky, "Merton as Method for Inter-Religious Engagement," 35.

that extends beyond the intellectual level. The current trend in contemporary Buddhist-Christian dialogue is to downplay the role of intellectual dialogue and to integrate the dialogue of spirituality and the dialogue of social engagement. The consequence of this development implies that those involved in the dialogue have realized the limitations of intellectual dialogue.[146] In his article "Theological Trends: The Buddhist-Christian dialogue," Michael Barnes argues that in order to achieve mutual transformation in Buddhist-Christian dialogue, purely intellectual dialogue is insufficient and must be complemented by dialogue at a more existential level.[147] James L. Fredericks, a specialist in Buddhist-Christian dialogue, also claims that from a Christian perspective, intellectual dialogue with Buddhists has reached its limit; thus, to develop new forms of solidarity with other religious traditions, especially Buddhism, Christians must focus on praxis and contemplation and continue to search for truth and service to the world.[148] Therefore, the new dynamic of Buddhist-Christian dialogue has to shift from theory to praxis. However, it needs to be made clear that praxis does not exclude theory, but focuses on

146. For instance, Ovey Mohammed points out that "Buddhists draw . . . attention to the fact that [the] Christian faith is too talkative. They remind us that words about God are authentic only if they flow from a profound experience of prayer." See Ovey N. Mohammed, "Buddhist-Catholic Dialogue," *Celebrate* 31, no. 6 (1992): 14. Nhat Hanh states that "all concepts have to be transcended if we are to touch the ground of our being deeply." See Thich Nhat Hanh, *Going Home: Jesus and Buddha as Brothers* (New York, NY: Riverhead Books, 1999), 12.

147. See Barnes, "Theological Trends: The Buddhist-Christian Dialogue," 60.

148. See James L. Fredericks, *Buddhists and Christians: Through Comparative Theology to Solidarity* (Maryknoll, NY: Orbis Books, 2004), 98–105. According to Winston King, merely doing meditation is "not a genuine existential encounter . . . but a kind of psychosomatic experiment," and "merely intellectual discussion of religious beliefs is not interreligious *dialogue* but merely interreligious discussion." See Winston L. King, "Buddhist-Christian Dialogue Reconsidered," 6; Winston L. King, "Interreligious Dialogue," in *The Sound of Liberating Truth: Buddhist-Christian Dialogues in Honor of Frederick J. Streng*, ed. Sallie B. King and Paul O. Ingram (Surrey, UK: Curzon, 1999), 49.

sharing experiences and the wisdom gained from spiritual practice as well as from social engagement. This new direction may be described as one of *integrated encounter*.

This current trend in Buddhist-Christian dialogue is what Merton was striving to accomplish. He did not approach Buddhism in merely conceptual, experiential, or socially engaged ways. He sought an *integrated encounter* that was anchored in his own self-transformation through the experience of enlightenment. His first encounter with Buddhism was at an intellectual level, but his interest in experiential Zen led him to realize the importance of religious experience and self-transformation in Buddhism. He believed that an existential and experiential focus on the inner self, spiritual practice, religious experience, and compassionate love would reveal the compatibility of the two religions and *promote a sense of solidarity*.

Through the quality of his immersion in Buddhism, Merton realized that there were parallels between Buddhist religious life and Christian contemplative life. Thus, he attempted to integrate Buddhist practical methods and teachings into Christian contemplative practice for spiritual renewal. For example, he integrated the "quiet meditation" practice of *Soto* Zen into his personal Christian meditation, since for him *Soto* Zen contained a "hidden and primitive form of theological faith."[149] Fredericks acknowledges that "since the pioneering efforts of Catholic monks like Thomas Merton, Roman Catholics in many parts of the world have taken up the serious practice of Buddhist meditation, to the extent that some Catholic monks have even received ordination as Zen teachers."[150] By embracing the conceptual, experiential, and practical dimension of Buddhism at a deep spiritual level, Merton exemplified a creative reinterpretation of his own tradition in the light of Buddhist wisdom.

149. MZM, 36, 37.
150. James L. Fredericks, "Off the Map: The Catholic Church and Its Dialogue with Buddhists," in *Catholicism and Interreligious Dialogue*, ed. James L. Heft (New York, NY: Oxford University Press, 2012), 139–140.

Second, Merton evolved into one of the pioneers in Buddhist-Christian dialogue by deep friendships and spiritual exchange. His direct meeting or correspondence with Buddhists revealed how important friendship is at the beginning of dialogue if one is to attain spiritual communion with them. True friendship between the adherents of two traditions, friendship marked by an open mind and mutual respect, enables the sharing of strengths and gifts as well as mutual encouragement for growth in the spiritual life. Indeed, friendship is a "source of great joy . . . [and] a way to enlightenment and to union" between God and humanity.[151] In such friendship "the love mediated between friends can flow over as generosity into acts of charity and friendship to others."[152] Merton noted, "Disinterested love is also called the 'love of friendship,' that is to say a love which rests in the good of the beloved, not in one's interest or satisfaction. "[153] Merton's "love of friendship" was rooted in his friendship with Christ and his love of God; through self-transcendence, he extended this friendship to others, especially Buddhists, in a love that went beyond his own interest or satisfaction. His friendship with Buddhists became a model for Buddhist-Christian dialogue.

Limitations of Merton's Dialogue with Buddhists and Buddhism

Recently, some scholars have suggested that Merton's understanding of Buddhism was imperfect, incomplete, and/or limited. For instance, MacCormick claims that "[Merton] was at times

---

151. William Johnston, *The Mirror Mind: Zen-Christian Dialogue* (New York, NY: Fordham University Press, 1990), 160.

152. John D. Dadosky, "The Church and the Other: Mediation and Friendship in Post–Vatican II Roman Catholic Ecclesiology," *Pacifica* 18 (October 2005): 316.

153. Thomas Merton, *Seeds of Destruction* (New York, NY: Farrar, Straus and Giroux, 1964), 261 (hereafter SD).

guilty of overstating and oversimplifying [Buddhist] positions, and erred in over-conceptualizing their beliefs."[154] John Keenan argues:

> [W]e cannot look to Merton for any adequate understanding of Buddhism. Because of the limitation of sources available to him in his time, his understanding of Zen Buddhism . . . was just too pure and too naïve, too simplistic. . . . Moreover, Zen is but one school of Buddhism among many.[155]

Dadosky responds with the belief that "Merton's knowledge of Buddhism is compromised because his reliance on Suzuki seems to be more of a residual effect of a backlash against the scholarship of Suzuki."[156] In fact, Suzuki, a lay student of the *Rinzai* Zen roshi Imakita Kosen, concentrated on *Rinzai* Zen, which emphasized *koans*, rather than on *Soto* Zen, which focused on *Zazen*, sitting meditation. Suzuki's view of Zen was merely one of many formulations or interpretations of Zen. Roger Corless, a cofounder of the Society of Buddhist-Christian Dialogue, criticizes not only Suzuki's problematical and idealized understanding of Zen in the Japanese context but also his limited knowledge or misunderstanding of Christianity.[157] Robert H. Sharf, a professor of Buddhist

---

154. MacCormick, "The Zen Catholicism of Thomas Merton," 802. For example, Merton's essay on *"Nirvana,"* according to MacCormick, is a striking instance of his overconceptualizing of Zen. Merton defined *nirvana* as "the wisdom of perfect love," but this attempt to conceptualize Reality appeared per se to be misconceived. See ibid., 812. See also ZBA, 84.

155. Keenan, "The Limits of Thomas Merton's Understanding of Buddhism," 123, 126–127.

156. Dadosky, "Merton's Dialogue with Zen: Pioneering or Passé?," 71. Dadosky claims that "many scholars now criticize Suzuki because they disagree with his interpretation of Zen and because his success as a popularizer has led to misconceptions by Western scholars. These critics not only believe Suzuki misrepresents Zen, but they believe he ignores the various complex lineages of various schools and the doctrinal aspects as well." See ibid., 54.

157. For example, according to Corless, Suzuki understood the term "mysticism" as *mikkyo*, Esoteric Buddhism. Thus, Suzuki stressed that there was no

studies, also criticizes Suzuki's Zen as an "intellectualized Zen" that also included Japanese nationalism. Furthermore, he says, it was frequently held in suspicion by the Zen tradition.[158] Nevertheless, Merton admired Suzuki as "the chief authority on Zen Buddhism" and broadly accepted his transcendental interpretation of Zen.[159]

In 1965, however, Merton confessed to William Johnston, SJ, that he had "no real knowledge of Zen as it actually is in Japan."[160] Merton realized that there were many Buddhist schools, each of which had its own spiritual depth and vast source material, but that he could not read these sources because he was not familiar with Asian languages.[161] Indeed, he could only rely on the limited number of Buddhist sources that had been translated from the original Chinese or Japanese texts prior to 1965. Moreover, since he was a cloistered contemplative monk, he would not have had many opportunities for direct experiences of the Buddhist life or for encountering various Buddhist schools.

Merton's knowledge of Buddhism was not, however, restricted to the Zen Buddhism of Suzuki or to Mahayana Buddhism, and his encounter with Buddhists and Buddhism was not limited to intellectual knowledge. Dadosky comments, "Keenan's claim that we cannot rely on Merton for knowledge of Buddhism is not really fair. Any serious student of Buddhism, including Merton himself, recognizes that our knowledge develops and continues

---

"mysticism" in Zen. See Corless, "In Search of a Context for the Merton-Suzuki Dialogue," 83–84.

158. Sharf, "Whose Zen?," 43, 46–48.

159. MZM, 207.

160. HGL, 441.

161. Yet, without knowledge of Chinese, Merton's translated book, *The Way of Chuang Tzu*, published in 1965, is praised by an expert on Chinese language and literature. See Lucien Miller, "Merton's *Chuang Tzu*," in *Merton & the Tao: Dialogue with John Wu and the Ancient Sage*, ed. Cristóbal Serrán-Pagán y Fuentes (Louisville, KY: Fons Vitae, 2013), 47–83.

to develop."[162] Indeed, Merton's knowledge of Buddhism grew throughout his lifetime and especially in his encounters with Tibetan Buddhism and Theravada Buddhism during his Asian pilgrimage. Many Tibetan Buddhists who met with Merton admired his rich knowledge of Buddhism and his interest in Buddhist meditation at a deep spiritual level. David Steindl-Rast, whose knowledge of Buddhism is extensive, and who met with Merton before his Asian journey, said that Merton had a "vastly superior theoretical knowledge [of] Zen."[163]

Leaving aside the question of the depth and breadth of Merton's knowledge of Buddhism, it must be said that his encounter with Buddhism was not limited to intellectual knowledge. For a true understanding of Merton's Buddhist-Christian dialogue, we must take into account his integrated approach to Buddhism and his various approaches to interreligious dialogue. Moreover, Merton's dialogue with Buddhism can become a model for interreligious dialogue. For instance, in his article, "Beyond the Birds of Appetite," Larry A. Fader claims that "Merton's encounter with Suzuki and with the Japanese scholar's interpretation of Zen is an example of what religious dialogue can be at its best and is testimony to Merton's courageous dedication to truth."[164] Furthermore, Dadosky suggests that Merton's life shows that he engaged in interreligious dialogue and friendship as a "method of mutual self-mediation."[165] Merton expanded the horizon for interreligious dialogue between Buddhists and Christians through mutual learning and the sharing of religious experience and spiritual practice, even though his vision of Buddhism was limited.

Keenan also believes that Merton's emphasis on our common humanity detracted from his understanding of interreligious

162. Dadosky, "Merton's Dialogue with Zen: Pioneering or Passé?," 72.

163. Cited in Thurston, "Footnotes to the Asian Journey of Thomas Merton," 219.

164. Fader, "Beyond the Birds of Appetite," 252.

165. Dadosky, "Merton's Dialogue with Zen: Pioneering or Passé?," 70–71.

dialogue. He claims that "after forty years of conversation, people tire of dialogue, because it so often rehearses the same old ground about our common humanity, offering no new insight and no new approach. . . . All well and good, but that does grow tedious."[166] He continually criticizes experiential dialogue, arguing that dialogue itself needs the mediation of language or words since there is no way to employ ineffable pure experiences for a shared experiential dialogue.[167] His evaluation of the last forty (now fifty) years of Buddhist-Christian dialogue is that it has grown tedious and superficial and has yielded little visible fruit. He believes that because of its insistence on the dimension of ineffability, experiential dialogue is seriously limited.

However, the main reason for the obstacles to some Buddhist-Christian dialogue may not be its focus on experience and our common humanity, but its overemphasis and overestimation of the value of intellectual dialogue. Few Buddhists are interested in Christian intellectual discussions that challenge Buddhist faith and practice. At an even more basic level, they believe that knowledge and truth-claims not gained through experience are not a valid base for spiritual growth. Beyond purely intellectual dialogue, solidarity needs to be established between religious traditions that are based on heart-to-heart dialogue between human beings who recognize their common or shared humanity. Archbishop Michael L. Fitzgerald claims that "the relationship of fraternity is based on the common origin of human beings, but also on the way God's Spirit is at work in human hearts."[168] Raab suggests that "a horizon [of anthropology] lends itself more readily to a discussion of the human journey, and its fulfillment, as a

166. Keenan, "The Limits of Thomas Merton's Understanding of Buddhism," 129.

167. See ibid., 129–130.

168. Michael L. Fitzgerald, "Pope John Paul II and Interreligious Dialogue: A Catholic Assessment," in *John Paul II and Interreligious Dialogue*, ed. Byron L. Sherwin and Harold Kasimow (Maryknoll, NY: Orbis Books, 1999), 218.

foundation for interreligious dialogue . . . [including] the 'religious' or 'spiritual' as a legitimate category of human experience, understanding, and reflection."[169] Dialogue through the sharing of common horizons may be the way that leads to transcendence or mutual transformation.

The mature Merton encountered Buddhists through heart-to-heart dialogue, beyond words. Carr claims that "Merton's conviction was that despite the significant differences among the religions, certain commonalities could be discovered. In the spiritual family . . . something beyond verbal differentiation and communication was possible."[170] Merton's contemplative dialogue with Buddhists exemplified the way we could move from verbal communication to spiritual communion beyond words. Keenan may be overlooking Merton's spiritual communion when he criticizes experiential dialogue. In addition, due to the dimension of ineffability of mystical experience, there are various expressions and interpretations regarding the experience, and through experiential dialogue, these differences can both provide mutual enrichment and a challenge for one another. In brief, Merton knew that the fruit of Buddhist-Christian dialogue was neither union between different religious systems, nor the acquiring of extensive knowledge about other religions, but spiritual communion and mutual transformation through spiritual exchange and sharing.

Beyond Merton's Encounter with Buddhism

Today, Merton's followers are attempting to develop his legacy. His concept of a universal consciousness beyond religious structures also invites discussion about the possibility of Buddhist-Christian dual-participation and/or dual-belonging. In order to go beyond his encounter with Buddhists, the above dimensions

---

169. Raab, *Openness and Fidelity*, 43.

170. Anne E. Carr, "Merton's East-West Reflections," *Horizons* 21, no. 2 (1994): 248.

of his explorations and legacy will be discussed as follows: 1) his limited exposure to Buddhism, 2) his notion of transcendent identity, and 3) his practical and monastic approach to Buddhism.

First, Merton's encounter with Buddhism was limited, for the most part, to Japanese Zen and Tibetan Buddhism. True, he did meet with several Theravada monks during his Asian pilgrimage and with the Vietnamese Buddhist monk Thich Nhat Hanh at the Abbey of Gethsemani; however, he did not engage with them to the same extent. Furthermore, he had no contact with Korean *Seon* Buddhism or Cambodian Buddhism, nor even with American Buddhism, all of which developed different political, spiritual, dogmatic, and cultic commitments. Like different Christian denominations, each Buddhist denomination conceives and speaks of religious experience differently. Because of these diversities, dialogue with specific denominations of Buddhism may lead to conflicting assessments and even misunderstandings of Buddhism. As the Swiss theologian Hans Küng notes, "There is not 'a' Buddhism, just as there is not simply 'a' Christianity."[171] There is no single Buddhist theology, no single Buddhist leader.

Since Buddhist-Christian dialogue progresses through intersubjective relationships between members of different schools, it cannot help being limited by the various branches of the two religions. Thus, Christians must avoid applying a single standard of dialogical methodology with Buddhists in general. Merton himself moved from a general understanding of Buddhism, gained through his increasing familiarity with Zen, to a more specific dialogue on spiritual practice, and he progressed similarly in his dialogues with Tibetan lamas and rinpoches.

Again, Merton's view of universal religious identity provides a new way of understanding dual religious participation and belonging, which is currently one of the relevant issues in

---

171. Hans Küng, "Foreword," in *Christianity and Buddhism: A Multicultural History of Their Dialogue*, trans. Phyllis Jestice (Maryknoll, NY: Orbis Books, 2001), x.

Buddhist-Christian dialogue. There are three possibilities of dialogue regarding this new phenomenon of double participation-belonging: 1) engaging in the practices of the other religion without losing one's original religious identity, 2) making a formal commitment to both religious communities, and 3) acknowledging a transcendent identity beyond specific religious identity.[172]

In a strict sense, the first level does not really define dual religious belonging, but rather speaks to dual religious participation. Many Christians are already crossing the boundaries of the two traditions. Those who are fascinated with Zen meditation tend to perceive Zen not as a religion but as a "meta-religion." For them, Zen is not exclusively an expression of Buddhism; rather, it is compatible with any religion. Thus, they may consider themselves as Zen Christians.

Religious practitioners at the second level of engagement unequivocally defend dual Buddhist/Christian identity. They identify themselves as both Buddhist and Christian, and they practice and worship within both traditions. The number of dual belongers has increased over the past several decades. Their commitment and openness may contribute to the creation of a new realm of religious identity and the advancement of Buddhist-Christian dialogue. For example, speaking of his Buddhist-Christian practice and hybrid identity, Paul Knitter, a leading theologian of religious

---

172. Regarding the possibility of dialogue pertaining to this new phenomenon of double belonging, George Kilcourse suggests that interchurch couples (and their families) through mixed marriage can be considered a "double belonging." He points out that "what evolves in *Foyers Mixtes* [mixed families] reflections on the unique identity of interchurch couples is a twofold conviction: (1) couples and their families claim a 'double belonging'; and (2) couples and their families do not create a 'mythical third church.' The first conviction raises ecclesiological questions and promotes a constructive theological and pastoral response. The second conviction, by contrast, seeks to rebut a recurring charge made against the implications and future directions of families who attempt to realize a 'double belonging.'" See George Kilcourse, *Double Belonging: Interchurch Families and Christian Unity* (New York/Mahwah, NJ: Paulist Press, 1992), 17.

pluralism, claims that by being on the cutting edge of his Christian community, he hopes to show how Buddhist-Christian dual belonging can lead the Christian community to "a new way of being church."[173] Rose Drew, author of *Buddhist and Christian?: An Exploration of Dual Belonging*, claims that the integration of these two religious practices is distinct from both their Buddhist and Christian orientations and cannot be replaced by either original tradition.[174] According to her, this integrated worldview and practice are not syncretistic, since "dual belonging involves only the *legitimate* integration of *reconcilable* truths."[175]

In spite of the favorable views expressed by some Christians, however, the possibility of dual religious identity is still in dispute among Christians.[176] From a Buddhist perspective, since religious identity depends on the evolving mind and on evolving religious experience, there is no fixed position on dual belonging.

Strictly speaking, the third level of dual Buddhist-Christian belonging is not about *belonging* to two religions, but of *going beyond* belonging. Through the experience of self-transcendence, one may attain a universal consciousness that transcends the boundary of one's religious identity, even though an explicit religious identity may still be maintained. For an awakened person, belonging to a religious structure is not the main issue. The person is free from religious structures and can cross over religious traditions at a deep spiritual level. Thomas Merton was neither an

---

173. Paul F. Knitter, *Without Buddha I Could not Be a Christian* (Croydon, UK: Oneworld, 2009), 216–217.

174. Rose Drew, *Buddhist and Christian?: An Exploration of Dual Belonging* (New York, NY: Routledge, 2011), 211–212. Drew points out that dual belongers are challenged to find a balance between the integration of religious thought and religious practice due to the difficulty of the compatibility of truths, the threat of a split personality, and the need to follow one path in each of the traditions. See ibid., 215–216.

175. Ibid., 215 (emphasis in original).

176. See William Johnston, *Mystical Journey: An Autobiography* (Maryknoll, NY: Orbis Books, 2006), 118.

unfaithful Catholic monk nor an explicit Buddhist monk, but an awakened monk who realized *the Sacred* in the other religion.[177] If Merton had not arrived at the experience of self-transcendence and enlightenment at a universal level, his monastic interreligious dialogue would have merely resulted in the intellectual or idealistic exercise of a Roman Catholic monk. However, his cross-religious experience and self-transcendence may have led him to consider a new level of religious identity beyond religious systems.

It is against this background that Merton's statement "I am a Buddhist" can be understood. In the 1960s, he frequently identified himself as a Buddhist. For example, in a letter to Marco Pallis, he wrote, "I think that I am as much a . . . Buddhist in temperament and spirit as I am a Christian."[178] In the preface he wrote for the Japanese edition of *Seeds of Contemplation*, published in 1965, he also noted that he felt himself "much closer to the Zen monks of ancient Japan than to the busy and impatient men of the West."[179] On the eve of his trip to Asia in 1968, he wrote, "I see no contradiction between Buddhism and Christianity. . . . I intend to become as good a Buddhist as I can."[180] These statements led some people to conclude either that he intended to change his religious identity or that he assumed a dual identity as both Buddhist and Christian.

177. Merton notes, "If I affirm myself as a Catholic merely by denying all that is Muslim, Jewish, Protestant, Hindu, Buddhist, etc., in the end I will find that there is not much left for me to affirm as a Catholic: and certainly no breath of the Spirit with which to affirm it." See CGB, 141.

178. HGL, 465. In 1962, he was referred to as a Buddhist by his community: "[Merton is] a hermit and a Buddhist and . . . in choir [he is] praying as a Buddhist." See ibid., 580.

179. IEW, 67.

180. Cited in David Steindl-Rast, "Man of Prayer," in *Thomas Merton, Monk*, ed. Patrick Hark (Garden City, NY: Image Books, 1976), 90. Merton also said, "I am much closer to Confucius and Lao Tzu than to my contemporaries in the United States." Cited in Lipski, *Thomas Merton in Asia*, 5.

However, Merton's statements relate neither to his specific religious identity nor call into question his Christian identity. Rather, they reveal his understanding—and achievement—of a different level of religious identity.[181] William Nicholls and Ian Kent describe this new identity as "transcendent Identity."[182] According to Merton, the goal of a contemplative is at a higher level, namely, "the transcendent ground and source of being, the not-being and the emptiness that [was] so called because it is absolutely beyond all definitions and limitation."[183] Merton saw that through the experience of self-transcendence or *satori*, one could discover an original identity in "a living contact with the Infinite Source of all being."[184] He noted, "This identity is not the denial of my own personal reality but its highest affirmation. It is a discovery of *genuine identity* in and with the One," as well as a recovery of "an older unity."[185] At the level of the unity with One, or the interdependence with all, one's original identity is not limited by religious structure but transcends it. His internalization of self-transformation between Buddhism and Christianity, his *satori*-like experience in Polonnaruwa, and his transcultural/religious consciousness reflect his attainment of transcendence beyond religious boundaries. Thus, Merton's religious identity as a Christian was not denied but enriched when he moved toward Buddhism. His new understanding of religious identity may be an example of what Whalen Lai and Michael von Brück suggest when they write,

---

181. Dennis McInerny claims that "if we want to call Merton a Buddhist, . . . I certainly see no harm in doing so . . . [since] his being a Buddhist was in no wise contradictory to nor a diminishment of his being a Christian." See Dennis McInerny, *Thomas Merton: The Man and His Work* (Spencer, MA: Cistercian Publications, 1974), 94.

182. William Nicholls and Ian Kent, "Merton and Identity," in *Thomas Merton: Pilgrim in Process*, ed. Donald Grayston and Michael W. Higgins (Toronto, ON: Griffin House, 1983), 110.

183. IEW, 69.

184. Ibid., 70.

185. MZM, 18 (emphasis in original); AJ, 308.

"Christians . . . discover their specifically Christian identity in a new way through encounter with Buddhists."[186] Merton exposed himself to "the entire universe of religious belief."[187] This new way of interpreting transcendent identity will need to be further developed for a better understanding of dual religious belonging.

Merton's practical and monastic approach to Buddhism has significant implications for current Buddhist-Christian dialogue. Near the end of his life, he was thinking about ways Christian monastics could learn about meditation from Tibetan Buddhists. He was also thinking about contemplative dialogue and inter-monastic exchanges. In the years following his death, some of his suggestions are gradually being implemented by Buddhist and Christian monastics. For example, there are the "Gethsemani Encounters," the first of which was suggested by the Dalai Lama and held at the Abbey of Gethsemani in 1996. Three more have been held since then, to give expression to and expand Merton's hopes for dialogue between Buddhist and Christian monastics. This topic will be dealt with in more detail in the following two chapters.

Merton's Aspiration in His Encounter with Tibetan Buddhism

Merton's encounter with Tibetan Buddhists was developed by heart-to-heart meetings with monks, lamas, masters, and rinpoches. When he encountered Tibetan Buddhists in 1968, he had a rich knowledge of Buddhism as well as the practical experience of being a contemplative monk for over twenty-five years. From the Tibetan Buddhists he wanted to learn practical ways for attaining an experience of enlightenment that went beyond intellectual knowledge. He recognized that Tibetan Buddhists

186. Whalen Lai and Michael von Brück, *Christianity and Buddhism: A Multicultural History of Their Dialogue*, trans. Phyllis Jestice (Maryknoll, NY: Orbis Books, 2001), 248–249.

187. Ian S. MacNiven, "More Than Scribe: James Laughlin, Thomas Merton and The Asian Journal," *The Merton Annual* 26 (2013): 53.

had "a certain depth of spiritual experience" and "a deeper attainment and certitude than . . . Catholic contemplatives."[188] His heightened interest in *dzogchen* also reflected his discovery of the practical and spiritual value of Tibetan Buddhism. In this context, he approached Tibetan masters for: 1) existential and experiential dialogue as a student and 2) contemplative dialogue as a monk.

First, in his writings while in Asia, he emphasized dialogue on the "existential level of experience and of spiritual maturity" and introduced himself as a pilgrim learner.[189] He noted, "I come as a pilgrim who is anxious to obtain not just information . . . but to drink from ancient sources of monastic vision and experience."[190] This reference to himself as a *pilgrim student* was a kind of paradigm shift since at that time, Western Christianity church tended to approach Asian religious traditions as their *teacher.* In order to become a better, more enlightened monk, he looked for enlightened mentors in Asia, desired to learn about their practical methods in depth, and wanted "to live and share [their] traditions, as far as [he could] by living them in their traditional milieu."[191] After his direct meeting with various Tibetan Buddhists and visiting their temples and hermits, Merton noted:

> Meeting the Dalai Lama and the various Tibetans, lamas or "enlightened" laymen, has been the most significant thing of all, especially in the way we were able to communicate with one another and share an essentially spiritual experience of "Buddhism" which is also somehow in harmony with Christianity.[192]

Merton asked many questions of the Tibetan Buddhists he met, and in doing so his view of Christian contemplation was enriched

188. AJ, 124.

189. Ibid., 312; see more, Jack Downey, "The Great Compassion: Thomas Merton in Asia," *American Catholic Studies* 126, no. 2 (2015): 120.

190. AJ, 312–313.

191. Ibid., 313.

192. Ibid., 148.

and extended. He showed by his example that Christians should be willing to approach Buddhism as students. As a pilgrim student Merton showed that Buddhist learning could help to renew and to enhance Christian contemplation and monasticism. This will be discussed further in the next chapter.

Second, Merton's "heart-to-heart" encounter with Tibetan Buddhists was through contemplative dialogue. Talbott reflected that "Merton's reception by each Lama brought about an instantaneous mutual recognition in an atmosphere of *'Cor ad cor loquitur.'* "[193] Merton frequently noted that a deep spiritual bond was established through these meetings. For example, after meeting with the Dalai Lama, he noted, "It was a warm and cordial discussion…. I feel a great respect and fondness for him as a person and believe, too, that there is a real spiritual bond between us."[194] This deep spiritual bond was made possible perhaps by the fact that both Merton and the Dalai Lama were contemplative monks who had similar spiritual practices, and both aimed at self-transformation through the experience of enlightenment. The spiritual bond between contemplatives was also present in Merton's subsequent meetings with rinpoches. For example, in the meeting between Merton and Chatral Rinpoche, they immediately recognized each other as persons who had attained and continually sought deeper inner experience. At the end of the meeting, "they embraced with tears in their eyes."[195] Merton's encounters with Tibetan Buddhists showed that dialogue between contemplatives, or monastics, could help to build a deeper sense of spiritual solidarity that went beyond religious traditions.

We do not know what Merton might have done, or become, after his Asian pilgrimage, but it is fair to state that his engagement with Tibetan Buddhists can certainly provide a model for

193. Harold Talbott, "From a Letter of September 14, 2000, to Bonnie Thurston," cited in *Merton & Buddhism*, 18–20.

194. AJ, 125.

195. Thurston, "Footnotes to the Asian Journey of Thomas Merton," 222.

contemplative dialogue between contemplatives and monastics. As has already been noted, Merton planned to learn from Tibetan monks after his Asian journey. Tibetan scholar Lobsang Phuntsok Lhalungpa, who met Merton in Delhi several times, reports that "before [Merton] left for Thailand he told me about his plan to bring some Tibetan monks to the United States and house them near Gethsemani so that he and the Trappist monks could learn about Tibetan meditation techniques from them."[196] Talbott also refers to Merton's plan to learn Tibetan meditation practices with Chatral Rinpoche. Talbott said that he "was curious about his Faith in Jesus Christ inhering in him along with his intention to train with Chatral Rinpoche in order to practice the Long Chen Nying Thig lineal transmission of the practice of Dzogpachenpo of the Nyingmapa Buddhists of Tibet."[197]

Merton went to Asia looking not for artifacts but for living witnesses in ancient sources and then discovered spiritual brothers and mentors in Asia. He felt especially comfortable with the Tibetan Buddhists. Through learning their meditation and his meetings with them, his consciousness was transformed by seeing himself and others "from the Tibetan side."[198] While Zen meditation helped him to discover a connection point between Buddhist and Christian contemplative practices, Tibetan meditation inspired him to find the way for further development of Christian meditation toward perfect spiritual freedom. This new insight offered his dream of contemplative dialogue between monastics or contemplatives of different religious traditions in spiritual communion at a deep spiritual and practical level.

196. Ibid., 223–224.
197. Ibid., 226. "Long Chen Nying Thig" is revealed scripture of the *Nyingma* school that gives a systematic explanation of *dzogchen*. "Dzogpachenpo" means someone who has achieved a high realization of *dzogchen*.
198. AJ, 152.

Conclusion

Thomas Merton was a pioneer in Buddhist-Christian dialogue in that he achieved an integrated level of dialogue with Buddhists based on self-transformation. Through his engagement in dialogue, he realized the dangers of a facile comparison and syncretism. He saw that Buddhists and Christians must dialogue at a profound spiritual level since those who experienced self-transcendence were no longer in isolation but were able to accept others with openness, freedom, and love, and to dialogue with them at a mature level. Merton noted, "The more I am able to affirm others, to say 'yes' to them in myself, by discovering them in myself and myself in them, the more real I am. I am fully real if my own heart says *yes* to *everyone*."[199] His openness to others and his scrupulous respect of significant differences in other traditions led him to learn from them and to attain deeper spiritual maturity.

Indeed, his enthusiasm for self-transformation and union with God in his own contemplative tradition was carried over into his dialogue with Zen Buddhism and contributed to the development of his new view of contemplation as well as to the attainment of a new spiritual awareness. His progress involved regarding the inner self not only as the connecting point between God or the Absolute and the human person, but as the point of intersection between East and West. He realized that the integration of one's inner self can bring about a new identity and a spiritual rebirth in Christ, in whom there is no Jew or Greek, male or female, slave or free (cf. Gal 3:28).

In his transformation of consciousness, Merton's encounter with Buddhists exemplifies the bonding of spiritual friendship, brotherhood, solidarity at a profound level, and the achievement of mutual enrichment through spiritual exchange in which one is both learner and teacher. Despite the limitations of his knowledge of Zen and the challenges inherent in Christian-Buddhist dialogue,

---

199. CGB, 140 (emphasis in original).

he achieved a new and spiritually mature regard for Buddhists and learned to appreciate the depths of their spirituality. He stated that "we have now reached a stage of . . . religious maturity at which it may be possible for someone to remain perfectly faithful to a Christian or Western monastic commitment, and yet learn in depth from . . . a Buddhist or Hindu discipline and experience."[200] He showed that the goal of dialogue between these two traditions was not conversion, proselytization, syncretism, or indifferentism, but deep exchange and spiritual communion, leading to mutual transformation.

At the end of his life, Merton was planning for further spiritual exchanges with Tibetan Buddhists. He was especially eager to learn more about their deep meditation practice. Talbott points out that "Merton had passed through . . . the stage of *kenosis*, self-emptying, and was spurning nothing. He possessed something of the 'pure perception' that is developed by practicing . . . Tibetan Buddhism."[201] Through his encounter with Tibetan Buddhists, his longing for attaining perfect self-emptiness was increased, and his desire to share their deep spirituality with Christian monastics and contemplatives was confirmed. He noted, "I have an immense amount to learn from Asia. . . . I am convinced that a rather superficial Christianity in European dress is not enough for Asia. We have lacked depth. We have lacked the breadth of view to grasp all the wonderful breadth and richness in the Asian traditions."[202]

Despite his spiritual depth in his own tradition, he longed to learn from Asian traditions in order to attain a deeper experience of enlightenment and to build a new and spiritually profound solidarity with Asian contemplatives. His spiritual yearning led him to integrate the Buddhist and Christian concepts of religious experience and practice. The inspiration he acquired from Buddhism encouraged him to propose that some of its teachings and

200. AJ, 313.
201. Cited in Thurston, "Unfolding of a New World," 21.
202. SD, 287.

practices might help the church come to a deeper understanding of Christian contemplation, in much the same way as the inspiration St. Thomas Aquinas acquired from Aristotelian philosophy led him to put forward some positions of Aristotle to help the church come to a deeper understanding of the Christian faith. Merton was not a systematic theologian, but he made a great contribution to the development of Christian contemplative life by bringing to it the light of Buddhist philosophy, practice, and experiences. In addition, through his encounter with Buddhist monastics and lay contemplatives, Merton saw possibilities for contemplative dialogue and inter-monastic exchange with them, and also with monastics or contemplatives in Hinduism, Judaism, Taoism, and Islam. The next chapter will deal with Merton's legacy in the areas of contemplative dialogue and inter-monastic exchange in more detail.

CHAPTER 3

Merton's Pioneering Work with Inter-Monastic/Contemplative Dialogue

Many of the world's great religions have monastic traditions that have been practiced for centuries. In the twentieth century, Christian monastics or contemplatives, especially Thomas Merton, realized that they could dialogue with other monastics through inter-monastic encounters, where they could experientially explore each other's monastic disciplines.[1] On November 21, 2014, Pope Francis encouraged inter-monastic dialogue and its development in his "Letter to All Consecrated People":

> Nor can we forget that the phenomenon of monasticism and of other expressions of religious fraternity is present in all the great religions. There are instances, some long-standing, of inter-monastic dialogue involving the Catholic Church and certain of the great religious traditions. I trust that the Year of

---

1. For Merton, "inter-monastic encounters" or "inter-monastic exchanges" means the contact between monastics of different religious traditions through the sharing of monastic life, spiritual practices, and contemplative experience. It is similar to "inter-monastic dialogue" but more focused on mutual exchange through actual meetings.

> Consecrated Life will be an opportunity *to review* the progress made, *to make consecrated persons aware* of this dialogue, and *to consider* what *further steps* can be taken towards greater mutual understanding and greater cooperation in the many common areas of service to human life.[2]

Pope Francis, who was aware of the value of monasticism for future interreligious dialogue, recommends a review of the progress already made by monastic men and women who have engaged in interreligious dialogue.

Merton was a pioneer of inter-monastic encounters with Buddhists. He first engaged in Buddhist-Christian dialogue with D. T. Suzuki. This encounter led him to enter into dialogue with Asian monastic traditions. He believed that inter-monastic dialogue could play a significant role for monastic renewal and could pave the way for dialogue with all contemplatives, whether lay or monastic. By the end of his life, he had become a promoter of an existential, experiential, and spiritual level of "contemplative dialogue" through "intermonastic communion."[3] His dialogue with monastics or contemplatives in other religions was focused on *spiritual communion* beyond the realm of doctrine. He believed that if inter-monastic encounters were anchored in monastic contemplative dialogue, it could lead to a true heart-to-heart dialogue and a mutual affirmation of the wisdom of other traditions. In a "state of trans-cultural maturity," he realized, "we are already one," and contemplative dialogue and inter-monastic exchanges could help to retrieve humanity's original *unity-in-diversity*.[4]

The few studies that deal with Merton's inter-monastic dialogue at the contemplative level reveal his striving to find God

---

2. Pope Francis, "To All Consecrated People: On the Occasion of the Year of Consecrated Life" (November 21, 2014), #4, http://w2.vatican.va/content /francesco/en/apost_letters/documents/papa-francesco_lettera-ap_20141121 _lettera-consacrati.html (emphasis added).

3. AJ, 316.

4. CWA, 206; AJ, 308.

in contemplation and in openness to monastics of other religious traditions. Although such authors as Pierre-François de Béthune, Fabrice Blée, and Peter Bowe refer to Merton's contribution to monastic interreligious dialogue, the specific role that Merton played in the development of inter-monastic exchanges has not yet been the subject of serious study and analysis.[5] The reason for this may be that Merton did not fully or concretely explore inter-monastic encounters in detail, and his interest in inter-monastic dialogue overlapped with his attraction to contemplative dialogue, which includes non-monastics, in Buddhist-Christian dialogue. In addition, his direct and indirect intentions regarding inter-monastic exchanges gradually evolved through his encounter with Buddhist monastics and contemplatives. References to those intentions and the methods he used to engage in such exchanges are scattered throughout his writings. Thus, with regard to both inter-monastic exchange and inter-contemplative dialogue, it is necessary to scrutinize Merton's journals, notes, and addresses, especially those in which he refers to his meetings with Buddhist masters, lamas, and rinpoches. Furthermore, in order to gain an insight into his unique contribution to monastic interreligious dialogue, it is necessary to examine his progress toward inter-contemplative dialogue through inter-monastic communion from a transcultural perspective.

This chapter will argue that Merton created a new paradigm for interreligious dialogue by means of inter-monastic exchange and inter-contemplative dialogue. I will first present his motives for interreligious dialogue with monastics and contemplatives. I will then explore the value of his inter-monastic exchange in

---

5. See Pierre-François de Béthune, *Interreligious Hospitality: The Fulfillment of Dialogue* (Collegeville, MN: Liturgical Press, 2010), xv, 6; Blée, *The Third Desert*, 8, 28–42; Peter Bowe, "Contemporary Witness, Future Configuration: Monastic Interfaith Dialogue," in *Catholics in Interreligious Dialogue: Studies in Monasticism, Theology and Spirituality*, ed. Antony O'Mahony and Peter Bowe (Leominster, UK: Gracewing, 2006), 10–25.

the light of various forms of interreligious dialogue and examine what the relationship between inter-monastic exchange and inter-contemplative dialogue will be. I will also attempt to show how Merton's inter-monastic exchanges proceeded from finding his own searching, to discovering friendship with other monastics and forming bonds in a cross-cultural monastic spiritual family. He believed that spiritual communion between monastics could lead to universal communion with all contemplatives. Further, I will deal with Merton's understanding of spiritual communion and the relationship between transcultural maturity and inter-monastic dialogue. After addressing the question of whether or not the concept of communion is to be found in Buddhism, I will conclude with an evaluation of Merton's inter-monastic exchange through the contributions he hoped to make and those he actually made.

Motives for Monastic and Contemplative Interreligious Dialogue

When we consider what motivated Merton to engage in inter-monastic dialogue between East and West, we may wonder what more precisely it was about Asian monasticism that he believed could be helpful for Catholic monastic renewal. Did he believe that Asian monasticism was perfect? If monasticism is not just a Christian phenomenon, and if a seed of contemplation is present in everyone, what did Merton find in the relationship between the monastic archetype and the hidden contemplative dimension of interreligious dialogue? Establishing Merton's motives for inter-monastic dialogue will provide answers to these questions.

The Renewal of Catholic Monasticism

Following the Protestant Reformation of the sixteenth century, the Catholic institution of monasticism went into decline, and monasticism all but disappeared in many predominantly Protestant regions.[6] Moreover, the growth of secularization, rationalism, and science in the modern period brought about a general loss of interest in contemplative life, and monasticism was thoroughly marginalized. This loss of interest in the contemplative life was still evident when Merton entered the Abbey of Gethsemani in 1941. However, through his own monastic experience and his rediscovery of the spirituality of the Desert Fathers and Mothers, he realized how important it was to revive contemplation within Christian monastic communities. Hence, in the 1960s, he devoted himself to the development of monastic renewal by returning to the original monastic charism, adapting it to the modern world and directing it to the inner transformation of all contemplative monks and nuns.

Merton's first concern for monastic renewal was "the clarification of monastic principles by a return to sources."[7] He believed that the monastic life should not be assessed according to norms that would be appropriate for evaluating the active religious life or apostolic ministry. He recognized—and disapproved of—the degree to which materialism and activism were penetrating monastic communities, causing monks and nuns to lose their true monastic vocation, namely, contemplation. He noted that monastic renewal "will not be possible if, in fact, those monastic institutions, which are active rather than contemplative, are taken as the norm. The monastic life as lived in the large active communities today devoted to education or to business is not fully normal."[8] To overcome this conflict between the interior and the exterior

6. There was also an abundance of new Catholic orders that emerged over the centuries that questioned the notion that contemplation had to mean withdrawal from society: the dialectic between action and contemplation, the rise of apostolic orders, and so forth.

7. Thomas Merton, "Monastic Renewal: A Memorandum," in *Thomas Merton: The Monastic Journey*, ed. Patrick Hart (Garden City, NY: Image Books, 1978), 214.

8. Ibid. See also SCL, 147–151; SS, 351.

life, Merton suggested rediscovering the "ancient tradition" rather than keeping a "rigid and stereotyped" monastic institution.[9] For him, to "return to sources" was to "concentrate on the *charism of the monastic vocation*" as well as to rediscover "the meaning and spirit of monasticism as it was understood and lived by the early monks."[10] In the third century, a time of great growth of monasticism, the charism of the ancient monastic way "centered in the witness of complete renunciation in obedience to the gospel" and aimed at "the freedom and peace of the wilderness existence, a return to the desert that [was] also a recovery of (inner) paradise."[11] Following the directive of the Second Vatican Council that religious orders should return to their original charism, his first principle for monastic renewal was to *let monks, inspired by their monastic forebears, be true contemplative monks.*

Merton also realized that ancient monastic spirituality was not just for monastics or hermits, but also for the church and for the world. He believed that the monastic was a person "who at once loves the world, yet stands apart from it with a critical objectivity which refuses to become involved in its transient fashions and its more manifest absurdities."[12] He did not reject ordinary human life and experience, for through them God could manifest himself. Rather, he pointed out that for Christian monastics, true *aggiornamento* did not mean mere social adjustment but *openness* to the world and also to non-Christian monastics, without "depriving them of the authentic riches of their mystical and prophetic tradition."[13] He noted, " 'Openness' is essential to renewal itself [and] is *necessary* for contemplatives, [who] are witnesses of Christ, of the new creation . . . of the Living God . . . by their

---

9. IE, 77–78.
10. CWA, 15 (emphasis in original), 126.
11. Ibid., 127, 18.
12. Merton, "The Monk Today," 241.
13. MZM, 214.

lives and by the transformation of their consciousness."[14] In the dynamic movement between a return to the original sources and openness to others, expressed through dialogue with other ancient monastic traditions and their spiritual disciplines, he saw the possibility of monastic renewal within Christianity.

Second, Merton insisted that genuine monastic renewal did not consist in changing or reforming monastic structures, but in a total inner transformation.[15] As he noted, "What is essential in the monastic life is not embedded in buildings, is not embedded in clothing, is not necessarily embedded even in a rule. . . . It is concerned with [the] business of total inner transformation. . . . All other things serve that end."[16] Fundamentally, monastics, who seek God, have to undergo the experience of inner conversion, namely, a total inner transformation whereby one becomes a new person in Christ. Merton stated that the identity of monastics "cannot be preserved without a discipline oriented to real inner transformation, to the development of a 'new man.' "[17] For him, true monastic renewal was interior and personal. In October 1964, he wrote to Father Columba Halsey, a Benedictine monk from Kentucky, "It is also true that no amount of change in the institution will matter if we do not grow and change ourselves. And I think the crucial thing in all this reform is the deepening of *faith* in the individual monk."[18] He saw that the renewal of individual

14. CWA, 133, 134 (emphasis in original). Merton noted, "The real purpose of openness is to renew life in the Spirit, life in love. A greater love and understanding of people is no obstacle to a true growth in contemplation, for contemplation is rooted and grounded in charity." See CWA, 140.

15. Merton distinguished a "renewal" from a "reform." For him, the renewal "requires active participation at every level," but the reform "starts at the top with the action of superiors and reaches the subject passively through new laws and new decrees to be accepted and obeyed." See ibid., 84.

16. AJ, 340; see more, Thomas F. McKenna, "Thomas Merton and the Renewal of Religious Life," *Merton Annual* 3 (1990): 117.

17. CWA, 106.

18. SCL, 249 (emphasis in original).

monks, brought about by an inner transformation through union with God, could contribute to monastic renewal as well as to a renewal of the Church.[19]

Through his encounter with monastics in other traditions, especially Buddhists, Merton realized that their monastic tradition could help him develop his two views for monastic renewal, that is, a return to sources and a total inner transformation. He did not enter into dialogue with Buddhist monastics simply to obtain information or to compare monastic disciplines; he did so for the purpose of Catholic monastic renewal.[20] His encounter with ancient Asian sources and monastic practices led him to realize that they could inspire Christian monastics who were pursuing a return to "simpler monastic ways" and the recovery of "a deeper life of prayer."[21] Of course, Merton did not consider Asian monasticism to be perfect. He saw that, like Western monasticism, Eastern monastic traditions were also faced with many problems, and indeed, were in crisis because of materialism.[22] However, he was fascinated by their ancient sources and practical ways, in both of which he discovered vast treasures of monastic wisdom concerning self-transformation and compassionate love. He realized that both East and West were "concentrated on what is really essential to the monastic quest: this . . . is to be sought in the area of true self-transcendence and enlightenment . . . in the transformation of consciousness in its ultimate ground . . . and most authentic devotional love of the bhakti type."[23] He also saw

19. See CWA, 105.

20. In 1968, before leaving Gethsemani, Merton noted, "Considering the crucial importance of the time, the need for monastic renewal, the isolation of our Asian monasteries, their constant appeals for help, I feel it a duty to respond. And I hope this will enable me to get in contact with Buddhist monasticism and see something of it firsthand." See AJ, 295. See also AJ, 312–313; CWA, 182; Thurston, "Why Merton Looked East," 47–48; Shannon, *Silent Lamp*, 272.

21. Merton, "Monastic Renewal," 215.

22. See AJ, 307; MZM, 231.

23. AJ, 316.

that these monastic values were developed differently in different religious and cultural contexts. Thus, Merton believed "that some of us need to [learn in depth from a Buddhist or Hindu discipline and experience] in order to improve the quality of our own monastic life and to help in the task of monastic renewal which has been undertaken within the Western Church."[24] Indeed, his exchanges with and learning from Eastern monks helped to revitalize Western monasticism and influenced the process of shaping "the new monasticism."[25]

The Discovery of Monkhood and the Contemplative Charism in All Religions

Merton's Christian understanding of monastic life gradually changed from a medieval Christian view to a more universalist view. Until the late 1950s, his view of the common life was limited to the traditional image of a monk as "a different species of being, pseudoangels . . . [and persons] of interior life."[26] This separate and superior understanding of monastic life, however, was transformed in Merton through his own religious experiences and inner conversion. In a later writing, he noted that "the monk belongs to the world, but the world belongs to him insofar as he has dedicated himself totally to liberation from it in order to

24. Ibid., 313. At the end of his Asian journey, Merton told Jean Jadot, a former President of the Vatican Secretariat for Non-Christians in Rome, "What . . . I think we have to learn from India, is the importance of the guru, the master, the spiritual master. . . . This is something we have lost in our Catholic tradition, and we have to return to it." See Jean Jadot, "Jean Jadot," in *Merton by Those Who Knew Him Best*, 156.

25. CWA, 13. Gregory J. Ryan argues that "the seeds lying dormant in Merton's ideas about monasticism have germinated, flowered, and borne fruit in the New Monasticism, in communities through America and Europe." See Gregory J. Ryan, "Merton, Main, and the New Monasticism," *Monastic Studies* 18 (1988): 120–121.

26. CGB, 154.

liberate it."[27] His early view of Asian monasticism and mysticism was also transformed and extended. For example, through his encounter with other monastic/contemplative traditions, Merton's understanding of the term "monastic" was no longer restricted to the Christian world. It now included: 1) a certain detachment from secular concerns of worldly life, whether partial or total, temporary or permanent, 2) a preoccupation with the radical inner depth of one's religious and philosophical beliefs, and 3) a special concern with inner transformation and the discovery of a transcendent dimension of life, even for those who did not adopt a celibate form of monasticism, as was the case, for example, in some Japanese Buddhist schools and Islamic Sufism.[28]

Moreover, through his meetings with contemplatives who were "experienced and fully qualified to represent such traditions as Raja Yoga, Zen, Hasidism, Tibetan Buddhism, Sufism," Merton recognized that "the question of contacts and actual communication between contemplatives of the various traditions no longer presents very great obstacles."[29] Thus, he did not hesitate to claim that Western contemplative monastics could become partners in dialogue with Asian contemplative monastics: "If anyone should be open to these Oriental traditions and interested in them, it should be the contemplative monks of the Western monastic orders."[30] His discovery of a common monastic way of life and the value of monastic exchanges with different religious traditions were closely related to his realization that God's call to contemplation is universal.

---

27. AJ, 341.

28. See ibid., 309–310. Michael W. Higgins points out that "one way Merton found to implode the constricting and reductionist definition of monkhood that identified it exclusively with Christian tradition was to view it from the perspective of the East, in whose spiritual tradition contradictions and negation cease and the contraries live in harmony." See Michael W. Higgins, *Thomas Merton: Faithful Visionary* (Collegeville, MN: Liturgical Press, 2014), 95.

29. MZM, 209.

30. Ibid., vii.

Across cultures and throughout history virtually every religious tradition has given rise to a monastic form of life. Raimon Panikkar, a Roman Catholic cleric with an academic interest in Eastern religious traditions, describes it as the *archetype of monkhood*, which can be realized in any human person who seeks a relationship with the transcendent through the mode of simplicity. He notes, "Monasticism is not a specifically Christian, Jaina, Buddhist, or sectarian phenomenon; rather, it is a basically human and primordially religious one. . . . Every human being has a monastic dimension that everyone must realize in different ways."[31] Although Merton did not explicitly speak of the archetype of monkhood, the concept corresponds to his realization that the contemplative call was addressed to everyone. He believed that the seeds of contemplation are present in people of every culture, but they are hidden. He described the hidden contemplative as one who practices a type of "masked contemplation" in daily life.[32] Lay contemplatives living in the world are not monks per se, but they can be true contemplatives. He noted:

> Although they are active laborers, they are also hidden contemplatives because of the great purity of heart maintained in them

31. Raimon Panikkar, *Blessed Simplicity: The Monk as Universal Archetype* (New York, NY: Seabury Press, 1982), 16. Panikkar made an important distinction between the "monk as archetype" and the "archetype of the monk." He did not discuss the monk as archetype, which meant the monk is an ideal of human life, but the archetypal character of monasticism, which is a universal pattern of spirituality in human persons. He considered monasticism as the archetype of human spirituality. See ibid., 7–9. By contrast, Terrence Kardong points out that "the monk does not authenticate himself in any absolute way. 'Monk' is a universally recognized cultural/religious archetype, and one either conforms to that template or one is not a monk." See Terrence Kardong, "Thoughts on the Future of Western Monasticism," in *A Monastic Vision for the 21st Century: Where Do We Go from Here?*, ed. Patrick Hart (Kalamazoo, MI: Cistercian Publications, 2006), 63.

32. Merton wrote, "The 'masked contemplative' is one whose contemplation is hidden from no one so much as from himself." See IE, 64.

by obedience, fraternal charity, self-sacrifice, and perfect abandonment to God's will in all that they do and suffer. They are
much closer to God than they realize. They enjoy a kind of a
"masked" contemplation.[33]

His description of the hidden contemplative shows that they are
not all that far from the monastic way of life, whose aim is "great
purity of heart" and union with God through various monastic disciplines. He believed that this hidden contemplative dimension had
to be awakened in everyone. According to Bowe, for Merton "the
monastic archetype, to be found in all sorts and conditions of men
and women, is marked by a special contemplative dedication . . .
and [by] a special concern for inner personal transformation."[34]
Joachim Viens, a Trappist monk who corresponded with Merton,
points out that for Merton, monkhood did not mean archetypal
in the sense of "some ideal form" but in the sense of that which
"lives in each of us."[35] For Merton, contemplation was essential
for the attainment of self-transformation, and the capacity for
contemplative experience is opened to everyone. He saw that the
search for an interior life, a longing for solitude, and contemplative
experiences could awaken a hidden contemplative.

The discovery of the capacity for contemplation and the hidden
monkhood in all human persons became one of Merton's motives
for the inter-monastic encounters. Monasticism highlights the
radical commitment to religious ideals and cultivates the experience of enlightenment in contemplation by means of common
spiritual practices, such as detachment, solitude, silence, worship,
meditation, and communal and/or hermitic life. Hence, Merton
saw that interreligious dialogue that brought together monastics of
different religions could facilitate mutual enrichment at a practical

33. Ibid.
34. Bowe, "Contemporary Witness, Future Configuration," 14.
35. Joachim Viens, "Thomas Merton's Final Journey," in *Toward an Integrated Humanity*, 223.

and deep spiritual level. Moreover, Merton believed that inter-monastic exchange could help to foster an awakening of "inner" monkhood or the hidden contemplative in everyone. He saw that through dialogue with hidden contemplatives, monastics could play a prophetic role in regaining the most basic human values: "personal integrity, inner peace, authenticity, identity, inner depth, spiritual joy, the capacity to love, the capacity to enjoy God's creation and give thanks."[36] He stressed that sharing the fruits of contemplative practices and monastic life was "a duty" of contemplative monastics in the modern world, one that was facing a crisis of faith and the loss of basic human values.[37]

Merton's Inter-Monastic Exchange and Contemplative Dialogue

At the Gethsemani Encounter in 1996, which can be thought of as one of Merton's most significant legacies for monastic interreligious dialogue, the Dalai Lama suggested to Buddhist and Christian monastics and contemplatives that "we should seek to be following the example that he [Merton] gave to us. If all of us followed this model, it would become very widespread and would

---

36. CWA, 82. Ephrem Arcement points out that "Merton saw that what was distinctive about this ideal of the monk as prophet was that it was an ideal that made itself real. . . . Merton likened the prophetic ideal of the monk to a type of Jungian archetype, with the prophet an archetype for the monk." See Ephrem Arcement, *In the School of Prophets: The Formation of Thomas Merton's Prophetic Spirituality* (Collegeville, MN: Cistercian Publications, 2015), 162. Merton noted, "[the] trope of the 'prophetic' life of the monk [is] a living witness to the truth of God's word, of His promises, and of His demand for penance. The monk is the man who has taken the word of the Lord literally." See Thomas Merton, *Pre-Benedictine Monasticism: Initiation into the Monastic Tradition 2* (Kalamazoo, MI: Cistercian Publications, 2006), 29.

37. CWA, 163.

be of very great benefit to the world."[38] His recommendation implies that Merton's model of inter-monastic encounters was welcomed by Buddhists, and that it could become an example and a model for a form of interreligious dialogue that would benefit the world. We therefore need to look more closely at Merton's actual involvement in inter-monastic exchanges, examine the kind of model or example he provided, and determine how his inter-monastic exchanges can benefit the world, especially those who have lost interest in contemplation and the interior life.

For Merton, inter-monastic *exchange* meant more than meeting with monastics of different religions for mutual understanding. It also meant sharing monastic life experientially and spiritually in different monastic milieus. "Mere sitting at home and meditating on the divine presence is not enough for our time," he wrote. "[Monastics] have to come to the end of a long journey and see that the stranger we meet there is no other than ourselves—which is the same as saying that we find Christ in him."[39] Beyond a doctrinal level of interreligious dialogue and traditional monastic life in the cloister, he discovered a new mode of dialogue between contemplative monastics. This inter-monastic exchange included contemplative dialogue, dialogue through life, and experiential dialogue in depth.

In the following section, I will explore Merton's interreligious dialogue on spirituality, religious experience, and life within the context of monasticism. Since I dealt with his dialogue at the level of religious experience with Buddhism in chapter one, this chapter will be more focused on dialogue at the level of monastic life. Next, his contemplative dialogue, which was alluded to in previous chapters, will be examined in depth in order to discover the essential principle underpinning his inter-monastic encounters.

---

38. The Dalai Lama, "A Tribute to Thomas Merton," in *The Gethsemani Encounter*, 260.

39. Thomas Merton, "From Pilgrimage to Crusade," in *Thomas Merton: Selected Essays*, 204.

Exchange on Spirituality, Experience, and Life through Monasticism

Through direct contact with other monastics and his under-standing of different monastic spiritualities, Merton recognized that inter-monastic encounters could involve three different forms of interreligious dialogue, namely: 1) existential dialogue, 2) experiential dialogue, and 3) practical dialogue.[40]

For Merton, the inter-monastic encounters were, first of all, dialogue at the existential level of experience. He stressed that "it is above all important for Westerners like myself to learn what little they can from Asia, *in* Asia. . . . We must seek not merely to make superficial reports *about* the Asian traditions, but to live and share those traditions, as far as we can, by living them in their traditional milieu."[41] Merton encountered Buddhist monastics or contemplatives and shared his contemplative monastic life with them at his monastery in Gethsemani, Kentucky, and especially during his pilgrimage in Asia. These encounters led him to the conviction that "[inter-monastic exchange] must take place under the true monastic conditions of quiet, tranquility, sobriety, leisure-liness, reverence, meditation, and cloistered peace."[42] Through a lived experience in the monastic milieus of other cultures, monastics can experience monastic practice, prayer, meditation, and the work of different traditions on an existential level. Merton believed that inter-monastic exchanges on this level could show that this was "precisely the most fruitful" and often the best possible way "to come to a very frank, simple, and totally satisfying

40. See AJ, 312–313; ZBA, 39; MZM, viii.

41. AJ, 313 (emphasis in original). Before his Asian pilgrimage, Merton wrote, "I am convinced that it is very important for me to meet some Eastern monks and also see some of our own Christian monasteries out there." See Thomas Merton and Jean Leclercq, *Survival or Prophecy?: The Letters of Thomas Merton and Jean Leclercq*, ed. Patrick Hart (New York, NY: Farrar, Straus and Giroux, 2002), 164.

42. AJ, 313.

understanding in comparing notes on the contemplative life, its disciplines, its vagaries, and its rewards."[43] He saw that despite cultural and doctrinal differences, dialogue at this level could offer real contact between Eastern and Western monastics. In his notes "Monastic Experience and East-West Dialogue," Merton stated, "Cultural and doctrinal differences must remain, but they do not invalidate a very real quality of existential likeness. . . . On this existential level of experience . . . it is possible to achieve real and significant contacts and perhaps much more besides."[44] Although many monastics or contemplatives were "devoted to a somewhat hidden and solitary mode of life," he suggested that having "an opportunity to visit monasteries where other . . . contemplative traditions" existed could contribute to genuine dialogue with other contemplatives.[45]

Second, Merton discovered that inter-monastic encounters could become a forum for sharing religious experience in depth. He saw that Christian monastics have a specific position from which to dialogue with Asian Hindu and Buddhist monastics about spiritual experiences. He stated, "Catholic monasticism . . . is in a better position for dialogue with Asia at the moment because of the climate of openness following Vatican II. Catholic monasticism . . . could also apply very well to Hindu and Buddhist philosophies, disciplines, [and] experiences."[46] His encounter with Buddhist monasticism made clear to him the central role that monasticism played in Asian religions. He therefore realized that it would be insufficient to interact with them simply at the intellectual level; interaction needed to take place at the experiential level of monasticism and contemplation. He noted, "The values hidden in Oriental thought actually reveal themselves only on the plane of spiritual experience . . . [and] a

43. MZM, 209.
44. AJ, 312.
45. MZM, 208.
46. AJ, 311.

dialogue with Oriental wisdom becomes necessary."[47] Merton saw that the monastic life in different religious traditions was commonly organized to attain self-transformation through the various spiritual practices and experiences that are essential to monastic life. Monastic traditions throughout the world have treasured the religious experiences of the great monastics or masters of their own traditions, but there is no uniform contemplative experience. Thus, Merton saw that sharing monastic riches at the level of spiritual experience could contribute to mutual enrichment by recontextualizing one's own monastic spirituality.[48] Through his inter-monastic encounters in Asia, Merton shared in the contemplative experience of Buddhist monastics or contemplatives in order to deepen his own contemplative life, and to attain new horizons of religious experience.

The third element of Merton's inter-monastic encounters was the sharing of spiritual disciplines and contemplative practices. He saw that "the great contemplative traditions of East and West . . . agree in thinking that by spiritual disciplines a man can radically change his life and attain to a deeper meaning, a more perfect integration, a more complete fulfillment, a more total liberty of spirit."[49] In fact, the goals and methods of Buddhist and Christian monastic practices are neither totally the same nor totally different. Merton respected different monastic disciplines and desired to learn from them without losing his own monastic commitment. He noted, "I think that we have now reached a stage of (long overdue) religious maturity at which it may be possible for

47. Merton, "Christian Culture Needs Oriental Wisdom," 112.

48. Merton noted, "The classics of monasticism and contemplation are there to be reinterpreted for modern readers. . . . Oriental ways of contemplation (Zen, Yoga, Taoism) can no longer be completely neglected by us." Although Sufism and Hassidism are not strictly monasticism in the Christian sense, Merton considered that they are "closely related to a monastic type of spirituality." See CWA, 113.

49. MZM, viii.

someone to remain perfectly faithful to a Christian and Western monastic commitment, and yet learn in depth from, say, a Buddhist or Hindu discipline or experience."[50] He saw that Christian monastic spirituality could be developed by the study and practice of Asian monastic disciplines. For example, the insights offered by Zen monasticism led him to conclude that the monastic practices of Christianity and Zen have in common the elements of guidance by a spiritual director or a master and the utilization of practical tools, such as meditation, to attain spiritual insights. He stated, "In Asian traditions as well as in Christian monasticism, there has been considerable stress on the need for a guide or spiritual father, an experienced elder who knows how to bring the less experienced to a decisive point of breakthrough where this 'new being' is attained."[51] However, Merton saw that the relationship between a master and a disciple had become weak in the Christian monastic tradition. He stated, "Christian monasticism . . . might compensate, to some extent, for the lack of an experienced and charismatic teacher."[52] In this regard, Merton attempted to seek a spiritual mentor on his Asian trip. He noted, "If I were going to settle down with a Tibetan guru, I think Chatral would be the one I'd choose."[53] He intended to learn Tibetan foundational practices (*ngondro*) and *dzogchen* meditation from Chatral Rinpoche, and even envisioned learning Tibetan practical ways at the Abbey of Gethsemani along with his fellow monks.[54] He also discussed with Harold Talbott "the possibility of getting Sonam Kazi or

50. AJ, 313.

51. CWA, 202. Merton notes that "strictly speaking, Christian monasticism is less dependent on the aid of a guide than some of the other traditions. In Sufism and Zen the spiritual master is as essential as the analyst in psychoanalysis." See ibid., 202.

52. Ibid.

53. AJ, 144.

54. See Thurston, "Footnotes to the Asian Journey of Thomas Merton," 223–224.

someone to set up a good Tibetan meditation center in America, perhaps in New Mexico, in some indirect connection with Christ in the Desert."[55] Merton saw that Christian monastics could become partners in dialogue with Asian monastics who practice various ways of meditation: *Yoga* in Hinduism, *Zazen* in Zen Buddhism, *Vipassana* in Theravada Buddhism, and *Dzogchen* in Tibetan Buddhism.[56] His inter-monastic encounters were focused on actually learning various spiritual disciplines from monastics or contemplatives of different religious traditions and sharing his monastic daily practices with them.

Contemplative Dialogue: The Principle of Inter-Monastic Encounters

Merton's inter-monastic encounters opened a new era for interreligious dialogue by discovering the value of contemplation as a basis for dialogue between Eastern and Western religious traditions. Before Merton, the mystical or contemplative tradition tended to be thought of almost as belonging exclusively to the spiritual domain of Christianity. In addition, beginning with the Parliament of the World's Religions in Chicago in 1893, interreligious dialogue seemed to be solely concerned with intellectual or theological discussions in order to prove the superiority of Christianity. In the post–World War II era, however, some Christian academics and religious began to realize the value of Eastern religion and spirituality. At that time, Merton played a pioneering role by rediscovering the Christian contemplative tradition and by

---

55. AJ, 166. Merton visited the Benedictine Monastery of Christ in the Desert at Chama Canyon, New Mexico, in May and in September 1968.

56. His inter-monastic dialogue through meditation practice was not a reductionist view that merely tried to find a way for situating other monastic practice into a Christian framework. He took up an Asian meditation practice, first of all, for his own spiritual enlightenment since he believed that there were specific methods for attaining enlightenment in different cultural or religious contexts.

coming to an appreciation of the depth of Eastern contemplative traditions.[57] He noted, "One of the most important aspects of inter-faith dialogue . . . is the special contribution that the contemplative life can bring to the dialogue, not only among Christians but also between Christians and the ancient religions of the East."[58] He was convinced that interreligious dialogue could be brought to a deeper level by including the contemplative dimension, and so he promoted "contemplative dialogue" between the Eastern and Western contemplative traditions. He noted:

> [T]he great contemplative traditions of East and West, while differing sometimes quite radically in their formulation of their aims and in their understanding of their methods, agree in thinking that by spiritual disciplines a man can radically change his life and attain to a deeper meaning, a more perfect integration, a more complete fulfillment, a more total liberty of spirit. . . . Far from being suspicious of the Oriental mystical traditions, Catholic contemplatives since the Second Vatican Council should be in a position to appreciate the wealth of experience that has accumulated in those traditions.[59]

For Merton, contemplative dialogue did not primarily focus on "institutional structure, monastic rule, traditional forms of cult and observance," but on "enlightenment itself" and "interior development."[60] The Second Vatican Council authorized and em-

---

57. Simmer-Brown points out that "in the decades since Merton's untimely death, there has been tremendous change in contemplative communities in Buddhism and Christianity, change that has affected the abilities of the practice communities to survive at all." See Judith Simmer-Brown, " 'Wide Open to Life': Thomas Merton's Dialogue of Contemplative Practice," *Buddhist-Christian Studies* 35 (2015): 195.

58. MZM, 203.

59. Ibid., viii.

60. AJ, 317.

powered his radical commitment to interreligious dialogue with contemplatives in Asian traditions.[61]

As a condition for fruitful contemplative dialogue, Merton stressed the necessity of spiritual maturity through a long period of discipline within a contemplative tradition. His contemplative dialogue was rooted in spiritual maturity obtained through contemplative experience shaped by daily monastic disciplines, a contemplative experience that was infused with a longing for union with God. Buddhist contemplatives are also continually involved in the practice of spiritual disciplines in order to obtain enlightenment. Merton knew that these spiritual disciplines did not completely guarantee the realization of contemplative experience in either tradition, but they could cultivate "certain inner conditions of awareness, of openness, of readiness for the new and the unexpected" religious experience.[62] In addition, the contemplative practice could promote the spiritual maturity and openness to others at a deeper spiritual level. For authentic contemplative dialogue, Merton suggested that "contemplative dialogue must be reserved for those who have been seriously disciplined by years of silence and by a long habit of meditation."[63] He saw that without serious spiritual discipline and preparation in one's own tradition, contemplative dialogue could remain at the superficial level of subjective or provincial immaturity.

---

61. For instance, the Second Vatican Council declared, "The Catholic Church rejects nothing of what is true and holy in these [Asian] religions. . . . The Church therefore has this exhortation for her sons: prudently and lovingly, through dialogue and collaboration with the followers of other religions, and in witness of Christian faith and life, acknowledge, preserve and promote the spiritual and moral goods found among these men, as well as the values in their society and culture." See "Declaration on the Relationship of the Church to Non-Christian Religions" (*Nostra Aetate*), no. 2, in *Interreligious Dialogue*, 44. See also MZM, viii–ix.

62. CWA, 101.

63. AJ, 316.

Merton saw that Buddhist and Christian monastics were in a better position for contemplative dialogue.[64] Through encounters with Buddhist contemplative monastics, he realized that inter-monastic dialogue could facilitate spiritual communion with them. Thus, he considered contemplative dialogue to be a basic principle of inter-monastic encounters. Merton did not distinguish inter-monastic dialogue from contemplative dialogue, nor did he exclude lay contemplatives from inter-monastic dialogue. Although his use of the term "monastic" was extended to various forms of contemplative life in the great religions, he noted that not all contemplatives are monastics.[65] Considering this overlap and his insistence that inter-monastic dialogue was not merely for

64. Merton saw the value of Hinduism through Aldous Huxley's book *Ends and Means*, and the *Bhagavad-Gita*, the *Upanishads*, the *Yoga Sutras* of Patanjali, and the life of Mahatma Gandhi, and he also corresponded with the Hindus and wrote about the holiness of a Hindu monk, Brahmachari, in the essay, "Dr. M. B. Brahmachari: A Personal Tribute." Despite all positive impressions, Merton was more interested in Buddhist monasticism than the Hindu. Through encounter with Buddhist tradition, he realized "its deep contemplativeness and stress on experience and awareness, and its ability to transform the monks whom he met into persons of evident holiness." See Rachel F. McDermott, "Why Zen Buddhism and not Hinduism?: The Asias of Thomas Merton's Voyages East," *The Merton Annual* 23 (2010): 32. Hinduism also has the same religious elements, such as contemplation, meditation, nonduality, and self-transformation, but McDermott argues that three elements of Hindu tradition influenced Merton to prefer a closer focus on Buddhist monasticism in his inter-monastic dialogue: 1) the Hindu emphasis on the *guru* and *yogi*: Merton thought that Christians did not need a *guru* "in the flesh" since they have a Jesus, a living master, and thus he preferred Buddhist monastic communities to the Hindu *yogi* or *swami*, who has a tendency to be itinerant and to wander in the streets begging; 2) the Hindu emphasis on image worship: Merton was not interested in all their exuberant but somewhat "laughable" image worship; 3) the Hindu emphasis on the caste: Merton saw the poor in Calcutta and may have attributed this problem to caste consciousness. See McDermott, "Why Zen Buddhism and not Hinduism?," 37–40; cf. AJ, 238.

65. See AJ, 309–317.

monastics, a new phrase, *inter-monastic/contemplative dialogue,* can be used to describe his model of interreligious dialogue.

Merton's Paths of Inter-Monastic/ Contemplative Dialogue

Thomas Merton was not the first Christian monk to engage in monastic interreligious dialogue. Throughout the twentieth century, Christian monastics or contemplatives had sought an encounter with monastics and contemplatives of different religious traditions. For example, Henri Le Saux (Abhishiktananda, 1910–1973), a French Benedictine monk, tried to adapt Benedictine monasticism to the Hindu ascetical tradition of *sannyasa* (renunciation of material desires and prejudices). Le Saux immersed himself totally in Hindu mysticism by living in India. Bede Griffiths (1906–1993), an English Benedictine monk, devoted much of his ministry in India to applying elements of *sannyasa* to Western monasticism. Although Louis Massignon (1883–1962) was not formally a monk, he approached Islam from a mystical and monastic perspective.[66]

Like them, Merton saw that monasticism and contemplation could be useful for interreligious dialogue. He noted, "There is a real possibility of contact on a deep level between this contemplation and the monastic tradition in the West and the various

---

66. See Pierre-François de Béthune, "Monastic Interreligious Dialogue: A History," in *Catholics in Interreligious Dialogue*, 4–5; Blée, *The Third Desert*, 33–42. Bowe points out that Louis Massignon "felt that Islam, up to then deeply suspicious of monasticism, would one day be able, in reaching out to a new mystical reality, to discover its need for full integration and completion in precisely that forbidden . . . monastic ideal. . . . For the monastic ideal, shared across the boundaries of religion and of lifestyles within the various religious traditions themselves, pertains and points in some way indeed to the end time, to the fulfillment of all things." See Bowe, "Contemporary Witness, Future Configuration," 14.

contemplative traditions in the East—including the Islamic Sufis
. . . [and] the better-known monastic groups in Hinduism and
Buddhism."[67] In this regard, we may analyze Merton's unique
approach to inter-monastic dialogue at the level of contemplation
and indicate how he implemented his approach.

For him, the spiritual family, spiritual communion, and transcultural maturity are deeply interconnected in successful inter-
monastic/contemplative dialogue. The spiritual family facilitates
the progress and points to the goal of his dialogue. Spiritual communion expresses the method of his dialogue on spiritual maturity.
The state of transcultural maturity helps one understand the final
integration of his dialogue. These themes were the fruits of his
own contemplative experiences as well as his own inter-monastic/
contemplative dialogue.

The Spiritual Family

Merton's inter-monastic/contemplative dialogue progressed
from an exclusive concern with the self to friendship. He saw that
many monks and contemplatives usually concentrate on seeking
their true self and enlightenment, and that awakened persons are
open to others in friendship. Friendship was a basic dynamic of
Merton's interreligious dialogue. Furthermore, from a universal
perspective, he realized that inter-monastic/contemplative dialogue could facilitate the bonding of the spiritual family of all
contemplatives beyond both religious and cultural boundaries.

Merton's metaphor of the *spiritual family* was deeply related
to his spiritual journey, especially in terms of his search for his
spiritual home. During his premonastic period, he had no home
of his own. He moved from one relative's home to another's and
then to a dormitory. The Abbey of Gethsemani was his home on
earth but not his "true" home. He noted:

67. AJ, 311.

My monastery is not a home. It is not a place where I am rooted and established on the earth. It is not an environment in which I become aware of myself as an individual, but rather a place in which I disappear from the world as an object of interest in order to be everywhere in it by hiddenness and compassion.[68]

Although Merton described his pilgrimage to Asia by saying "I am going home, to the home where I have never been in this body," Asia was also not his eternal dwelling place.[69] Throughout his monastic life, he had sought a spiritual home. For him, home was a symbol of wholeness which had many layers of meaning: from a dwelling place on earth to God's dwelling place in the very center of the human heart.[70] Thus, Merton sought a spiritual home in his self, which was centered "on God, the one center of all, which is 'everywhere and nowhere,' in whom all are encountered, from

---

68. IEW, 45. For Merton, there were two meanings of home: a person's residential home and a spiritual home. He did not merely consider home as a physical place; rather, it pointed to a spiritual meaning. For example, he described the meeting with Suzuki as his home: "In meeting Dr. Suzuki and drinking a cup of tea with him I felt I had met this one man. It was like finally arriving at one's own home." See ZBA, 61. Merton's comment that drinking tea with Suzuki was like arriving at his home demonstrates one of his tendencies for a rather enthusiastic expression of the new insights that occurred to him. See George Kilcourse, *Ace of Freedoms: Thomas Merton's Christ* (Notre Dame, IN: University of Notre Dame Press, 1993), 1–2. Merton's comparison between a residential home and a spiritual home can be compared with the meaning of stability, which is one of the vows of Benedictine monastics. Stability means that the monk or the nun pledges lifelong commitment not only to a particular community, but also to abide in Christ.

69. AJ, 5.

70. Shannon argues that for Merton, " 'Home' is a rich symbol with many layers of meaning. . . . 'Home' can designate the place from which we come (paradise) and the place to which we ultimately return (paradise regained). . . . Understood in this sense, 'home' *roots us in eternity*. It is the symbol of our final integration: we achieve perfect wholeness in God. This is the deepest meaning of 'going home.' " See Shannon, *Silent Lamp*, 8–9 (emphasis in original).

whom all proceed."[71] Through union with God in Christ, he realized that his home was nowhere and everywhere. Regarding the spiritual meaning of home for Merton, his personal friend Deba P. Patnaik points out that "the home [Merton] refers to is the ground of being/becoming of mystical contemplation, ecstatic faith, and spiritual enlightenment."[72]

Merton saw that looking for one's spiritual home was grounded in many monastic or anchoritic traditions. The beginner in monastic life leaves his or her family and home and lives in a new community under a rule or alone under the direction of a master. The novice avoids a stable place and comfortable life and practices spiritual disciplines in order to attain spiritual freedom and detachment from the ego. The experience of enlightenment leads him or her to realize the interdependence of all things. Then, the awakened person begins to see others as spiritual brothers and sisters and to enter a fuller communion with the divine, other persons, and nature, as members of the spiritual family.

With this understanding of the spiritual family, Merton called monastics from different traditions brothers. For example, in 1966 Merton met Thich Nhat Hanh when the Vietnamese monk visited the Abbey of Gethsemani during a lecture tour urging the end of the Vietnamese War. He wrote, "Nhat Hanh is *my brother*. . . . We are both monks, and we have lived the monastic life about the same number of years. . . . I have far more in common with [him] than I have with many Americans. . . . [These] are the bonds of a new solidarity and a *new brotherhood*."[73] In his dialogue with Buddhist monks, Merton found his spiritual family in the brotherhood that called him to be one with his Buddhist brothers in addressing grave social problems in the world of the twentieth century. When he visited the Abbey of Gethsemani in 1996,

---

71. ZBA, 24.

72. Debra P. Patnaik, "Syllables of the Great Song: Merton and Asian Religious Thought," in *The Message of Thomas Merton*, 74.

73. PP, 261–262 (emphasis added).

the Dalai Lama said, "I always consider myself as one of [Thomas Merton's] Buddhist brothers."[74] These examples show that monastics who have attained self-transformation and spiritual maturity consider other monastics, including those of different traditions, comembers of the monastic household. Merton noted, "There is a wider 'oikoumene,' the household and the *spiritual family* of man seeking the meaning of his life and its ultimate purpose."[75] He believed that inter-monastic/contemplative dialogue could become a witness for the divided global village, whose members need to find their true selves and create bonds of friendship with the other members the spiritual family.

From Communication to Communion

Merton's method for inter-monastic/contemplative dialogue was not primarily for the purpose of the communication of monastic knowledge or truths arrived at through contemplation, but first and foremost it was for the achievement of true interpersonal communion. In 1968, when he spoke to Eastern monastics at Calcutta regarding his new path of interreligious dialogue, he said that "the deepest level of communication is not communication, but *communion*. It is wordless. It is beyond words. . . . My dear *brothers*, we are already *one*. . . . And what we have to recover is our *original unity*."[76] Striving for universal and ultimate unity through spiritual communion was the main feature of his approach to interreligious dialogue.

In order to understand his path of inter-monastic/contemplative dialogue through spiritual communion, we will explore 1) the

74. The Dalai Lama, "A Tribute to Thomas Merton," 260.

75. MZM, x (emphasis added). Classical Greek words: *oikos*, meaning a "house," "family," "people," or "nation"; *oikoumen⬚*, "the whole inhabited world"; and *oikoumenikos*, "open to or participating in the whole world." Merton interpreted it as the *spiritual family*.

76. AJ, 308 (emphasis added).

relationship between communion with the divine and inter-monastic communion, 2) the interaction between communication and communion, and 3) examples of Merton's inter-monastic communion.

First, Merton's spiritual communion with Eastern and Western monastics or contemplatives was rooted in his own contemplative experience of communion with Christ. He realized that in contemplation one recovered the original state of paradise. According to Merton, Adam would have known God through contemplation in the garden of paradise, but he lost his existential communion with reality through the Fall. However, the New Adam, Jesus Christ, redeemed humanity and restored our relationship with God, thereby manifesting a "mystical union of all . . . transformed and deified members of regenerated humanity with one another and with God."[77] Through union with God in Christ, the New Adam, the contemplative person can become a *New Man* and can enter into the original contemplative state, which is God's paradise. Merton wrote, "We see that we ourselves are Adam, we ourselves are Christ, and that we are all dwelling in one another, by virtue of the unity of the divine image reformed by grace. . . . We are [God's] new Paradise."[78] This recovery of one's original existential communion with God in contemplation is not the end of our spiritual journey, but a new beginning for *universal communion*. Consequently, Merton's communion with the divine evolved into a spiritual communion with all beings and became a universal communion, a new wholeness, transcending all boundaries in God.[79]

77. NM, 158.

78. Ibid., 161.

79. For example, Merton noted, "With You [God] there is no longer any dialogue, any contest, any opposition. You are found in communion! Thou in me and I in Thee, Thou in them and they in me; dispossession within dispossession, dispassion within dispassion, emptiness within emptiness, freedom within freedom. I am alone. Thou art alone. The Father and I are One." See Thomas Merton, *Dialogues with Silence: Prayers & Drawings*, ed. Jonathan Montaldo (San Francisco, CA: HarperSanFrancisco, 2001), 95. He also stated in his last talk at Bangkok, "I am just saying that somewhere behind our [Christian] monas-

Merton realized that spiritual communion with other monastics or contemplatives of different traditions was possible, and that it could bring about deep spiritual solidarity with them. He saw that spiritual communion was "the awareness of participation in an ontological or religious reality: in the mystery of being, of human love, of redemptive mystery, of contemplative truth."[80] In many great religious traditions, mystical communion with Divine Reality or Being was deeply connected to communion with persons and nature in love and truth. He noted that "the higher religions all point to this deepest unity, because they all strive after the experience of this unity. . . . The experience of unity for the Christian is unity in the Holy Spirit. For Asian religions it is unity in Absolute Being (Atman) or in the Void (Sunyata)."[81] He saw that in many monastic traditions, spiritual communion was rooted in self-emptiness and an openness to others in compassionate love. He remarked that "the state of insight which is final integration implies an openness, an 'emptiness,' a 'poverty' similar to those described in such detail not only . . . by St. John of the Cross . . . but also by the Sufis, the early Taoist masters and Zen Buddhists."[82] In short, beyond religious systems, contemplative experience brought about awareness of a new being and unity, and at the same time, an openness to others in universal communion. At this deep spiritual level, Merton claimed that the way of inter-monastic/contemplative dialogue can bring about spiritual communion.

Second, by means of inter-monastic encounters, Merton hoped to achieve spiritual communion through communication. He saw that communication on the verbal level was the first step toward

---

ticism, and behind Buddhist monasticism, is the belief that this kind of freedom and transcendence is somehow attainable." See AJ, 342.

80. Thomas Merton, "Symbolism: Communication or Communion?," in *Thomas Merton: Selected Essays*, 250.

81. Ibid., 253.

82. CWA, 206.

a deeper communion. True communication at the deepest level was what he called "communion, beyond the level of words, a communion in authentic experience that [was] shared not only on a 'preverbal' level but also on a 'postverbal' level."[83] On the preverbal level, monastic or contemplative experience prepares the minds and hearts of monastics or contemplatives in different contexts for communion with other monastics or contemplatives. For example, when Buddhist monastics visit a Christian monastery (and vice versa), a "preverbal" welcoming, such as a warm hospitable welcome (for example, smiling, embracing, clasping hands, bowing, and possibly exchanging gifts), helps to establish communion between different monastics even before any serious discussion takes place. Inter-monastic/contemplative encounters could lead them to spiritual communion on a postverbal level, "beyond their own words and their own understanding in the silence of an ultimate experience which might conceivably not have occurred if they had not met and spoken."[84]

Broadly speaking, spiritual communion may correspond to the Buddhist understanding of a "heart-to-heart transmission" (以心傳心 *Ishindenshin,* or 拈華微笑 *Nengemishō*). For example, in Zen Buddhism, the Flower Sermon by Shakyamuni Buddha may be considered as a kind of spiritual communion. Buddha gave a wordless sermon to his disciples (*sangha*) by holding up a white flower. The only one who could understand the Flower Sermon was Mahakasyapa, who smiled and remained silent. Without words, he experienced a heart-to-heart transmission and directly grasped the Buddha's teaching. In this regard, Merton noted, "the whole aim of Zen is not to make foolproof statements about experience, but to come to direct grips with reality without the mediation of logical verbalizing."[85] He saw that a heart-to-heart relationship between awakened persons and the awareness of the

---

83. AJ, 315.
84. Ibid.
85. ZBA, 37.

interdependence of all things in Buddhism were close to what is called universal communion in Christian contemplation. At this point, he realized the possibility of inter-monastic/contemplative dialogue with Buddhist monastics on the level of spiritual communion. Simmer-Brown argues that the word used by Merton, "communion," is not a Buddhist term. Rather, "transmission" or "mind-to-mind, heart-to-heart" may more accurately describe the contemplative dialogic relationship.[86] Merton believed that inter-monastic communion could lead to heart-to-heart transmission or spiritual communion on the preverbal as well as the postverbal level. He knew that if communication was regarded as primary, communion would not take place, and dialogue would remain superficial.[87] Merton's encounters with other monastics and contemplatives created a new mode of interreligious dialogue at the level of spiritual depth: that new mode was communication that led to communion.

Third, spiritual communion was at the heart of Merton's dialogue with Buddhists. In his meeting with Suzuki, who was not a monk, Merton was deeply moved by the silent tea ceremony. He described it this way: "It was at once as if nothing at all had happened. . . . A very old deaf Zen man . . . had drunk a cup of tea, as though with the complete wakefulness of a child and yet as though at the same time declaring with utter finality: 'this is not important!' "[88] Beyond a verbal level, this kind of spiritual communion led him to dialogue with Suzuki on a deeper level: "I am deeply gratified to find, in this dialogue with Dr. Suzuki . . . [that] we can so easily and agreeably communicate with one another on the deepest and most important level."[89] Merton's heart-to-heart meeting with Tibetan Buddhists, especially Chatral Rinpoche, also

86. Simmer-Brown, "Wide Open to Life," 198–199.

87. See Merton, "Symbolism: Communication or Communion?," 249.

88. Thomas Merton, "Learning to Live," in *Thomas Merton: Selected Essays*, 441.

89. ZBA, 138.

manifested in spiritual communion. Merton and Chatral discovered basically the same deep inner experience and began to draw close to something real. Merton noted, "The unspoken or half-spoken message of the talk was our complete understanding of each other as people who were somehow on the edge of great realization and knew it and were trying . . . to go out and get lost in it—and that it was a grace for us to meet one another."[90] James George, who was the High Commissioner of the Canadian Embassy in New Delhi and hosted Merton, reported that during the meeting between them "Chatral smiled broadly and replied softly 'It's the same with me,' and they embraced with tears in their eyes. This was perhaps the most intimate contact he had with any of the Tibetans."[91]

Merton's spiritual communion between contemplatives of different religious traditions could become a model for universal communion for others. He invited all people into universal communion through true love, which contemplation could awaken at the core of everyone's being. He believed that in this love, hidden contemplatives could unite with one another beyond religious and cultural boundaries.

Transcultural Maturity

Theologians differentiate three approaches to other religions: exclusivism, inclusivism, and pluralism.[92] As we saw in chapter 1, in the 1940s, Merton's attitude toward other religions was *exclu-*

90. AJ, 143.

91. Cited in Thurston, "Footnotes to the Asian Journey of Thomas Merton," 222.

92. For example, Paul F. Knitter provides helpful models for exploring Christian attitudes toward other world religions: the replacement model (exclusivism: there is only one true religion), the fulfillment model (inclusivism: one model fulfills many religions), the acceptance model (pluralism: there are many true religions: so be it), and the mutuality model (many true religions called into dialogue). In the mutuality model, he introduces the concept of a "religious-mystical bridge," which supposes that the same Divine Mystery or Reality is experienced

sivist. He believed that Roman Catholicism was the one true religion. In the 1950s, he came to the conviction that God is present in non-Christian religions and all humanity is *included* in the divine salvific will. In the early 1960s, it seems that he began to draw closer to a *pluralistic* approach as he recognized in other religions the truth and love of the Cosmic Christ, and as he gradually abandoned his sense of superiority and started to learn from them.[93] Nonetheless, he did not espouse the pluralistic view that held that all religions are equally true. He neither agreed with religious syncretism nor abandoned Christian uniqueness.[94] He approached other religions as a contemplative monk and as a theologian. After 1965, he was more interested in how the resources of Eastern and Western monasticism could be directed to the transformation of human consciousness beyond a theological view.[95] From the uni-

---

differently within the different religious traditions. See Paul F. Knitter, *Introducing Theologies of Religions* (Maryknoll, NY: Orbis Books, 2002), 125.

93. See Jacques Goulet, "Thomas Merton's Journey toward World Religious Ecumenism," *The Merton Annual* 4 (1991): 115–125.

94. Merton stated that the feature of religious dialogue is "no syncretism, indifferentism, the vapid and careless friendliness that accepts everything by thinking nothing." See CGB, 141. See also AJ, 316; MZM, 207; ZBA, 43. Raab points out that "[t]hough Merton never wrote a systematic theology of religious pluralism, the evidence he leaves us suggests that if he had, it would not have been a pluralistic model that abandons Christian uniqueness, but a model of religious pluralism based on a Trinitarian Theism, affirming other sapiential traditions in terms of the universal presence of the Spirit beyond the boundaries of the visible Church but holding fast to Christ crucified and risen as the fullness of divine revelation." See Raab, "Insights from the Inter-Contemplative Dialogue," 91.

95. Shannon claims that Merton's transcultural consciousness had developed from his staying at the hermitage since 1965. Hilary Costello argues that during the last three or four years of Merton's life, when he was more insistent on the transformation of consciousness to which monastics were called, his consciousness was gradually transformed to a state of transcultural maturity. See Shannon, *Silent Lamp*, 4–6; Hilary Costello, "Pilgrim: Freedom Bound," in *The Legacy of Thomas Merton*, ed. Patrick Hart (Kalamazoo, MI: Cistercian Publications, 1986), 67–79.

versal, transcultural perspective, he began to move toward the *final integration* of contemplative monastic life. Merton noted, "Final integration is a state of transcultural maturity. . . . The man who is 'fully born' has an entirely 'inner experience of life.' He apprehends his life fully and wholly from an inner ground. . . . He is in a certain sense 'cosmic' and 'universal man.' "[96] He saw that those who achieved the stage of transcultural maturity were no longer limited by their own culture or religion because they had become free from all boundaries that would limit one from embracing the totality of life. Merton's self-transformation in contemplation and his encounter with Asian traditions contributed to a deeper transcultural consciousness.

The notion of the final integration comes to Merton from his study of a Persian psychologist, Dr. Reza Arasteh. Arasteh argues that "to become a fully integrated personality . . . one must be born again and again experience numerous spiritual rebirths."[97] Merton also saw that through spiritual rebirth in Christ, Christian consciousness was transformed into divine consciousness. He wrote, "Dr. Arasteh is interested . . . in the final and complete maturing of the human psyche on a transcultural level."[98] Although Arasteh's study was purely psychological in the language of Sufism, Merton saw the possibility of human "reintegration and new life on a totally different level."[99] Merton reframed the insight of Arasteh in the Christian context. He saw that if Christians consider the final integration only in terms of psychology, they could not fully understand it. He noted, "For a Christian, a

---

96. CWA, 206. Shannon comments that in his essay "Final Integration," Merton wrote that "the fully integrated person has experienced qualities of every type of life: ordinary human existence, intellectual life, artistic creation, human love, and religious life." See Shannon, *Silent Lamp*, 287.

97. A. Reza Arasteh, *Rumi the Persian: Rebirth in Creativity and Love* (Tucson, AZ: Omen Press, 1972), 25.

98. CWA, 203.

99. Ibid., 209.

transcultural integration is eschatological. The rebirth of man and of society on a transcultural level is a rebirth into the transformed and redeemed time . . . the time of the Spirit."[100] Eschatologically, he saw that on the transcultural level, the cultural particularity of each religion gave way before God or Ultimate Reality, which is truly universal and all in all. From the universal perspective, as Merton clearly stated in "Marxism and Monastic Perspectives," his last Bangkok address, "there is no longer Asian or European for the Christian. . . . [All] dialectical approaches go beyond the thesis and the antithesis . . . black and white, East and West. We accept the division, we work with the division and we go beyond the division."[101] This lecture showed that through deep inner freedom and universal consciousness, transcultural persons were not limited to their own particular religion or culture, or to any other human category. These people could bring a new "perspective, liberty and spontaneity into the lives of others."[102]

Merton saw that Christian monastic life aimed at achieving the state of transcultural maturity through reintegration of the self in Christ. He noted, "[Transcultural] maturity is exactly what the monastic life should produce. The monastic ideal is precisely this sort of freedom in the spirit, this liberation from the limits of all that is merely partial and fragmentary in the given culture."[103] However, he saw that transcultural maturity was seldom accepted among monastics who believed that to stay in their own monastery would guarantee their full spiritual development. Since monastics were called to a "universality of vision that [saw] everything in the light of the One Truth," he stressed that monastics must concentrate on developing transcultural consciousness.[104] For Merton,

---

100. Ibid., 210–211. See also William M. Thompson, "Merton's Contribution to a Transcultural Consciousness," in *Thomas Merton: Pilgrim in Process*, 163.

101. AJ, 340–341.

102. CWA, 207.

103. Ibid.

104. Ibid.

transcultural maturity was also essential for "a readiness to enter into dialogue with all that is pure, wise, profound, and humane in every kind of culture."[105] From the perspective of *homo universalis*, he claimed that the peculiar vocation of monastics for interreligious dialogue in the modern world was not only to attain the "element of inner transcendent freedom," but also to grow "toward the full maturity of universal man."[106]

Merton discerned that the attainment of transcultural consciousness was not the exclusive prerogative of Christian monastics but the common goal of monasticism in the great religions. His viewpoint indicates a kind of paradigm shift at a time when many Christians did not allow for the possibility of transforming union and universal freedom outside a totally Christian milieu. Yet, Merton came to the opinion that Christian spiritual rebirth, Hindu self-realization of *Atman*, Buddhist *Sunyata*, Taoist *Wu-wei*, and Sufis *Baqa*, which were related to transformation of human consciousness, could become sources for inter-monastic/contemplative dialogue. According to Carr, Merton's new state of transcultural maturity includes "the openness, emptiness, and poverty described by the Christian mystics, by the Sufis, the Taoist masters, and Zen Buddhists, attitudes which point to docility to the Spirit and to a potency for an authentic creativity that is universal, not limited by the person's own culture."[107] In and through contemplative dialogue, Merton found within himself the final integration, the state of transcultural maturity, and recognized that such maturity is common to awakened persons regardless of their religion or culture. Thus, he foresaw that inter-monastic/contemplative dialogue at the level of transcultural maturity could lead to "the growth of a truly universal consciousness in the modern world."[108]

105. Merton, "Christian Culture Needs Oriental Wisdom," 112.
106. AJ, 317.
107. Carr, *A Search for Wisdom and Spirit*, 105.
108. AJ, 317.

Merton's Contributions and Development of His Legacy

Thomas Merton opened a new era of monastic and contemplative interreligious dialogue. His fascination with Asian religious traditions propelled him to develop his inter-monastic/contemplative dialogue, a form of dialogue that went beyond intellectual dialogue and dealt with experience, spirituality, and life. His direct encounter with various Buddhist monastics and contemplatives and his visits to their dwellings in Asia significantly deepened his interest and involvement in monastic and contemplative interreligious dialogue. Although his unexpected and sudden death prevented him from fully developing his ideas regarding inter-monastic/contemplative dialogue, he became a model for all who are engaged in this type of dialogue. In order to advance his legacy, we shall first evaluate his contributions to and plans for inter-monastic/contemplative dialogue by comparing them to the current status of monastic interreligious dialogue. Second, the prophetic role of monasticism will be made clear by showing that Merton did not think of inter-monastic/contemplative dialogue as an esoteric activity for a spiritual elite but a mission for all contemplatives. Third, whether his monastic encounter with Asian monastics was idealistic and/or romantic, or not, will be evaluated. Finally, we will move beyond his legacy to propose the development of inter-monastic pilgrimage and spiritual solidarity between monastics and lay contemplatives.

Merton's Contributions to Inter-Monastic/ Contemplative Dialogue

Merton's first contribution to inter-monastic/contemplative dialogue was to discover the crucial role of sharing contemplative experiences and monastic life with other religious traditions. Although monastics and contemplatives were viewed by society as marginal persons, he realized that dialogue between them, even when it took place in a monastery or hermitage, could become a way of sharing the whole of religious life, including spirituality, religious experience, spiritual discipline, and individual and communal problems. His direct meetings with other monastics and contemplatives in Asia show us the importance of concrete experience in dialogue. Blée points out that "the main reason Merton continues to be an inspiration for monks involved in dialogue is that he was so convinced of the importance of absorbing Eastern religions *in situ*."[109] Merton frequently stressed the importance of actually experiencing their living situations. For example, he noted, "One cannot understand Buddhism until one meets it . . . in a person in whom it is alive. Then there is no longer a problem of understanding doctrines which cannot help being a bit exotic for a westerner, but only a question of appreciating a value which is self-evident."[110] Merton read many Buddhist writings and corresponded with Buddhists, yet his direct meetings with them and his pilgrimage to the places they lived were most influential to his newfound understanding of Buddhism and his attainment of cross-religious experience in Asia.

Merton showed that sharing monastic/contemplative life in depth could lead to working together to achieve their common contemplative goal, including the transformation of human consciousness for all contemplatives who genuinely seek it. According to him, many monastics or contemplatives commonly strove to attain "a deepening of consciousness toward an eventual breakthrough and discovery of a transcendent dimension of life beyond that of the ordinary empirical self and ethical and pious observance."[111] Merton's affirmation of the value of direct encounter with monastics from other religions and sharing monastic discipline and experience with them coincides with a statement Pope John Paul II made at a later date. The pope said, "By sharing their experience of affective prayer, meditation, and contemplation,

---

109. Blée, *The Third Desert*, 42 (emphasis in original).
110. ZBA, 62.
111. AJ, 309–310.

[contemplatives] help to forge closer bonds between the followers of Christianity and Buddhism, which opens the way for greater cooperation in the promotion of integral human development."[112] Merton showed that inter-monastic/contemplative dialogue that went beyond formal and superficial encounters could contribute to mutual transformation in depth and become an incentive for the promotion of integral human life.

Second, Merton contributed to the development of new paths for monastic interreligious dialogue at a deeper spiritual level. From a universal perspective, he aimed at bonding the spiritual family of contemplatives through communion with other monastics, who attained or were pursuing spiritual maturity in their own monastic contexts. He believed that inter-monastic communion could provide a proper answer to the question of how Christian monasticism could approach Asian monasticism in the new era of religious pluralism. For example, regarding his encounter with Buddhist monastics in Asia, he stated, "So far my talks with Buddhists have been open and frank, and there has been full communication on a really deep level. We seem to recognize in one another a certain depth of spiritual experience, and it is unquestionable."[113] The foregoing does not claim that Merton possessed an unusual ability for spiritual communion beyond words, but he shows us the possibility of inter-monastic encounters at a deeper level. He was convinced that "communication in depth, across the lines that have hitherto divided religious and monastic traditions, is now not only possible and desirable but most important for the destinies of Twentieth-Century Man."[114] The method Merton promoted was to bond in spiritual communion with Asian monastics in mutual respect by learning from them and by sharing some of

112. John Paul II, "To the Bishops of Thailand" (1996), in *Interreligious Dialogue*, 621.

113. AJ, 124.

114. Ibid., 313.

the various spiritual experiences and monastic treasures they had accumulated.[115]

Merton's model of spiritual communion has largely influenced current monastic interreligious dialogue. For example, at the Gethsemani Encounter I, Pascaline Coff, a Benedictine nun, pointed out that "now we have gathered together in . . . friendship to take the next step on the journey of spiritual dialogue. In the prophetic words of Thomas Merton, the very raison d'être for our presence here at Gethsemani is to realize 'communication' that has become 'communion.' "[116] Béthune claims that spiritual communion is "dialogue's ultimate task" and that it "effects a remarkable renewal in our spiritual life."[117] Merton came to the realization that inter-monastic communion was relevant to the destiny of all persons at the deepest level of encounter. The participants of the Gethsemani Encounter, who experienced the "surprising dimension of spiritual communion" in the gathering, realized that Merton's prophetic words, "communication to communion," were not "a utopian dream."[118] They also realized that the Gethsemani experience was "an epiphany for all humankind: a profound unity, peace and harmony in the midst of the rich diversity of humankind."[119]

---

115. Catherine Cornille points out that Merton's inter-monastic dialogue contributed to "the shift from a purely missionary relationship to other religions to one defined more by reciprocal interest and respect [and] was largely inspired by a respect for the mystical depth of those traditions." See Catherine Cornille, *The Im-Possibility of Interreligious Dialogue* (New York, NY: Crossroad, 2008), 115.

116. Pascaline Coff, "How We Reached This Point: Communication Becoming Communion," in *The Gethsemani Encounter*, 5.

117. Béthune, "Preface" to *The Gethsemani Encounter*, xv. Walter E. Conn points out that "Merton was convinced that such communion would be of singular importance at this moment of crucial in human history when we are in grave danger of losing the spiritual heritage of thousands of generations." See Walter E. Conn, "Merton's Religious Development: The Monastic Years," *Cistercian Studies* 22 (1987): 286.

118. Béthune, "Preface" to *The Gethsemani Encounter*, xv.

119. Donald W. Mitchell and James Wiseman, "Introduction," in *The Gethsemani Encounter*, xxii.

Merton's contribution to spiritual communion bloomed at the Gethsemani Encounter and became a model of inter-monastic/contemplative dialogue.

Finally, Merton proposed that inter-monastic/contemplative dialogue could contribute a spiritual dimension to the dialogue of action directed toward the promotion of human society. He believed that monasticism and contemplation could offer "a different angle" in dealing with human problems.[120] He argued that since Buddhist and Christian monastics agreed that the root of human problems was human consciousness, they both sought to bring about a transformation of human consciousness and "in their sort of ideal setting and the ideal way of looking at them" they "fulfill this role in society."[121] The goals of great compassion (*mahakaruna*) in Buddhism and of selfless love (*agape*) in Christianity were both rooted in the recognition of the interdependence of all beings. Buddhist and Christian monastics could share with each other their ways to reach this goal and could cooperate to awaken the hidden contemplatives who live in the secular world. Merton saw that the spiritual solidarity between contemplative monastics was urgently needed for the modern materialized world. The Dalai Lama and Merton both agreed that the Communist model of institutional change in the socioeconomic realm could not achieve true and deep social transformation, but "it [*could*] be done in the monastery."[122] Consequently, Merton stressed a new vocation for monastics in the modern world: "It is the peculiar office of the monk in the modern world to keep alive the contemplative experience and to keep the way open for modern technological man to recover the integrity of his own inner depths."[123]

Historically, Eastern and Western monasticism alike have contributed to education, healthcare, agricultural techniques, art, and

---

120. AJ, 332.
121. Ibid., 333.
122. Ibid., 125, 334 (emphasis added).
123. Ibid., 317.

music to society. Today, however, these works are performed within secular institutions, and contemporary men and women seek to satisfy their spiritual thirst through monastic or contemplative methods regardless of the religious tradition in which these methods were developed. To respond to these spiritual searchers, monastics must recover the contemplative dimension of their monastic vocation. In the global village, it would be helpful if all monastics could incorporate Merton's notion of the spiritual family through inter-monastic/contemplative dialogue for their contemporary societies, which are largely dominated by materialism as well as divided by religion, race, culture, and economics.[124] Wayne Teasdale, who had been a member of the North American Board for East-West Dialogue, pointed out that "the contemplative and monastic contribution to interreligious dialogue and the evolving sense of universal responsibility and collaboration has been significant."[125] Cooperation for spiritual solidarity between monastics of different religious traditions can become an example for making peace in the divided world. Of course, the monastery is not a perfect community and monastics also have to deal with external or internal problems, yet, as members of a spiritual family, they can stand in solidarity with their brothers and sisters outside the monastery. Merton wrote that "the monastery is not an 'escape' from the world. On the contrary, by being in the

124. Merton offered an example of the role of monastics for the contemporary society. He noted, "You find, for example, the Cistercians of the 12th century speaking of a kind of monastic therapy. Adam of Perseigne has the idea that you come to the monastery, first, to be cured. The period of monastic formation is a period of cure, of convalescence." See ibid., 333.

125. Wayne Teasdale, "Interreligious Dialogue since Vatican II: The Monastic Contemplative Dimension," *Spirituality Today* 43, no. 2 (Summer 1991): 120. Teasdale maintains that "Because [the human] family is one, global, and interrelated, our actions must be consistent with this identity. . . . We have an obligation to promote a new vision of society, one in which war has no place in resolving disputes between and among states, organizations, and religions." See ibid., 131.

monastery I take my true part in all the struggles and sufferings of the world."[126] Monasticism could not solve all external social problems, but he showed that monastics and contemplatives, as members of the human family who have a responsibility for the world, could work together for transformation of human consciousness. And this cooperation could perhaps resolve social problems from a monastic and contemplative perspective based on encounter, dialogue, and the sharing of peaceful exchanges. In essence, this is the model used by Merton for inter-monastic/ contemplative dialogue.

Is Inter-Monastic/Contemplative Dialogue an Esoteric Activity for the Spiritually Elite?

Merton's inter-monastic/contemplative dialogue may appear to be an esoteric activity for some monastics or contemplatives who deliberately withdraw to the margins of society. His emphasis on a long-term spiritual discipline and the attainment of spiritual maturity for contemplative dialogue may suggest that only the spiritual elite are suited for this type of dialogue. In addition, not all monastics are interested in interreligious dialogue. Merton's inter-monastic/contemplative dialogue, however, was not just for vowed Christians but was intended for all contemplatives, both lay and vowed religious, who are concerned with their inner transformation and have a compassionate love for others. Through his encounter with other monastic traditions, Merton came to an experiential awareness that there were many different types of monastic life and contemplative life that were connected to the world. His partners in the dialogue were not limited to monastics or the spiritual elite but included all contemplatives, including hidden contemplatives in society. Since the contemplative experience is open to all persons, Merton believed that inter-monastic/contemplative dialogue

126. IEW, 45.

could become a place for all contemplatives to share their spiritual experiences and practices with them.[127] Blée claims that "the dialogue of spiritual experience is not a higher form of dialogue, an esoteric activity for a spiritual elite."[128] Béthune also argues that "monastics are not alone in endeavoring to pursue this 'dialogue of spiritual experience.' . . . All Christians are called to reach this level in their meetings with believers of other religions."[129] Christians are called to interreligious dialogue, and they are also called to contemplation and spiritual experience.

In this regard, Merton frequently stressed the prophetic role of monastics for the church and the world.[130] Historically, early Christian monastics or hermits left the city and went to the desert to follow Christ because they wanted to be free of a church that had become secularized after it had been officially recognized by Constantine. When Christianity became the official religion of the Empire, it brought with it the temptations of power and prestige. Amid these temptations, some visionaries, wanting to steer themselves away from the corruption that was erupting everywhere, began exploring new ascetic lifestyles in their attempt to live a life rooted in the gospels.[131]

In a similar way, Merton suggested that the monastic life might be a model for his contemporaries who had lost the true path to a

127. Merton stated, "The capacity for contemplative experience and the fact of its realization . . . are therefore implicit in all the great religious traditions, whether Asian or European, whether Hindu, Buddhist, Moslem, or Christian." See MZM, 209.

128. Blée, *The Third Desert*, 5.

129. Béthune, "Preface" to *The Gethsemani Encounter*, xiv–xv. See also Thompson, "Merton's Contribution to a Transcultural Consciousness," 159–160.

130. For instance, Merton wrote, "The vocation of the monk in the modern world . . . is not survival but prophecy." See Merton and Leclercq, *Survival or Prophecy?*, 175.

131. See IEW, 46; Thomas M. Gannon and George W. Traub, *The Desert and the City; An Interpretation of the History of Christian Spirituality* (New York, NY: Macmillan, 1969), 20–33.

spiritual life because of the materialism of the USA. In the 1960s, he brought a contemplative perspective to bear on his criticism of war, nuclear arms, racism, and materialism. In his article "A Spirituality for the Advent City: Thomas Merton's Monasticism without Walls," Jeffrey F. Keuss comments, "For Merton, the monastic life was not an escape or refuge from the modern city but a *prophetic form* of spirituality that he offered to the 'urban uncloistered' time and time again."[132] When Merton directed his contemplative experience to social engagement, he became a prophetic voice in the world.

Merton's view of the prophetic role of Christian monasticism in the world could be extended to collaboration with other monastic traditions. Although interreligious dialogue between monastics did not involve large numbers of people, he believed that such a dialogue could become "a witness of life" at a deep spiritual level for the modern world.[133] Béthune points out that "the monastic orders, Buddhist and Christian, are now able to recognize themselves as forerunners of a spiritual unity that is prophetic for all humankind."[134] This recognition was influenced by Merton's realization that for those of his contemporaries who had lost interest in the contemplative life, contemplative encounters between different monastic traditions could promote their spiritual growth and an openness to other religious traditions. The Buddhist monk Havanpola Ratanasara, who took part in the Gethsemani Encounter I, said, "I believe our gathering here at Gethsemani is a giant step on [the] path for the benefit of humanity. . . . [We] Buddhists are ready to dialogue so that we may contribute thereby to the spiritual transformation of humanity that today's world so

132. Jeffrey F. Keuss, "A Spirituality for the Advent City: Thomas Merton's Monasticism without Walls," *The Merton Journal* 10, no. 2 (Advent 2003): 2 (emphasis added).

133. AJ, 306.

134. Béthune, "Preface" to *The Gethsemani Encounter*, xii.

badly needs."[135] Merton contributed to the development of the prophetic role of inter-monastic/contemplative dialogue for society. His view of *monasticism without walls* and his exchanges with other monastic traditions produced a model whereby inter-monastic/contemplative dialogue could become a witness to the postmodern world.

Was Merton's Monastic Encounter with Asian Monasticism Idealistic and/or Romantic?

Even though Merton contributed many elements belonging to the model of inter-monastic dialogue, he did not see the model's completion. He set foot in Asia for only two months near the end of his life.[136] In his fewer than two months in Asia, Merton did not have sufficient time for a direct lived experience of various Asian religious contexts or of life in an Asian monastery. Lipski offers the criticism that "Merton's idealistic presuppositions colored his images of Asia and his interpretation of Asian religions, and thereby blurred his view of Asian reality."[137] For example, as Trungpa Rinpoche pointed out regarding "spiritual materialism" in Tibetan Buddhism, Asian monasticism is *not perfect*.[138]

135. Havanpola Ratanasara, "Dialogue and Unity: A Buddhist Perspective," in *The Gethsemani Encounter*, 15, 17.

136. Whereas other pioneers of monastic interreligious dialogue, Abhishiktananda and Griffiths, for example, had lived in India for several decades. Abhishiktananda was present at Shantivanam from 1950 to 1968, and Griffiths took up residence there from 1968 to 1993. During the long period, they incorporated Eastern forms of meditation into Christian spiritual practice. See Blée, *The Third Desert*, 43.

137. Lipski, *Thomas Merton and Asia*, iv.

138. Simmer-Brown, "The Liberty That Nobody Can Touch," 58. Chögyam Trungpa claims that there are the three lords of materialism: physical materialism, psychological materialism, and spiritual materialism. According to Trungpa, spiritual materialism is the belief that a certain particular emotional state of mind can lead to a refuge from our daily suffering although it could actually lead to

It is faced with various problems and is in crisis due to spiritual materialism. Although Merton recognized this problem, he still tended to have an idealized and romantic view of Asian religions and monasticism due to his lack of a real Asian monastic experience. Perhaps his many dreams of Asia also reflected his romantic view of Buddhism. For instance, on November 5, 1968, in Asia, he wrote, "Last night I dreamed that I was, temporarily, back at Gethsemani. I was dressed in a Buddhist monk's habit. . . . I met some women in the corridor . . . students of Asian religion, to whom I was explaining I was a kind of Zen monk and Gelugpa together."[139] One could interpret this dream as unconscious desire of a Trappist monk to be assimilated as a Buddhist monk.

In his spiritual exchanges with Asian monastics, however, Merton did consider that they might also be faced with the same kind of monastic crisis in the modern world.[140] For example, he noted, "Zen monasticism is currently in crisis, as is monasticism everywhere, and doubtless the question of poverty and living on alms as well as work will be a matter of urgent concern to them as well as among us."[141] In other words, he did not simply admire and praise Asian monasticism. Corless points out that although Merton

---

more long-term suffering. Spiritual materialism comes from "a distorted, ego-centered version of spirituality," and those who fall into it use spiritual practices to promote their own personal benefit, status, and reputation. See Chögyam Trungpa, *Cutting Through Spiritual Materialism*, ed. John Baker and Marvin Casper (Boston, MA: Shambhala, 2002), 1–26.

139. OSM, 255. Prophetically, after his death his dream of meeting with Asian religious students in the monastic corridor was eventually achieved at least in part at the Gethsemani Encounter in 1996, when Buddhist nuns stayed at his monastery.

140. Merton noted, "In the West there is now going on a great upheaval in monasticism, and much that is of undying value is being thrown away irresponsibly, foolishly, in favor of things that are superficial and showy, that have no ultimate value. . . . The time is coming when you [the Eastern monastics] may face the same situation." See AJ, 307.

141. MZM, 231.

had a "romance with Orientalism," it was ended through contacts with Tibetan Buddhists and the Polonnaruwa experience.[142] After the experience, Merton noted, "The thing about all this is that there is no puzzle, no problem, and really no 'mystery.'"[143] Any misconceptions he had of Asian religions were dispelled and he could see Asian and Christian traditions from a more integrated and universal perspective beyond structures. In his last lecture in Bangkok, he stated, "the question of Asian monasticism for Christians should not be interpreted in terms of just playing . . . an Asian role. . . . For a Christian—as also, I believe, for a Buddhist—there is an essential orientation that goes beyond this or that society, this or that culture, or even this or that religion."[144]

From the transcultural perspective, Merton believed that for renewal in both Western and Eastern monasticism to occur, inter-monastic exchanges were imperative if monastics were to rediscover the value of their ancient spiritual traditions and be able to share their contemplative spirituality with their contemporaries. His approach to inter-monastic/contemplative dialogue might be regarded as an idealized view by those who focus solely on intellectual dialogue or those who expect to see visible results. His interest in ancient sources was not an idealization of Asian monasticism, but for the discovery of the sources of monastic renewal as well as for inter-monastic dialogue. It did not mean that Merton neglected contemporary problems faced by monastics. It was simply his basic method for monastic renewal. In response to the emphasis on ressourcement that was so evident in the Second Vatican Council's documents, which he read, Merton rediscovered the value of Western ancient monastic sources and then turned to the ancient monastic sources of the East. He believed that Asian monasticism could contribute to the renewal of Catholic monas-

---

142. Roger Corless, "Fire on the Seven Storey Mountain," in *Toward an Integrated Humanity*, 214.
143. AJ, 235.
144. Ibid., 340.

ticism and that it could also provide a basis for spiritual solidarity with the monasticisms of other religious traditions.

Furthermore, his interest was not focused merely on the theory of Asian monasticism but was primarily focused on its concrete monastic experience and discipline. However, he did not simply accept Asian spiritual practices, but discerned their credibility and practicality in his spiritual maturity. For instance, he seemed unimpressed by Rato Rinpoche's teaching of "calm abiding (*shamatha, shi-ne*) meditation," which is a way of getting into meditation by recognizing "that there is always an aspect of the mind that is watching the watcher—that is watching the meditative mind."[145] Merton told Talbott, "We know that already, and we don't want the watcher to watch it, so that's of no use to us."[146] Although he was fascinated by Asian contemplative practices, he did not merely admire them without discernment.

Merton seemed to have an idealistic or romantic view of Asian traditions in his early thought, but his spiritual maturity in contemplation and his longing for becoming an enlightened monk facilitated the shift from his romance with Asian traditions to one of critical engagement. Although the profound experience he had several weeks before his death would have affirmed the genuine value he intuited all along in Asian monasticism beyond any more superficial romanticism that may have tempted him along the way.

Development of Merton's Legacy

Merton's legacy of inter-monastic/contemplative dialogue has been developed by Dialogue Interreligieux Monastique/Monastic Interreligious Dialogue (DIMMID). The next chapter will explore this development in greater detail. In this section, following Merton's example, two ways of inter-monastic/contemplative dialogue

---

145. Simmer-Brown, "The Liberty That Nobody Can Touch," 67; Tworkov, "The Jesus Lama," 17.

146. Tworkov, "The Jesus Lama," 17.

will be suggested: 1) inter-monastic pilgrimage and 2) spiritual solidarity between monastics and lay contemplatives.

Merton's Asian pilgrimage can be seen as a model for the development of inter-monastic pilgrimages involving monastic communities from the East and the West. For Merton, pilgrimage had geographical as well as spiritual dimensions.[147] Pilgrimage might seem to be contrary to St. Benedict's emphasis on stability, which has been interpreted to mean that one is to remain in one's own monastery for a whole lifetime, even though the Rule itself contains a chapter that deals with monks who go on a journey.[148] Today's context is quite different from that of St. Benedict, when undisciplined roaming monks (*gyrovagi* or *circumcelliones*) were a real problem for the monasteries of Europe. Today, Benedictine and Cistercian monastics can engage in an inter-monastic pilgrimage to a different culture and religion. It is seen as a way of attaining new horizons within monastic spirituality without compromising one's vow of stability to a particular monastic community. It can involve freely making a pilgrimage between different monasteries regardless of the Monastic Exchange Programs developed by the DIMMID.

Pilgrimages by Christian monastics to monasteries of different religions are considered a form of spiritual pilgrimage by the Catholic Church. Pope John Paul II stated that "all monastic life is a pilgrimage. . . . As pilgrims of the infinite, you invite all men and women to strengthen their inner life so as to make it a dwelling place of God. On your path you meet other seekers

---

147. See Merton, "From Pilgrimage to Crusade," 187; John D. Barbour, "The Ethics of Intercultural Travel: Thomas Merton's Asian Pilgrimage and Orientalism," *Biography* 28, no. 1 (Winter 2005): 16.

148. See St. Benedict, *RB 1980: The Rule of St. Benedict in English*, ed. Timothy Fry (Collegeville, MN: Liturgical Press, 1982), 20–21, 78–79; in the Rule of St. Benedict, Chapter 50, "Brothers Working at a Distance or Traveling," shows that monastics can work in locations a long distance from the monastery and can also be sent on a journey. See ibid., 72.

of the absolute, which enables you to establish a respectful and profound dialogue with them."[149]

Merton saw that the spirituality of pilgrimage was more developed in Buddhist monastic life. He noted:

> The Buddhist monastic life is essentially a life of pilgrimage (*angya*). It is as a pilgrim that the newcomer presents himself at the monastery door, whether he be a monk already experienced and trained in another monastery, or a postulant newly arrived from secular life. . . . He comes on foot as a "homeless one". . . . The purpose of *angya*, or pilgrimage, is to convince the monk of the fact that his whole life is a search, in exile, for his true home. . . . [If monastics] return to the world, they must live in it with the mentality of pilgrims.[150]

Merton believed that Western monastics "must . . . consider" the spirituality of monastic pilgrimage as developed in Zen monasticism.[151] The understanding of monastic life as a pilgrimage can be extended to one of the paths of inter-monastic exchange. For example, Blée points out that "the approach by which monks involved in dialogue honor their calling is by becoming pilgrims. . . . Being a pilgrim means walking alongside other believers towards a common destiny."[152] Griffiths describes the importance of *monastic pilgrimage* and points to Merton's example of being a pilgrim in Asia:

149. John Paul II, "To the Faithful in the General Audience" (2000), in *Inter-religious Dialogue*, 781.

150. MZM, 225–226.

151. Ibid., 225. Merton was aware that monastic forms in Asian traditions were not the same as those in Christian monasticism. For example, in his article "Zen Buddhist Monasticism," he noted that unlike Christian contemplative monastics, Buddhist monastics were free to leave for another monastery. See ibid., 215–217. He knew that to attain enlightenment, Buddhist monks should be spiritually free from the "religious framework" or "the conceptual apparatus," even from the teaching of Buddha. See ZBA, 44, 77; MZM, 282.

152. Blée, *The Third Desert*, 201.

> Could we not conceive of a Benedictine monk who should be given this freedom to wander, to go to India, it may be, to Sri Lanka, to Thailand, to Japan, visiting Hindu ashrams and Buddhist monasteries, not as an escape from the restrictions of community life or as a vacation, but as an integral part of his monastic vocation? Did not Thomas Merton point to something like this both in his life and in the manner of his death?[153]

If Merton's example of monastic pilgrimage were to be followed through visits to monasteries of other religious traditions by Christian monastics, then Hindus, Buddhists, and other Christian monastics would be able to share mutually their understanding and practices of the mystical or contemplative life. Moreover, a spirituality of hospitality, which is found in many different monastic traditions, can enhance the practice of inter-monastic pilgrimage.

Second, Merton's inter-monastic/contemplative dialogue can encourage spiritual solidarity between monastics and lay contemplatives beyond religious boundaries. He engaged in dialogue with lay contemplatives at the Abbey of Gethsemani and in Asia.[154] His unfinished plan for learning Tibetan spirituality from

---

153. Bede Griffiths, "The Monastic Order and the Ashram," *American Benedictine Review* 30, no. 2 (June 1979): 142.

154. Through the development of his new view of contemplation, Merton modified his perspective concerning lay contemplatives and celebrated their value. He called such lay people "hidden" or "masked" contemplatives. See IE, 64. He met or corresponded with them at the Abbey of Gethsemani as well as his hermitage. For example, Etta Gullick, a lay married woman and mother in Oxford, England, who was giving courses to Oxford Anglican ordinands, visited Merton with her husband and enjoyed a picnic at Monks Pond. Merton and Etta corresponded regularly and shared "other spiritual writers, problems of prayer, the pains and joys of a dedicated spiritual life, the issues of war and peace." See HGL, 340. Although in Merton's time, lay Christians could not consider themselves as "lay contemplatives" (the term was developed much later), Merton urged that "lay contemplatives should not withdraw and meditate while others struggle to make a living" and that they should "fuse their creative love with God's love to fulfill their true vocation to divinity as sons and daughters

Chatral Rinpoche, a lay contemplative, is being partly realized through the Gethsemani Encounters. However, the majority of the participants in these gatherings are still Catholic and Buddhist monastics. It now seems reasonable to increase the participation of lay contemplatives to foster spiritual bonding between them and monastics.

Today, traditional monastics need to find ways to promote contemplative experience for the laity. Merton stated that contemplative monastics in our day must prepare to share "something of their own solitude and their own awareness of the Mystery of Christ with those who come to their monasteries."[155] Coff argues that "the lay contemplative is on the move, searching, testing, seeking, loving and longing for the Lord, using everyday life as a spiritual exercise. The monk beyond the monastery is striving . . . to be a channel of the Divine Presence . . . and to awaken all to the grasp of the Spirit."[156] For further development of Merton's contemplative dialogue between monastics and the lay contemplative, monasteries need to become *channels* of the Divine Presence and places for sharing and promoting contemplative experience. Béthune claims that "the monastic world is certainly a favourable environment. . . . It is the setting where the dialogue of spiritual experience can flourish."[157] Merton noted:

> Thus, there are contemplatives not only in the monasteries but also in the midst of secular life. But in all contemplative traditions, it has been found necessary that those who have attained to some depth of religious insight should to some *extent guide*

---

of God." See Paul R. Dekar, *Thomas Merton: Twentieth-Century Wisdom for Twenty-First-Century Living* (Eugene, OR: Cascade Books, 2011), 58.

155. CWA, 193.

156. Pascaline Coff, "The Universal Call to Contemplation: Cloisters beyond the Monastery," *The Merton Annual* 16 (2003): 210.

157. Pierre-François de Béthune, "Monastic Inter-Religious Dialogue," in *The Wiley-Blackwell Companion to Inter-Religious Dialogue*, ed. Catherine Cornille (Malden, MA: Wiley Blackwell, 2013), 43.

others who seek to attain the same experience of truth in their own lives.[158]

In his monastery and his hermitage, Merton was a great promoter and catalyst of lay contemplatives. At the same time, he did not hesitate to learn about contemplative meditation from lay contemplatives in a different tradition. He exemplified the mutual enrichment that is possible when monastics and lay contemplatives enter into dialogue.

Today, many monasteries open their doors to lay contemplatives who wish to share monastic life and receive spiritual direction within monastic walls. What still needs to be developed is the willingness of Christian monastics to put aside their attitude of superiority and to learn from lay contemplatives within and outside their own religious traditions. To achieve spiritual solidarity between monastics and lay contemplatives, the monastery has to become a platform for spiritual exchange in the local community. In the next chapter, we will see examples of this from South Korea in more detail.

Conclusion

Thomas Merton's interreligious dialogue moved from a traditional Christian monastic perspective toward a transcultural perspective and inter-monastic/contemplative communion. His longing for union with God through contemplation instigated his attraction to interreligious dialogue. His contemplative experience opened his mind and heart to other religions, especially Buddhism. His openness to Zen Buddhism and his dialogue with Buddhists led him to spiritual maturity and an interest in Buddhist monasticism.

---

158. CWA, 162 (emphasis added).

Merton, the contemplative monk, recognized that Buddhism was originally a form of monasticism and that it came into existence well before Christian monasticism. His discovery of the value of Buddhist monasticism and contemplation led him to make an Asian pilgrimage that provided him with an opportunity to meet many Buddhist monastics or contemplatives of different schools. He said that his Asian pilgrimage was "not concerned with talking, but with learning and with making contact with important people in the Buddhist *monastic* field."[159] To deepen his understanding of his own monastic tradition, he met with other religious monastics or contemplatives in order to learn from their ancient monastic sources and to experience contemplative life with them in their own monastic contexts. He believed that inter-monastic/contemplative encounters could cultivate monastic renewal and also provide a way of bringing together a spiritual family of contemplatives from different religions and cultures. At the end of his life in Asia, he made the case for supporting the cause of interreligious dialogue between monastics of the great world religions, and between contemplatives beyond religious and cultural boundaries for the modern world. His notion and methods for inter-monastic/contemplative dialogue may possibly be summarized by the words of Corless for this type of dialogue: "Do visit and exchange often; Do live together in openness; Do cooperate on common projects; Don't debate rather than meditate; Don't assume doctrinal similarities; Don't recommend dual practice to unprepared persons."[160]

Merton's encounter with different monastics and contemplatives at the Bangkok Conference in 1968 has inspired subsequent gatherings for monastic interreligious dialogue. His legacy has blossomed indirectly through the Spiritual Exchange program in Europe and directly through the Gethsemani Encounters in

159. AJ, 320 (emphasis added).
160. Roger Corless, "Sense and Nonsense in Buddhist-Christian Intermonastic Dialogue," *Monastic Studies* 19 (1991): 19.

North America, sponsored by the European and North American commissions of DIMMID. Official Catholic documents and papal statements have also encouraged this form of dialogue with Asian traditions. For example, Pope John Paul II stated, "Monasticism can make a valuable contribution to interreligious dialogue as well, since in some non-Christian religions important forms of monastic life are known and practiced."[161]

Asian monastics and contemplatives have also welcomed these expressions of monastic and contemplative interreligious dialogue. For example, Thomas L. Kirchner, a Buddhist monk in Japan, states, "A notable feature of the rich exchange between Christians and Buddhists has been the importance of the role played by contemplatives. . . . The dynamic force behind Buddhist-Christian dialogue has been provided largely by men and women in monastic orders."[162]

Merton's contemplative, existential, experiential, and universal approach to non-Christian monastics and lay contemplatives has provided a model for fostering and promoting dialogue with them. The path he took provides a road-map for interreligious dialogue on various levels, such as monastic hospitality, spiritual exchange, spiritual maturity, the transformation of human suffering, monastic discipline, monastic pilgrimage, and monastic ecology. His example has also inspired monastic experience programs for lay contemplatives.

Merton was in a unique position to engage in monastic and contemplative interreligious dialogue with Buddhists and was, indeed, a pioneer of this type of dialogue. It is true that because of his limited monastic experience of different Asian monasticisms, he tended at times to idealize Asian monasticism. However, this

161. John Paul II, "To the Abbot's Congress of the Benedictine Confederation" (1996), in *Interreligious Dialogue*, 624.

162. Thomas L. Kirchner, "Dialogue, Intermonastic: Buddhist Perspectives," in *Encyclopedia of Monasticism*, ed. William M. Johnston (Chicago, IL: Fitzroy Dearborn, 2000), 380.

tendency does not seem so objectionable when compared to the present situation of monastic interreligious dialogue. Fifty years after the death of Merton, there are still only a few monastics who are engaged in interreligious dialogue. Part of the reason for this is a decrease in monastic vocations in the Western world and a lack of interest in dialogue among many Eastern monastics. Since 2000, there have been only a few monastic exchange programs between Eastern and Western monastics, and the number of participants has declined considerably. Another reason for the decline is the high cost of travel. Although many monastics who engage in inter-monastic dialogue acknowledge the role Merton played in establishing the fundamental principles and methods for monastic dialogue, they are faced with these practical difficulties and will have to adapt to current situations if they are to follow his legacy. One way of adapting to current exigencies would be to focus more on *intra*-monastic dialogue in the same regions. Doing so would help reduce traveling costs as well as solve the language problem. Another issue is that the practice of monastic interreligious dialogue between Buddhist and Christian monasteries in Asia is still underdeveloped. Finally, cooperation between monastics and lay contemplatives in the spiritual communion will also further the kind of inter-monastic/contemplative dialogue that Merton envisaged.

CHAPTER 4

Merton's Legacy: Beyond His Encounter with Buddhism

In June 2018, the Monastic Institute at Sant'Anselmo, the international Benedictine University in Rome, hosted a symposium on "Thomas Merton: Prophecy and Renewal."[1] One of the areas that scholars were invited to address is the prophetic vision Merton brought to interreligious and inter-monastic dialogue, a vision that has continued to inspire the members of Dialogue Interreligieux Monastique/Monastic Interreligious Dialogue (DIMMID) as they have engaged in dialogue with Buddhist and Hindu monastics and with Muslims over the years following Merton's death.

Prior to the establishment of European and American commissions for interreligious dialogue in 1978, Aide à l'Implantation Monastique (AIM) initiated monastic interreligious dialogue with Asian monastics, especially through a meeting in Bangkok in 1968 and another in Bangalore in 1973. The two subcommissions were known as the "North American Board for East-West Dialogue" (NABEWD)—the name was subsequently changed to "Monastic Interreligious Dialogue" (MID)—and "Dialogue Interreligieux

---

1. See Merton Symposium, "Thomas Merton: Prophecy and Renewal" (June 12–15, 2018), http://www.anselmianum.com/facolta-di-teologia/istituto -monastico/merton-symposium-welcome/.

Monastique" (DIM) in Europe. In 1994, Dialogue Interreligieux Monastique/Monastic Interreligious Dialogue was established as an independent secretariat of the Benedictine Confederation in order to give greater emphasis and visibility to its particular work on behalf of the Benedictine Confederation and the Cistercian Order. Through local and regional commissions in Europe, North America, and Australia, DIMMID has developed monastic exchange programs between Western monastic men and women and their Eastern counterparts.[2] It is presently looking for ways to continue the work of Merton's legacy through the establishment of commissions for monastic interreligious dialogue in Asia as well as in Africa.

In order to bring Merton's legacy to bear on existential and experiential dialogue between Asian Buddhist and Christian monastics, DIMMID has drawn inspiration for *inter-* and *intra*-monastic dialogue in an Asian context from Raimon Panikkar's concept of "*intra-religious* dialogue," which is an inner dialogue within one's self and an encounter with another religious experience on an intimate level. Béthune and Blée suggest that Panikkar's notion of intra-religious dialogue is especially applicable to the monastic approach to interreligious dialogue. I will further develop their suggestion by speaking of "*intra-monastic* dialogue," in which I will include Merton's contemplative dialogue at the intimate level as well as his call for dialogue between monastics within the same culture and region of different religions.

This chapter aims to demonstrate why further development of monastic interreligious dialogue is urgently needed in Asia, and how it could greatly benefit from the patterns and goals that Merton proposed in his reflections on dialogue between Buddhist and Christian monastics. To this end, the chapter will explore Merton's legacy within the context of current monastic interreligious dia-

2. There is also a commission for monastic interreligious dialogue in India/Sri Lanka, but its activity has rarely extended beyond inviting a Hindu or Muslim to speak at the annual gathering of the Indo–Sri Lankan Benedictine Federation.

logue. It will be helpful to determine how his contribution can be expanded and taken beyond the models he proposed.

First, I will present the history and the activities of AIM and DIMMID and will evaluate them in the light of their value for the future of monastic exchange programs and the Gethsemani Encounters. These programs, which were initiated under the direct or indirect influence of Merton, have focused on contemplative dialogue in a spirit of openness, spiritual friendship, communion, and concrete collaboration by *living* and *sharing* the monastic life of different religious traditions.

Second, I will suggest that Merton's legacy needs to be developed in an Asian context through an intra-monastic exchange program involving Asian monastics of different religious traditions. In order to show further examples of current trends in intra-monastic dialogue within the same cultural setting, I will explore the history and experience of the Benedictine monastic community of St. Joseph in South Korea. Beginning in 1987, St. Joseph's Monastery has attempted to blend a Christian lifestyle with a Korean Buddhist lifestyle. I will also examine the "Samsohoe" gathering, which is the intra-religious gathering of religious women in South Korea that began in 1988. Next, the Buddhist *Temple Stay* program and the Benedictine *Monastery Stay* program in South Korea will be studied as examples of exchanges between monastics and the laity that put into practice Merton's original conception of contemplative dialogue. These examples will provide the backdrop to my own attempt to foster Buddhist-Christian inter-monastic exchange in South Korea taking Merton as an inspiration and model, while seeking to go further.

The History of Interreligious Monastic Encounter: From AIM to DIMMID

At the Bangkok Congress in 1968, Merton recommended monastic experience as the basis for dialogue between Eastern and Western monasticism. In the years following the Second Vatican

Council (1962–1965) and Merton's death (1968), however, there were only a few monks and nuns engaged in Buddhist-Catholic dialogue.[3] But Catholic monastics gradually began to realize the value of monasticism and contemplation for dialogue with Asian monastic traditions, and their efforts blossomed at the 1996 Gethsemani Encounter. In the years following, various meetings among Catholic monastics and exchange programs with Buddhist monastics sponsored by DIMMID developed Merton's legacy for a new dimension of interreligious dialogue.

In this section, I will explore the activity of AIM in the area of inter-monastic dialogue by examining the Congresses that took place in Bangkok and Bangalore. I will consider the evolution that led to the establishment of DIMMID from the two subcommissions for inter-monastic dialogue of AIM. I will also look at the main themes of Merton's pioneering works in monastic interreligious dialogue and I will show how he influenced its subsequent development.

The Congresses of Bangkok and Bangalore

In 1961, the Benedictine Confederation, in collaboration with the two branches of the Cistercian Order, established AIM in order to be of assistance to their new monastic communities in Asia, Latin America, and Africa.[4] Following the Second Vatican Council, how-

3. According to Professor Ovey N. Mohammed, this is probably due to the fact that "the 'Declaration on the Relationship of the Church to Non-Christian Religion' did not specify suitable areas for dialogue between Catholics and Buddhists." See Ovey N. Mohammed, "Catholicism in Dialogue with World Religions: The Value of Self-Denial," *Toronto Journal of Theology* 20, no. 1 (2004): 47–48.

4. Before the establishment of AIM, in the 1957 encyclical *Fidei Donum* Pope Pius XII requested Catholic monks and nuns to work enthusiastically for the spreading of the Christian faith. In 1959, at the Congress of Benedictine abbots meeting in Rome, Dom Benno Gut, the Abbot Primate, encouraged the creation of a Secretariat for coordination of monastic life in the mission lands of Africa, Asia, and Latin America. In 1961, the Abbot Primate officially established the Secretariat for the Missions with the name Aide à l'Implantation Monastique.

ever, AIM realized that these new monastic communities, founded on Western monastic principles and practices, especially in Asia, needed to become deeply inculturated, and therefore needed to be in dialogue with local cultures and religions. Thus, in 1968, the AIM Secretariat sponsored the first pan-Asian monastic Congress in Bangkok, Thailand, a Buddhist country, and, on the recommendation of Jean Leclercq, invited Thomas Merton to be a presenter. About seventy participants were drawn from countries in the Far East as a first step in promoting dialogue between Christian and non-Christian monastics. This pioneering event marked "a decisive step in the development of monastic dialogue."[5] John Moffitt, who wrote the proceedings of the Congress, said that it proposed "a new charter for monasticism" since "it is not only in the Far East that Christian monasticism is in need of rethinking [but] in the West, curiously enough, the situation is not very different from that on the other side of the world."[6] However, the Congress tended to focus on theoretical and intellectual issues, and most of the speakers were Christian monastics. Blée argues that in the Congress, "the concern for dialogue was quite weak and still theoretical. . . . [Nonetheless,] Bangkok's main contribution was to provide intellectual preparation for the actual practice of dialogue."[7]

In 1973, a second pan-Asian Congress was held in Bangalore, India. The theme was the search for God and spiritual experience in every religion, and the climate of this Congress was more experiential. Buddhist, Hindu, Jain, and Christian monastics and contemplatives, including Western lay contemplatives who lived in ashrams, took part in the meeting. More nuns participated and spoke in this

---

Dom Sortais OCSO, Abbot General of the Cistercians, gave his support. In 1962, the Synod of Benedictine Presidents confirmed the work of AIM.

5. Blée, *The Third Desert*, 28.

6. John Moffitt, *A New Charter for Monasticism: Proceedings of the Meeting of the Monastic Superiors in the Far East, Bangkok, December 9 to 15, 1968* (Notre Dame, IN: University of Notre Dame Press, 1970), xiv.

7. Blée, *The Third Desert*, 28.

Congress than at Bangkok. The schedule included three gatherings each day for prayer, meditation, and eucharistic celebration. One result of the meeting was the realization by Christian monastics that if Christian monasticism was to take root in Asian soil, the essential contemplative dimension of monasticism had to be evident. In line with Merton's stress on emphasizing the importance of the contemplative life for monastic interreligious dialogue, the participants focused more on spiritual experience and inner transformation. Blée points out that "[r]ecovering the essence of monasticism was one of the principal concerns of the Congress in Bangalore."[8] Because it dealt with religious experience through contemplation, the Congress was described as "the Pentecost of the monastic world."[9] The Congress contributed to openness and a new understanding of other forms of monasticism. According to Leclercq, "The most encouraging result of Bangalore was that some of those who had come without any interest in meeting the [monastics] of other religions, or even with prejudices against it, were, so to speak, converted and opened their eyes to the need for such an effort."[10]

However, Leclercq also acknowledged that a lack of spiritual exchange between Christian and non-Christian monastics limited what the Congress was able to achieve.[11] Non-Christian monastics did not sufficiently recognize the spiritual dimension of Christian monasticism. For example, Suzanne Siauve, a Hindu nun who took part in the Congress, commented, "We have to learn from you Christians organization and efficiency, but you have to learn from *our*

8. Ibid., 30.

9. Ibid., 25.

10. Jean Leclercq, "Introduction: The Second Meeting of the Monks of Asia," *Cistercian Studies* 9, nos. 2/3 (1974): 84. Abbot Primate Rembert Weakland said in his closing remarks, "Perhaps the most encouraging aspect of this meeting, in comparison with the meeting of Bangkok, was that it provided a genuine and real contact with non-Christian monasticism. This contact was more than just 'official.' We experienced here a real exchange." See Rembert Weakland, "Final Remarks," *Cistercian Studies* 9, nos. 2/3 (1974): 321.

11. See Leclercq, "Introduction: The Second Meeting of the Monks of Asia," 85.

spirituality."[12] At that time, there were few Christian monastics in Asia, and as a result, Buddhists and Hindus had limited opportunities for encountering Christian monastic spirituality. Moreover, Christian monasticism tended to be implanted in Asia in its Western form, giving little if any consideration to Asian cultural contexts. This lack of contact between Christian and non-Christian monastics, along with Christian monasticism's failure to adapt to the cultural context of Asia, made it difficult to engage in mutual and deep spiritual exchanges at that time. Furthermore, Asian Christian monastics could not see any urgent need for spiritual exchanges with Buddhist or Hindu monastics. They believed that they needed to focus more on being settled, establishing their financial independence from their Western mother monasteries, and increasing the number of monastic vocations. The Congress left two tasks to be undertaken at subsequent meetings: real inter-monastic exchange at a deep spiritual level, and the development of a type of dialogue that would be suited to the cultural setting of Asian Christian monastics.

The Congresses in Bangkok and in Bangalore represented the first opportunity for Hindu, Buddhist, and Christian monastics to meet, listen to one another, and enter into a spiritual relationship. These meetings, however, were only the beginning of monastic interreligious dialogue for mutual understanding and enrichment—and even for mutual transformation.

The Role of NABEWD and DIM in Establishing Contacts between Western and Asian Monastics

The recognition of the important contribution of monasticism to interreligious dialogue that came to the fore in the Bangkok and Bangalore Congresses was further developed through efforts undertaken in the Benedictine family with the official backing of the Catholic Church. In 1974, Cardinal Sergio Pignedoli, President

---

12. Suzanne Siauve, "Experience and Love of God in the Vaishnava Vedanta," *Cistercian Studies* 9, nos. 2/3 (1974): 135 (emphasis added).

of the Vatican Secretariat for Non-Christians, wrote to the Abbot Primate Rembert Weakland to stress the crucial role of monastics in the dialogue with Asian religions and to encourage interreligious dialogue at the level of spiritual experience for contemplative renewal in the church.[13] The letter influenced the founding of two subcommissions of AIM. In 1977, North American and European monastics gathered in Petersham, Massachusetts, USA, and in Loppen, Belgium, for the purpose of providing a structure to promote and organize monastic interreligious dialogue between the West and Asia. The two meetings created two subcommissions of AIM, NABEWD in North America and DIM in Europe.

The foundation of these two subcommissions constituted the beginning of an institution dedicated to the promotion of monastic interreligious dialogue through exchanges and collaboration between Western and Asian monasticism. Béthune points out that "the new commissions developed various projects to sensitize monks and nuns to [this] new dimension of Christian life . . . [for example,] to organize encounters with Buddhist or Hindu monastics in their monasteries or in Christian monasteries."[14] During the 1980s and 1990s, many Buddhist and Christian monastics shared their experience of monastic life through the "East-West Spiritual Exchange" program in Europe and the "Monastic Hospitality" program in North America. Both subcommissions recognized that monastic interreligious dialogue was becoming more and more important in a religiously pluralistic world, and therefore it would be advantageous to establish a structure independent from AIM that was dedicated to the "separate and legitimate activity" of monastic interreligious dialogue.[15]

---

13. See Sergio Pignedoli, "Dialogue Interreligieux Monastique," *Bulletin of AIM* 17 (1974): 61–63. Cardinal Pignedoli believed that "monasticism can be like a bridge between Christian and other spiritualities." See Béthune, "Monastic Interreligious Dialogue: A History," 5.

14. Béthune, "Monastic Interreligious Dialogue: A History," 6.

15. Blée, *The Third Desert*, 106.

In 1994, the recognition of the need for an institution to support the specific and autonomous mission of monastic interreligious dialogue prompted Abbot Primate Jerome Theisen, with the agreement of the two Cistercian Abbots General, to establish an organizational structure for DIMMID that was similar to that of AIM, in other words, to make DIMMID a permanent secretariat of the Benedictine Confederation. Pierre-François de Béthune, a monk of Clérlande in Belgium, was appointed as the Secretary General of the European and American commissions for Monastic Interreligious Dialogue; other continental commissions could and would be added to ensure that monastic interreligious dialogue would be global. DIMMID now includes two other commissions: Benedictine Interfaith Dialogue (BID) for India and Sri Lanka, and the Australian Monastic Encounter (AME) for Australia. The members of the AME include Hindu and Buddhist monastics as well as Benedictine and Cistercian monastics. Work is also under way to create commissions in Asia, Africa, and South America. The interdependent monastic organization of DIMMID meant that monastic interreligious dialogue could now take place at an international level. Its mission is to promote and support monastic encounter at the deep spiritual and practical levels between Christian monastic men and women and followers of other religions.

Today, DIMMID is challenged on both the local and international levels to promote interreligious dialogue with the adherents of religious traditions beyond Buddhism and Hinduism. In recent years, it has begun to engage in dialogue on spirituality with Muslims, especially Sufis and Shi'ites.

The Paradigm Shifts in Monastic Interreligious Dialogue

The period before the foundation of DIMMID was a transitional one for interiorizing and implementing the contributions of pioneers in monastic interreligious dialogue and the teachings of the Second Vatican Council on the relation between the church and other religions. Christian monastics and church leaders needed time to recognize and actualize the crucial role that monasticism and contemplation needed to play in interreligious dialogue with Asian traditions. Through the Congresses in Bangkok and Bangalore and the monastic exchange programs of NABEWD and DIM, Christian monastics made two paradigm shifts in their approach to monastic interreligious encounter: 1) from Westernized monasticism to pancultural monasticism and 2) from monasticism at the service of missionary proclamation to monasticism at the service of interreligious dialogue at the level of spiritual experience and practice.

The inter-monastic gatherings and actions sponsored by AIM revealed the importance of *pancultural* monasticism. Through an encounter with other forms of monasticism Christian monastics realized that monasticism was not the exclusive property of Christianity but actually predated Christianity and had developed in the cultural contexts of the great religions of the East. In his opening speech at the Bangkok Congress, Abbot Primate Weakland emphasized the need of establishing pancultural monasticism in a pluralized and globalized modern world. He said:

> Each area of the globe, by reason of these local differences, will of necessity develop a different monasticism. The beauty of these divergent expressions is our wealth. We should *no longer expect to transplant a tropical flower to Europe* or vice versa. On the other hand, such a concept, which I feel sure is integral to the whole genius of monasticism, demands greater responsibility and awareness on the part of those engaged in the actual living. Our monasticism now must also, in its pluralism, seek to be *pancultural*.[16]

The paradigm shift to pancultural monasticism became the framework for dialogue with Asian monastics. In the period between

---

16. Rembert Weakland, "Transplanting Ourselves or Just Finding Old Roots?," in *A New Charter for Monasticism*, 22 (emphasis added).

the Bangkok and Bangalore Congresses and the foundation of DIMMID, Christian monastics came to realize the need for a new spiritual solidarity in an emerging global culture, a solidarity that monasticism could help to bring about. They focused on "the question of transforming particular cultures into a world culture, with monks in dialogue addressing the place of religious experience in such a transformation."[17] This paradigm shift to pancultural consciousness echoed Merton's teaching on transcultural maturity and the transformation of human consciousness in monastic interreligious contemplative dialogue. In Calcutta, his emphasis on the recovery of original unity through spiritual communion was implemented at the subsequent pan-Asian Congresses and in the activities of the European and American subcommissions. According to Blée, "the words Merton spoke in Calcutta provided the key to understanding the meaning of dialogue and putting it into practice."[18]

Merton also contributed to the paradigm shift from monasticism as simply a transplant of Western culture to a monasticism in dialogue, a shift that came about through the recognition that monasticism is a transcultural phenomenon, through the achievement of greater transcultural maturity, and through the actual experience of spiritual exchanges with Asian monastics. Understanding monasticism as a pancultural phenomenon does not mean ignoring the specificity of the monastic way of life in different religious traditions, but being free of clinging to a particular culture and recognizing that genuine interreligious dialogue can only happen when one accepts that different forms of monasticism have developed in different cultural and religious contexts.

17. Blée, *The Third Desert*, 53. Cornelius Tholens states that different monastic traditions will have "to confront together the crucial questions raised by the cultural mutation currently experienced by all humanity, a mutation that challenges all religions." See Cornelius Tholens, "Une Enquête auprès des monastères d'Occident pour la poursuite du dialogue inter-religieux," *Bulletin de l'A.I.M.* 19 (1975): 49 (this part is translated by William Skudlarek).

18. Blée, *The Third Desert*, 54.

Merton's view of the need for a de-Westernized or de-Hellenized version of Christianity also influenced the new awareness of pan-cultural monasticism. Through encounters with Asian monasticism, Christian monastics realized that Asian monasticism could contribute to the creation of Christian cultures and a Christian monasticism that was different from the de-Europeanized or Benedictinized monasticism of the West. At the Bangkok Congress, Leclercq spoke of the need to "de-Hellenize" Western monasticism and declared that Christian monasticism needed to be "de-Benedictinized" if it was to take root and grow in Asia.[19]

In the past, St. Paul and many fathers of the church down to St. Augustine attempted to express Christianity in the language and symbolism of Hellenism, and St. Benedict wrote the Rule in and for his own cultural context. Although Hellenism and the Rule of St. Benedict have enriched Christian monasticism, they also hinder current Christian monastics from engaging in interreligious dialogue with monastics of other cultures. For inculturation of the Rule, Leclercq said, "We must maintain the riches and go beyond the limitation. We must set Christianity free from a particular cultural form in order to open it up to other forms—those of the scientific world, those of the Far East, those of Africa."[20]

What it might mean to de-Hellenize Christian monasticism was a topic reflected on in the subcommissions of AIM as Western monks attempted to gain new insight into Western monasticism through spiritual exchange with Asian monastics. As Blée points out, "The members of AIM provided a rationale for ridding mo-

---

19. Jean Leclercq, "Present-Day Problems in Monasticism," in *A New Charter for Monasticism*, 30–44. For Leclercq, "de-Benedictinized" does not mean discarding the Rule but inculturating it.

20. Ibid., 38. Leclercq also said, "If we cease making Christianity dependent on one specific culture in its forms of thought, its expression, its conduct, we shall open it out to other cultures; we shall give it a chance to become richer, to assume new elements, to communicate itself, in Asia and elsewhere, to whole peoples entirely different from those who received Hellenized Christianity." See ibid.

nasticism of Western accretions that were nonessential or—even worse—got in the way of experiencing and expressing the divine mystery. Rediscovering the essence of monasticism led to a program of de-Westernization."[21] During this period, the commissions of AIM established contacts with Asian traditions in order to discover another dimension of Christian monastic spirituality as well as to build a new spirituality for the postmodern world that drew on the wisdom of both East and West.

The second paradigm shift in monastic interreligious dialogue was the recognition of the significance of *dialogue* with Asian monastics. Although Merton and other pioneers stressed monastic interreligious dialogue at the contemplative level, many Christians during the 1970s did not fully realize the value of interreligious *dialogue* in relation to *mission* in Asia. However, following up on the work of the pioneers of interreligious dialogue, the Bangalore Congress and the subcommissions of AIM stressed that Benedictine monastic life should contribute to dialogue with Asian monastics through lived experience and spiritual exchange and not just be involved in missionary work for conversion. Weakland insisted that Christian monastics must overcome the spirit of conquest: "We come, not to 'civilize,' nor to 'conquer,' nor to 'convert,' but to *live*. We hope to find here, in a deeper way, what we are and to grow more deeply in our monasticism by our contacts here."[22] Therefore, one of the first concerns of the subcommissions of AIM was that they spend time in Buddhist monasteries or Hindu ashrams and learn about spiritual practices such as yoga or Zen meditation. This concern reflected a radical change in the way Christian monks thought about other religions and other forms of monasticism, since the almost universal opinion had been that engaging in the spiritual practices of different religious (that is, "pagan") traditions would be a form of idolatry.

21. Blée, *The Third Desert*, 31.
22. Weakland, "Transplanting Ourselves or Just Finding Old Roots?," 20 (emphasis added).

The efforts of the subcommissions of AIM contributed to the realization that monastic interreligious dialogue on the *experience of life* was a new way of encounter with Asian religious traditions at a deep spiritual level. As Cornelius Tholens, a Dutch Benedictine Abbot, put it, "We have left behind the familiar way of apologetics and mission and a new horizon has opened up— not that of a new missionary approach, but that of living together with the members of other religions and sharing what we have in common!"[23] Although monastics did not have a monopoly on dialogue at the level of spiritual experience, they were in a better position to continue and deepen this type of dialogue by living in another monastic milieu.[24] The monastic exchange programs organized by DIM and MID were fruits of this idea. They believed that various forms of interreligious dialogue, such as the dialogue of life, of action, of theological and spiritual exchange, would benefit from the experience of participating in different forms of monastic life. We will treat this realization in more detail in the following section.

Merton's Legacy and DIMMID

DIM developed an East-West Spiritual Exchange program between Japanese Zen and European monastics, while MID carried out a Monastic Hospitality program between Tibetan and

---

23. This is in an unpublished text written in 1979 and cited in Blée, *The Third Desert*, 198.

24. For example, Francis Acharya, one of the participants in the Bangkok Congress, stated, "Our [Christian] monastic life should grow under the enriching presence of our non-Christian brethren, and this mainly at three levels: study, friendly relations and dialogue, and ultimately an actual sharing in the experience of the monastic life as it is lived by our [Asian] people." See Francis Acharya, "Reorientation of Monastic Life in an Asian Context," in *A New Charter for Monasticism*, 116.

North American monastics. Both monastic exchange programs were indirectly inspired by Thomas Merton. On the other hand, the Gethsemani Encounters can be considered his direct legacy. The plan that Merton devised during his Asian journey—to learn from Tibetan monastics at the Abbey of Gethsemani—was realized through the first Gethsemani Encounter, which took place in 1996. Asian and Western monastics gathered in his monastery in order to look for ways to implement his legacy as they shared their monastic life in spiritual communion.

In this section, we will look at these monastic exchange programs and the Gethsemani Encounters in order to show how Merton's legacy has been developed by DIMMID for advanced monastic/contemplative interreligious dialogue.

Monastic Exchange Programs: An Indirect Legacy

History and the Progress

The East-West Spiritual Exchange program and the Monastic Hospitality program offered opportunities for the *dialogue of life* and the *dialogue of religious experience*. Many Buddhist and Christian monastics have appreciated the value of different monastic traditions as well as the possibility for mutual enrichment by embracing difference in a loving spirit of reverence. Thus, they began to share their different traditions by staying at each other's monasteries for several weeks or months. This new attempt at monastic dialogue flows out of the common monastic tradition of hospitality. Basing his teaching on the hospitality of Abraham (Gen 18) and the teaching of the Gospel of Matthew (25:35), St. Benedict taught that monastics should see Christ in the guest: "All guests who present themselves are to be welcomed as Christ" (RB 53.1). Similarly, Buddhist monasteries have also treasured the tradition of hospitality. For example, the tradition of *chadō*, the Buddhist tea ceremony, serves as a valuable contribution to the art of hospitality. Through participation in the tea ceremony, the guest may attain a "gradual awakening through the discreet chant and ritual and the quality of the host's presence."[25] Buddhists welcome everyone since they see that each person not only has the potential for Buddhahood but is also interdependent with all humanity and all nature.

In 1979, under the spirituality of hospitality of both traditions, the first Spiritual Exchange between Japanese Buddhist and Christian monastics took place in Europe. About forty Buddhist monastics lived in different Catholic monasteries of Germany, Holland, Belgium, France, and Italy for three weeks. Pope John Paul II encouraged this program by commenting: "I congratulate those among you who have lived in small groups in the great Christian monasteries and have shared fully their life of prayer and work for three weeks. Your experience is truly an epoch-making event in the history of interreligious dialogue."[26] In 1983, the Reverend Hirata Seiko, President of the Institute of Zen Studies, invited seventeen Christian monastics to spend time in Zen monasteries in Japan for the second Spiritual Exchange. Subsequent exchange programs have followed a similar pattern for interreligious monastic exchange. There have been twelve East-West Spiritual Exchanges through 2011, and more than two hundred Buddhist, Christian, and Hindu monastics have taken part in them.[27]

The most significant part of the Spiritual Exchange program is living in a different monastic community and following the monastic way of life of another religious tradition. It has led monastics to share their experiences of prayer and contemplation and their ways of searching for enlightenment or self-transcendence. By so doing, monastics could appreciate a different monastic tradition and reach a deeper level of spiritual communion beyond the

---

25. Pierre-Francois de Béthune, *By Faith and Hospitality: The Monastic Tradition as a Model for Interreligious Encounter* (Leominster, UK: Gracewing, 2002), 14.

26. John Paul II, "To the Lay Monks of the Various Buddhist Schools" (1979), in *Interreligious Dialogue*, 256.

27. See Béthune, *Interreligious Hospitality*, 95.

limitations of verbal exchange.[28] For example, Kadowaki Kakichi, a Japanese Zen Buddhist monk and a Jesuit priest and a participant in the program, said, "It seems that there can be a *wordless dialogue*, which is more effective in some sense. For instance, waking up early in the morning and living in accordance with the strict time schedule itself brings the participants closer."[29] As Morris J. Augustine wrote about his experience of the Spiritual Exchange, "[The program] gives us a better hold on that spiritual poverty which is a joy. . . . It consists in being better able to discern the essential and disengage it in a precise manner from the dogmatic and ritual formulae that express it."[30] The program has become a wellspring of a true spiritual enrichment for monastic communities. Today, it hopes to expand to include various countries in the East and West, as well as various lineages of Buddhist monasteries and Benedictine and Cistercian monasteries.

Another monastic exchange program, the Monastic Hospitality program, involved Tibetan and North American monastics. In 1981, NABEWD arranged for a program in which Tibetan Buddhist monastics stayed in Christian monasteries in the United States.[31] Three more such programs followed, and by 1988,

28. See Béthune, "Monastic Inter-Religious Dialogue," 38. As Béthune notes, "During such a stay verbal exchanges are of little value. It is the sharing, most often carried out in silence, of the details of daily life that makes up the essential aspect of the encounter. . . . This is a setting that makes possible greater awareness of the common destiny that binds together all those engaged in monastic life." See Béthune, *Interreligious Hospitality*, 93.

29. Jikai Fujiyoshi and Kadowaki Kakichi, "Interaction between Buddhism and Catholicism Sources of Eastern and Western Cultures," *Young East* 7, no. 1 (Winter 1981): 7 (emphasis in original).

30. Morris J. Augustine, "The Buddhist-Christian Monastic and Contemplative Encounter," *Buddhist-Christian Studies* 9 (1989): 251.

31. The groundwork for the Monastic Hospitality program "was laid in August 1981 at a Buddhist-Christian conference sponsored by the Naropa Institute in Boulder, Colorado. At a semiprivate audience with His Holiness the Dalai Lama, who was also attending this conference, Sr. Pascaline Coff, OSB, and Abbot Lawrence Wagner, OSB, asked His Holiness if he would like to send some of

groups of Tibetan monastics had visited twenty-five Benedictine and Cistercian monasteries and convents. At each monastery, they took part in the monastic life and shared their spiritual experience and life. After participating in one of these programs, the Venerable Kunchok Tsering recalled that the most admirable trait he observed in the American monasteries he visited was "the kindhearted, loving care and sharing among the members of the communities."[32]

In phase III in 1986 and phase V in 1992, two small groups of American monastics were received by Tibetan monasteries in India. For six weeks, they visited more than twenty Tibetan monasteries and nunneries and had an audience with the Dalai Lama at Dharamsala. They followed the daily *horarium* of their Tibetan hosts or witnessed particular ascetic practices. The Americans did not follow the example of the Europeans, who "opted for a radical hospitality that made it possible for them to follow the rule and extreme rigor of Zen monastic life."[33] Rather, their idea "was not so much to have an experience of the monastic life of the Tibetans as to visit them in a spirit of attentiveness and friendship."[34] They agreed, however, that the program helped them enter into the monastic observance of the Tibetan community and to learn from them.[35]

MID created a program that focused on educational support for Tibetan monastics, doing so in response to the suggestion of the Dalai Lama that new ways be developed to bring together

---

his monks to North America to visit monasteries here. As Sr. Pascaline writes, the Dalai Lama beamed a delighted 'yes,' and the cycle of exchanges was set in motion." See Aaron Raverty, "Monastic Interreligious Dialogue: Tibet, Nepal, and Northern India," *Cistercian Studies* 32, no. 2 (1997): 259–260.

32. Cited in Augustine, "The Buddhist-Christian Monastic and Contemplative Encounter," 252.

33. Blée, *The Third Desert*, 82.

34. Ibid.

35. See Teasdale, "The Ocean of Wisdom as Human and Spiritual Presence," 105–107.

Buddhist and Christian monastics.[36] As we shall see in the next section, the Monastic Hospitality program was transformed into the Gethsemani Encounter in 1996.

Development in the Face of Resistance and Doubt

The development of a new way of monastic interreligious dialogue was not welcomed by all Benedictine communities. Some conservative abbots were of the opinion that Asian monasticism could not be a substitute for the renewal of Christian contemplation.[37] They worried that some Western monastics tended to idealize Eastern spirituality. During the transition period there were also some problematic incidents, for instance, a controversy around an instance of intercommunion during the celebration of the Eucharist at a meeting sponsored by NABEWD. There were also some who believed that interreligious dialogue was a responsibility "outside the monastic institution," and others were suspicious of "the role of Centering Prayer" in monastic dialogue.[38] According to Blée, between the late 1970s and the mid-1980s, problems arose not because monastics did not understand the type of dialogue appropriate to them, but because of "the occurrence of avant-garde experiments in dialogue."[39] In the movement toward a new way of relating to the monastic traditions of other religions,

---

36. Phase VI in 1994 and phase VII in 1995 took place in Tibetan and in Christian monasteries. In 1996, "going beyond hospitality and exchange, MID developed an educational focus that has occasionally brought Tibetan monastics to the U.S. to study health care, computer skills, and English, and at other times funded such training for them at Benedictine communities in India." See Donald W. Mitchell and James A. Wiseman, "An Interview with Donald Mitchell and James Wiseman," *Buddhist-Christian Studies* 23 (2003): 198–199.

37. See Blée, *The Third Desert*, 67.

38. Ibid., 88, 90. The members of NABEWD agreed to promote programs such as Centering Prayer, but they also wondered whether promoting this form of prayer was essential to their goal of promoting, supporting, and engaging in monastic interreligious dialogue. See ibid., 90–92.

39. Ibid., 84.

the tension between old and new ways of regarding this relationship was bound to occur.

Between the mid-1980s and the mid-1990s, however, the tensions between the more conservative church leaders and scholars with the monastics who were involved in monastic interreligious dialogue lessened, and a new controversy arose. The latter was occasioned by Cardinal Joseph Ratzinger's 1989 *Letter to the Bishops of the Catholic Church on Some Aspects of Christian Meditation* in which he cautioned against the adaptation of Asian methods of meditation to Christians:

> With the present diffusion of eastern methods of meditation in the Christian world and in ecclesial communities, we find ourselves faced with a pointed renewal of an attempt, which is not free from dangers and errors, *to fuse Christian meditation with that which is non-Christian.* . . . [The] proposals to harmonize Christian meditation with eastern techniques need to have their contents and methods ever subjected to a thorough-going examination so as to avoid the danger of falling into syncretism.[40]

Cardinal Ratzinger presented an apology (*apologia*) for Christian spirituality and its methods, insisting that they were different from Eastern methods of meditation, and arguing that the latter were not only inferior but could be dangerous. Catholic monastics and others who had experienced the value of Asian methods of meditation strongly resisted the cardinal's admonition. For instance, Blée criticized the letter, saying that "it cast doubt on the validity of apophatic contemplation . . . [and] tended to lump together the great Asian traditions with recent derivations."[41] According to

40. Joseph Ratzinger, "Letter to the Bishops of the Catholic Church on Some Aspects of Christian Meditation" (October 15, 1989), http://www.vatican.va /roman_curia/congregations/cfaith/documents/rc_con_cfaith_doc_19891015 _meditazione-cristiana_en.html (emphasis in original).

41. Blée, *The Third Desert*, 115.

Béthune, "The document recalled some fundamental aspects of Christian prayer, but an overall tone of suspicion regarding the spiritual practices of other religions and a haughty ignorance of these practices prevented it from being very useful."[42] Béthune, then president of DIM, presented the critique of the document to the staff of the Pontifical Council for Interreligious Dialogue, and its president, Cardinal Francis Arinze, wrote Béthune an official letter requesting that DIM undertake a study of the use of Asian methods of meditation by Catholic monks and nuns. In 1993, DIM synthesized the responses to this study in a document entitled "Contemplation and Interreligious Dialogue: References and Perspectives Drawn from the Experience of Monastics." In that report, DIM confirmed that the encounter with the East had been a blessing for Western monasticism in that it had encouraged a reawakening of the contemplative tradition that is at the heart of the monastic call.[43]

Another remarkable example of coming to the defense of monks as well as of other Christians who adopted Eastern methods of meditation was occasioned by the Swiss theologian Hans Urs von Balthasar's denunciation of this practice. He referred to the use of Asian meditation techniques by some Benedictine monks as "the absolutely ridiculous dilettantism that brings counterfeited Asian methods to Europe."[44] In his view, the methods of Asian meditation were deeply rooted in the Asian worldview, and therefore, adopting their spiritual practices could be construed as an acceptance of that worldview and thus constitute a "betrayal"

---

42. Béthune, "Monastic Inter-Religious Dialogue," 40.

43. See Pierre-François de Béthune, "Contemplation and Interreligious Dialogue: References and Perspectives Drawn from the Experience of Monastics," in *The Attentive Voice: Reflections on the Meaning and Practice of Interreligious Dialogue*, ed. William Skudlarek (Brooklyn, NY: Lantern Books, 2011), 143–164.

44. Hans Urs von Balthasar, *Des Bords du Gange aux Rives du Jourdain* (Paris, France: Saint Paul, 1983), 161 (this part is translated in Blée, *The Third Desert*, 116).

of Christian faith.[45] He also insisted that true Christians, who believe in the incarnate and crucified love of Christ and the personal grace of God, could never truly practice Zen meditation since God is absent from the Buddhist tradition.[46] Balthasar's thought reinforced the anxiety of some Benedictine abbots regarding the monastic interreligious dialogue's more positive approach to some of meditation methods developed within Buddhism, and to express their disapproval, they discontinued their financial support of NABEWD.

Ironically, both the Letter of Ratzinger and the writings of von Balthasar led Catholic monastics to put even more effort into becoming familiar with Asian methods of meditation and acquiring a more accurate understanding of them. It also had an impact on the development of solidarity between the European and American subcommissions of AIM. As Blée points out, "While the subcommissions may have aroused suspicion and incomprehension among those who were more conservative, they always enjoyed the backing of Catholic authorities concerning their involvement in an in-depth and existential dialogue with other spiritual and ascetic paths."[47] In their response to the Letter of Cardinal Ratzinger, the monks who were involved the inter-monastic dialogue came to a deeper understanding of Asian spirituality and of what it means to engage in interreligious dialogue at the level of spiritual experience and practice. Their personal experience of Asian spiritual disciplines, including meditation, demonstrated the possibility of mutual enrichment between monks of different religious traditions. In short, the suspicions and debates led to the development

---

45. Hans Urs von Balthasar, "Meditation als Verrat [Meditation as Betrayal]," *Geist und Leben* 50 (1977): 261.

46. See ibid., 266; see also Ernest M. Valea, *Buddhist-Christian Dialogue as Theological Exchange: An Orthodox Contribution to Comparative Theology* (Eugene, OR: Pickwick Publications, 2015), 94–95.

47. Blée, *The Third Desert*, 118.

of "a new religious consciousness within the church" and made "intrareligious dialogue a common monastic concern."[48]

Evaluation and Prospect

During his Asian journey, Merton was convinced that the experience of other monastic traditions could become the vehicle for inter-monastic exchange that went beyond conceptual communication. Aaron Raverty, who, as a member of MID, took part in a monastic exchange program, points out that:

> Thomas Merton was and continues to be the great inspiration for interreligious dialogue. His contact with the Dalai Lama and others paved the way for continued exchange between monastics of the East and West. . . . The flame for dialogue that he lit remains unquenched and burns through those networks like MID or DIM that still carry the torch.[49]

The monastic exchange programs of DIMMID have implicitly developed Merton's example and pioneering work for inter-monastic encounters in two ways: 1) live-in monastic experience programs have developed from his pioneering existential and experiential dialogue; 2) the spirituality of monastic hospitality has developed from his notion of monastic pilgrimage.

First, Merton's emphasis on involvement in staying in the monastic milieu of other religious traditions and his personal example of Asian pilgrimage indirectly influenced the monastic exchange programs. In the existential dialogue, the participants of the programs on both sides report that they feel at *home* in the host monastery because in it they find similar monastic simplicity, love of silence, the practice of prayer and meditation, and even the tension between solitude and openness to the secular world.[50]

48. Ibid., 126, 127.
49. Raverty, "Monastic Interreligious Dialogue," 260.
50. See Béthune, "Monastic Inter-Religious Dialogue," 42.

Through the programs, they also come to appreciate other forms of monasticism. For example, after staying in the Buddhist monastery of Sogen-ji in 1983, Béthune reported that "we realized that we had taken part in a *reunion* of separated brethren. 'How is it that we ignored one another for so long?' "[51] One of the Japanese Buddhist monks who lived in a Trappist monastery for two weeks said, "The monks work hard. They don't eat very well, nor do they get a lot of sleep. So where does this joy come from that I see in their faces?"[52] Despite the difficulty of communicating in a foreign language, this Buddhist monk sensed the essence of Christian monastic life through following the monastic daily schedule and engaging in manual labor.

Hosting monks from another monastic tradition also helped correct misunderstandings. For example, commenting on the sojourn of Japanese Zen monks at his home monastery, Abbot Primate Notker Wolf said:

> In my own monastery of St. Ottilien, near Munich, our monks were greatly astonished to see that these Zen monks are not just pagans, as some stupid people might think. In fact, they showed great respect for our way of life. They were curious about our spirituality and were very eager to know what we do and why we do it. When they returned to Japan, they said, "Those Europeans who come to Japan and tell us that in Europe there is no spirituality." . . . It's not true![53]

Monastic exchange programs have offered a new view of different religious traditions and shown the value of the lived monastic experience. Béthune states that "*monasteries are privileged places*

---

51. Pierre-François de Béthune, "Interreligious Monastic Hospitality," *Monastic Studies* 16 (1985): 229 (emphasis in original).

52. Cited in Béthune, "Monastic Inter-Religious Dialogue," 47.

53. DIMMID, *Strangers No More*, DVD, directed by Lizette Lemoine and Aubin Hellot (Paris, France: Les Films du Large, 2016). Abbot Notker Wolf's comment has been slightly edited for the sake of clarity.

for dialogue and . . . this dialogue is a precious opportunity for monasteries."[54] Monasteries that participate in these programs become a place where Buddhist and Christian monastics can share their spiritual and monastic experiences at a deeper contemplative level.

Second, Merton's existential and experiential dialogue through monastic pilgrimage influenced the development of the practice and spirituality of interreligious monastic hospitality. When he was in Asia, Merton, who introduced himself as a pilgrim student, was warmly received by Buddhist monastics and contemplatives, although he was not able to stay in their monasteries very long. After his death, those who participated in monastic exchange programs not only became monastic pilgrims, but they were also able to experience another expression of monastic spirituality over a longer period of time.

Béthune played a crucial role in developing a program to extend interreligious hospitality for the purpose of dialogue. Historically, he saw that although hospitality held a place of honor in many religions, hospitality was normally not extended to other religions. Rather, hostility or rejection between religions was prevalent until the middle of the twentieth century.[55] Béthune rediscovered the value of monastic hospitality for interreligious dialogue. As he writes, "Hospitality . . . appears as a privileged way to meet the follower of another religion. This is all the more true since hospitality is known and respected as sacred in all cultures and religions."[56] He states two reasons why interreligious hospitality is the better way to encounter other monastics:

> Firstly, [the] approach through hospitality . . . offers an environment for verbal exchanges. In this existential context words

---

54. Béthune, "Interreligious Monastic Hospitality," 235 (emphasis in original).
55. See Béthune, *Interreligious Hospitality*, 11–15.
56. Pierre-François de Béthune, *Welcoming Other Religions*, trans. William Skudlarek (Collegeville, MN: Liturgical Press, 2016), 37.

and explanations can come into their own. Secondly, what characterizes hospitality is precisely that it is always designed for strangers. They are warmly welcomed, but with respect for their otherness, with no intention of ignoring their difference or of exploiting them.[57]

Interreligious hospitality can facilitate a more existential involvement with another form of monastic life in very concrete ways and can help to develop a closer relationship in which a stranger becomes a member of the spiritual family. As Béthune explains, "Hospitality consists of . . . allowing another person to come into one's home. . . . It is an existential form of experience . . . that occurs at the level of 'being.' "[58] This acceptance of religious strangers in a monastic community allows friendships to develop, and a deeper encounter with the religious *other* creates a bond of brotherhood.

Of course, hospitality can involve a risk; the word "host" is at the root of both "hospitality" and "hostility." Welcoming monastics of different traditions into a monastery may cause fear or confusion in the host community. Even St. Benedict taught that before guests were received, there was need of prayer for discernment because of "the delusions of the devil" (RB 53.5). However, many spiritually mature Buddhist and Catholic monastics who accepted other monastics into their monasteries came to realize that their guests were neither devils nor pagans, but spiritual friends in mind and heart. Wayne Teasdale, one of the pioneers in the interreligious movement, points out that "as time passed, more in-depth dialogue occurred. An organic evolution happened as the inter-monastic hospitality exchange became monastic interreligious dialogue and these dialogical exchanges became a communion of hearts and

---

57. Béthune, "Monastic Interreligious Dialogue," 8.
58. Béthune, *Interreligious Hospitality*, 101.

minds."[59] The spirituality of monastic hospitality made it easier for monastics to become a spiritual family that included other monastics, which was the goal of Merton's monastic interreligious dialogue, and could lead to the realization that, in Merton's words, "There are no strangers!"[60]

The Gethsemani Encounter: A Direct Legacy

History and Progress

A comment made by His Holiness the Dalai Lama at the 1993 Parliament of the World's Religions in Chicago is what led to the Gethsemani Encounter. The Tibetan leader thought that *interreligious* dialogue should continue in a monastic milieu and suggested that it take place at Thomas Merton's Abbey in Kentucky for a full week and involve just twenty-five Christian and twenty-five Buddhist monastics. He believed that a gathering of a small number of *spiritually mature* Buddhist and Christian monks and nuns could be an apt setting for dialogue on spirituality. His friendship with Merton and his sense of Merton's prophetic role for monastic interreligious dialogue undoubtedly inspired him to open a new era for interreligious dialogue at Merton's home monastery.

MID began to organize the first Gethsemani Encounter. Fifty participants—Buddhists, including Theravadin, Zen, and Tibetan monastics from Asia, along with lay contemplatives from the emerging American Buddhist communities, and Benedictine and Cistercian monastics, as well as one hundred observers, were invited to gather at the Abbey of Gethsemani in July 1996. For six days, the participants attended the liturgies of the Gethsemani monastic community, meditated together in silence, and shared their monastic way of life and their spiritual experiences and practices with one another.

---

59. Wayne Teasdale, *Catholicism in Dialogue: Conversations across Traditions* (Lanham, MD: Rowman & Littlefield, 2004), 117.

60. CGB, 155.

They spoke with one another about dialogue, ultimate reality, spirituality, prayer and meditation, spiritual growth and development, community and guidance, and the goals of personal and social transformation. As Donald W. Mitchell, one of the coordinators of the meeting, noted, "Each day there was a different topic addressed in five sessions. Two sessions were devoted to the Christian tradition, and there was one session each on the Theravadin, Zen, and Tibetan traditions."[61]

There were many lectures on various topics, but the presentations were very short and ample time was devoted to discussion. William Skudlarek, who was present as an observer, noted that "the Gethsemani Encounter was primarily a monastic rather than a theological interreligious dialogue . . . [The] reason for meeting was not to discuss doctrine but to describe their own praxis and to learn about other expressions of the monastic life."[62] Dialogue on spiritual practices can accompany the "conceptual dialogue" and the "social dialogue" that Merton also engaged in.[63] Using monasticism as a bridge to other religions, monastics of various religions can engage in mutual sharing and learn from each other at a spiritual level to facilitate "mutual creative transformation."[64] The first Gethsemani Encounter was a milestone, a new stage in monastic interreligious dialogue at the level of spiritual experience and practice.

In 2002, about twenty Buddhist monastics from different schools and thirty-five Catholic monastics again gathered at Merton's monastery for Gethsemani Encounter II. For six days, they con-

61. Donald W. Mitchell, "The Gethsemani Encounter on the Spiritual Life," *Buddhist-Christian Studies* 17 (1997): 206.

62. William Skudlarek, "Refashioning the Likeness, Playing with the Differences: Monastic Interreligious Dialogue at the Abbey of Gethsemani," *The Japan Christian Review* 63 (1997): 83.

63. Paul O. Ingram, " 'Fruit Salad Can Be Delicious': The Practice of Buddhist-Christian Dialogue," *Cross Currents* 50, no. 4 (Winter 2000/2001): 546–547.

64. Ibid., 543.

sidered the theme of "Suffering and Its Transformation." Mitchell points out that the topic "reminded the Christian members of the group of Thomas Merton's challenge to monastic communities to make their walls thin enough to share their spiritual riches with the world, to share with those in need of guidance, support, and inspiration for daily living."[65] By discussing suffering, which is a common human problem as well as a common theme for self-transformation in both traditions, the encounter led the participants to cooperate in offering spiritual support to persons facing suffering in the world. Each day, they focused on one of the principal causes of suffering: a sense of unworthiness and alienation, greed and consumerism, structural violence, and sickness, aging, and death. While for Buddhists *dukkha* (suffering) is a reality that needs to be overcome in order to achieve liberation from suffering, for Christians the Cross (embracing the reality of suffering) is the way to salvation.[66] Despite this fundamental difference, both Buddhist and Christian monastics recognized that in suffering there was "a potential occasion for bringing us closer to salvation (or enlightenment) depending on how we respond to it."[67] Both agreed that the experience of suffering was a part of life, and that in and through the suffering they were seeking the path to transformation.

In the second Gethsemani Encounter, monastics also talked about current problems in their community. They did not attempt to solve these problems, but confronting them together and recognizing how similar these problems often were strengthened their sense of monastic solidarity.

65. Donald W. Mitchell, "Preface," in *Finding Peace in Troubled Times: Buddhist and Christian Monastics on Transforming Suffering*, ed. Donald W. Mitchell and James A. Wiseman (Brooklyn, NY: Lantern Books, 2010), xi.

66. See Thomas Ryan, "Gethsemani II: Catholic and Buddhist Monastics Focus on Suffering," *Buddhist-Christian Studies* 24 (2004): 249–251.

67. Ibid., 250.

The topic from Gethsemani II, "Suffering," was extended to the "suffering of nature" at the third Gethsemani Encounter in 2008, which was devoted to monasticism and the environment. Although monastics are not experts in the area of ecology, they believe that the spirituality of both the Buddhist and the Christian monastic traditions can contribute to overcoming the current ecological crisis. Through dialogue on this issue, Buddhist and Christian monastics agreed that it "is precisely because the monastic virtues of nongreed, contentment, and reconnecting to the interdependent web of life . . . address the root cause of our ecological crisis that monasticism can make a valuable contribution to the contemporary green movement."[68] The participants reflected on the complementarity of the basic Buddhist notion of the interdependence of all things and Merton's contemplative principle for ecospirituality, namely, the universal communion of persons and nature in God.[69] Skudlarek points out that "Merton . . . was one of the first spiritual writers to call attention to the importance of interreligious dialogue, especially for monks, in addressing the world's problems. The opening presentation at Gethsemani III was therefore devoted to Merton's analysis of the ecological catastrophe."[70] Merton believed that the whole world itself was "a transparent manifestation of the love of God" and that God was manifested "in all His creatures" and "in the most wonderful interrelationship between them."[71] The transformation of human consciousness through contemplation or enlightenment

68. William Skudlarek, "Introduction," in *Green Monasticism: A Buddhist-Catholic Response to an Environmental Calamity*, ed. Donald W. Mitchell and William Skudlarek (Brooklyn, NY: Lantern Books, 2010), 6.

69. See NSC, 290–297. Merton descried universal communion as "the cosmic dance." Many of his writings and poems were filled with descriptions and contemplation about the beauties of nature.

70. Skudlarek, "Introduction" to *Green Monasticism*, 3.

71. Thomas Merton, *Witness to Freedom: The Letters of Thomas Merton in Times of Crisis*, ed. William H. Shannon (New York, NY: Farrar, Straus, Giroux, 1994), 71.

can lead to awareness of God's magnification or interdependence with all things. At Gethsemani III, Merton's insistence that contemplation is the principal characteristic of the monastic path and that it points the way for overcoming the environmental crisis was seen as a rich source for monastic interreligious dialogue and practice. Furthermore, the participants at this conference recognized that one's awareness of interdependence could provide a new ecological conscience in "reverence, renunciation, gratitude, and generosity" to nature.[72]

In 2015, Buddhist and Christian monastics again gathered at the Abbey for Gethsemani Encounter IV on the theme of *Spiritual Maturation*. In his notes, "Monastic Experience and East-West Dialogue," Merton stressed that on the "experiential level of experience and of spiritual maturity, it is possible to achieve real and significant contacts [between monastics and contemplatives]."[73] Spiritual maturity was a basic principle of his approach to inter-monastic/contemplative dialogue. The participants at Gethsemani IV attempted to develop his dialogical principle by sharing the way the two monastic traditions understood the intentional process of spiritual maturation. Cyprian Consiglio, a Christian monk, spoke on the Christian understanding of self-fulfillment and the true self for spiritual maturity, and Bhikshuni Thubten Semkye, a Tibetan Buddhist nun, described how the example of the nuns in her community was itself training for spiritual maturity. I had the privilege of participating in this conference. In my own presentation, I suggested that Christian monastics could learn from Buddhist spiritual sources for the attainment of spiritual maturity, making use of the "Ten Ox-Herding Pictures" in Zen Buddhism as one of the sources for Christian learning about the contemplative

---

72. Skudlarek, "Introduction" to *Green Monasticism*, 8. See also Ezekiel Lotz, "Paradise Regained Re-lost," in *Green Monasticism*, 26–34.

73. AJ, 312.

life.[74] Becky Van Ness, a professor of spirituality at Saint John's University in Minnesota, spoke about Buddhist wisdom for Christian spiritual direction that nurtures spiritual maturation. Finally, Buddhist monk Heng Sure shared Buddhist scriptures as a template of spiritual maturity.

Gethsemani IV did not merely provide a forum in which to explain one's own monastic tradition; it offered a setting in which each tradition could learn about resources for spiritual maturity from another tradition. For example, in a discussion regarding the "Ten Ox-Herding Pictures" in Zen Buddhism, a Tibetan Buddhist nun, Bhikshuni Losang Drimay, shared the *shamatha* diagrams from her tradition that picture an elephant on a path in place of the ox. The exchange helped the participants become aware of the similarities and differences in understanding and describing the contemplative journey. The cordial interaction of the participants as they shared monastic practices and contemplative sources was "an effective way to promote mutual understanding and appreciation for each other's traditions."[75]

Evaluation and Prospect

In his notes "Monastic Experience and East-West Dialogue," Merton emphasized that contemplative dialogue must be reserved for those who have reached spiritual maturity through a long period of discipline in their own monastic tradition.[76] In 1993, twenty-five years after Merton's death, his Buddhist friend and brother, the Dalai Lama, responded to his conviction by suggesting a gathering of spiritually mature monastics at Merton's monastery.

---

74. See Jaechan Park, "A Christian Contemplative Approach to the Ten Ox-Herding Pictures of Zen Buddhism: Interreligious Dialogue as Mutual Self-mediation," *Dilatato Corde* 5, nos. 1/2 (2015): 132–157.

75. Margaret Michaud, "Gethsemani Encounter IV" (May 27–31, 2015), http://www.dimmid.org/index.asp?Type=B_BASIC&SEC={5D499F35-FDD6 -4A8D-A305-A365C99AD0F9}.

76. See AJ, 316.

This new beginning of a contemplative dialogue between *spiritually mature* monastics or contemplatives may be considered the foremost contribution of the Gethsemani Encounters.

Historically, Christians have been encountering Buddhists since the first century, but their understanding of Buddhism was inaccurate, and their response was more *monological* than *dialogical*.[77] In the nineteenth century, Western scholars gradually became interested in Buddhism, but they interpreted it using Western categories. In so doing, they understood it as a philosophy rather than as a religious belief system. However, the Second Vatican Council provided a new impetus for dialogue that looked at the similarities and differences between the two religions.[78] Christian theologians gradually came to recognize the strengths of the Buddhist traditions, but still maintained a somewhat biased stance toward

77. According to Hans Küng, the first textual reference to Buddha in Christian sources occurs around the year 200. It is found in the *Miscellany* (*Stromateis*) of Clement of Alexandria, who mentioned that Christian gnosis was superior to every other kind of wisdom: "And there are in India those who follow the commandments of the Buddha, whom they revere as a god because of his immense holiness." Despite attempts by Jesuit missionaries Matteo Ricci and Robert de Nobili to achieve a respectable adoption of Christianity into Asian traditions in the sixteenth century, political factors and European imperialism obstructed an accurate and informed understanding of Buddhism. See Hans Küng, *Christianity and the World Religions: Paths of Dialogue with Islam, Hinduism, and Buddhism* (Garden City, NY: Doubleday, 1986), 307–308.

78. Georg Siegmund notes that "the intellectual meeting of East and West received new impetus from Vatican Council II and from the personality of Pope John XXIII." See Georg Siegmund, *Buddhism and Christianity: A Preface to Dialogue* (Tuscaloosa, AL: University of Alabama Press, 1980), 2. The Second Vatican Council stated that Buddhism "proposes a way of life by which men can, with confidence and trust, attain a state of perfect liberation and reach supreme illumination either through their own efforts or by the aid of divine help. . . . [The Church] has a high regard for the manner of life and conduct, the precepts and doctrines [of other religions]. . . . The Church urges her sons to enter . . . into discussion and collaboration with members of other religions." See "Declaration on the Relationship of the Church to Non-Christian Religions," in *Interreligious Dialogue*, 44.

it.[79] In 1980, the best-known organized forum for an encounter between the two traditions, the International Buddhist-Christian Conference, was held at the University of Hawaii. It signaled a turning away from Christian monologue and a turning toward dialogical encounter with Buddhists.[80]

The International Buddhist-Christian Conference addresses various topics for dialogue and tends to focus on intellectual exchanges between scholars. Through their practice of monastic interreligious dialogue over the course of thirty or so years after Merton's death, monastics have become adept at the methods of dialogue as well as the spirituality of dialogue. The Gethsemani Encounters were the result of the spiritual maturity they brought to the dialogue and of their realization that spiritual communion between monastics of different religious traditions was possible. Since each Encounter focused on specific topics for spiritual exchange, the Gethsemani Encounters are different from the monastic exchange programs described above, which involve visiting other monastic communities to experience their way of life without specifying topics for dialogue. The Encounters revealed in "a remarkable way the profound communion that unites all seekers of the Truth" through sharing contemplative experiences with brothers and sisters in the monastic spiritual family.[81]

This contemplative dialogue can help Buddhist and Christian monastics become "co-contemplatives."[82] Becoming such

79. For example, Fredericks argues that after the Second Vatican Council, the Catholic theological positions of inclusivism or fulfillment theology are inadequate in interreligious dialogue, since they distort other religious traditions by continuing to see them through the lens of the Catholic Catechism. See Fredericks, *Buddhists and Christians*, 14–21.

80. See Ingram, *The Process of Buddhist-Christian Dialogue*, 30; Seiichi Yagi and Leonard J. Swidler, *A Bridge to Buddhist-Christian Dialogue* (New York/Mahwah, NJ: Paulist Press, 1990), 9.

81. Béthune, "Preface" to *The Gethsemani Encounter*, xii.

82. Roger Corless, "The Dialogue of Silence: A Comparison of Buddhist and Christian Monasticism with a Practical Suggestion," in *The Cross and the*

does not imply a syncretism of two contemplative traditions, but rather the development of a new contemplative spirituality through a mutual sharing of their rich spiritual treasures. This mutual spiritual exchange can be understood in terms of Bernard Lonergan's concept of "mutual self-mediation."[83] Interpreted from an interreligious perspective, this means that the church, as both teacher and learner, can be influenced and can learn from other religious traditions in a complementary relationship.[84] The Gethsemani Encounters show that through a relationship of mutual self-mediation, Buddhist and Christian monastics can be enriched, can be complemented by each other's perspectives, and can dialogue with others, as co-contemplatives. For example, the use of the "Ten Ox-Herding Pictures" of Zen Buddhism at Gethsemani IV to reflect on Christian contemplative life showed that spiritual sources from different traditions can be brought to bear on other religious perspectives. The Encounters also show that beyond the Word of God in Scripture and the church fathers, Christian *lectio divina* can be extended to Buddhist texts.

Lotus: Christianity and Buddhism in Dialogue, ed. G.W. Houston (Delhi, India: Motilal Banarsidass, 1985), 84.

83. Bernard Lonergan classifies various kinds of mediation: *simple mediation, mutual mediation, self-mediation,* and *mutual self-mediation.* See Bernard Lonergan, "Mediation of Christ in Prayer," in *Philosophical and Theological Papers 1958–1964*, ed. Robert C. Croken, Frederick E. Crowe, and Robert M. Doran (Toronto, ON: University of Toronto Press for Lonergan Research Institute, 1996), 160–182. Among the four kinds of mediation identified by Lonergan, "mutual self-mediation" is reinterpreted as "one of the hermeneutic keys to articulate the complex of relations between the Church and the Other." See Dadosky, "The Church and the Other," 309.

84. Dadosky suggests that "mutual self-mediating relations, as graced, express that the Church can learn from the Other and be enriched in her own self-understanding by that encounter." See John D. Dadosky, "Towards a Fundamental Theological *Re*-interpretation of Vatican II," *The Heythrop Journal* 49, no. 5 (2008): 748. See also Joseph Komonchak, "The Significance of Vatican II for Ecclesiology," in *The Gift of the Church: A Textbook on Ecclesiology*, ed. Peter Phan (Collegeville, MN: Liturgical Press, 2000), 89.

Furthermore, those who took part in the Gethsemani Encounters did not limit themselves to comparing Emptiness and God or Buddha and Jesus, but shared their monastic disciplines and spiritual resources with each other.

In addition to the foregoing, spiritually mature contemplative dialogue can play a prophetic role for persons in the secular world who long for a deep spiritual life and sense a need for spiritual direction. Today, both Buddhist and Christian monastic traditions need to find new ways to express their contemplative experience to their contemporaries. For example, the Gethsemani Encounter contemplative dialogues on human suffering and the environment may inspire new ways of understanding human life and provide new spiritual directions for the laity.

Over the course of four Gethsemani Encounters, Buddhist monastics have been more open to monastics from different traditions, willing to learn from them and to become more engaged in inter-monastic exchange. Thubten Chodron, a Buddhist nun who has participated in these Encounters, said, "I could feel the faith and the good intentions of the Catholic monastics there. . . . I also wonder how we Buddhists can learn from the Church's history and avoid such difficulties ourselves in the future."[85] Skudlarek, who has taken part in all four Gethsemani Encounters, commented:

> Some of us have been here before, Buddhists and Catholics, and there's a level of exchange this time, that we didn't have before, when people—I would say the Buddhists especially—feel free to talk about what led them to change from one tradition to another. I think, even at the last meeting here six years ago, that wouldn't have happened, but it's happening now! There's a sense that you can speak the truth without fear.[86]

85. Thubten Chodron, "The Second Gethsemani Encounter" (April 18, 2002), http://thubtenchodron.org/2002/04/conference-reflections.

86. DIMMID, *Strangers No More*.

I believe there are a few changes that should be considered for future encounters. First, consideration should be given to gathering in one of the Buddhist monasteries in North America. Although the Dalai Lama indicated the Abbey of Gethsemani as a special place for interreligious monastic encounter, it would be good to meet in a place that offers Christian monastics an opportunity to experience Buddhist monastic life. The MID board of directors might consider a Buddhist monastery such as Chuang Yen Monastery in New York, or Hsi Lai Temple in Los Angeles as a setting for a future encounter. Buddhist monastics who live in these monasteries would benefit from the opportunity to be present at these gatherings for monastic interreligious dialogue. If a future encounter is held at Gethsemani, a visit to Buddhist temples or monasteries near the Abbey of Gethsemani, such as the Tibetan Drepung Gomang Center for Engaging Compassion in Louisville, could be added to the program.

Second, I would suggest creating small or local encounters between monastics or contemplatives of different religious traditions who have participated in the Gethsemani Encounters. In fact, organizers of the first Gethsemani Encounter thought that it would lead to small or local inter-monastic encounters. For instance, Mitchell points out that "this large and historic gathering of Buddhist and Christian monastics from around the world has opened the door to what will be a number of smaller and more local dialogues on the particular issues in spirituality that were raised at Gethsemani."[87] However, since the first Gethsemani Encounter, such local interreligious encounters have not multiplied in Asian, African, or South American contexts.

Finally, the Gethsemani Encounter should become an occasion for encounters between monastics and lay contemplatives of various religious traditions in order to move beyond Western or monastic-centered contemplative dialogue. Recently, the MID

87. Mitchell, "The Gethsemani Encounter on the Spiritual Life," 208.

commission realized the need for more involvement of lay contemplatives. In the 2016 commission, they decided to cultivate Benedictine oblates as advisors to MID and planned to invite them for future MID gatherings as speakers and participants. In addition, I believe participation in future Gethsemani Encounters should be extended to Muslim adepts and Hindu monastics.

Extending the Legacy: Suggestion for Future Inter-Monastic Exchange and Contemplative Dialogue

Interreligious dialogue has bridged various separations, whether of location (North America or Europe and Asia), of culture (West and East), or of religion (Christianity and several Asian religions). Up to now, Western Christian monastics have tended to take the lead in the dialogue, while Asian Buddhist and Christian monastics have adopted a passive stance. In addition, some Asian Christian monastics are confused by contemporary Western monks and nuns who, unlike many of their predecessors, are well disposed to Asian Buddhists and Hindus. In this regard, Blée argues that:

> Western monks may have been experts in the area of dialogue but Asian monks had serious reasons for not being very receptive to collaborating with them. . . . Asian Christian monks were not very happy about being told how to enter into dialogue with the local religions they themselves had come from especially since it was Westerners who some centuries earlier had insisted that their relationship to Christ had to be stripped of every trace of another religion. The role of their American and European counterparts would remain secondary.[88]

Although Western monastics realized the value of encountering Asian religions on a spiritual level, it has proven difficult to enter into dialogue with the many different Asian religions. Over

88. Blée, *The Third Desert*, 65.

the past few decades, DIMMID in the West has focused on monastic exchange at an international level with Asia, in particular with Tibetan and Japanese Zen Buddhism. Today, if monastic interreligious dialogue is to develop *within* Asia and *between* Asian monastics, DIMMID and the Asian Benedictine family have to consider undertaking four activities: 1) establishing an East Asian commission for monastic interreligious dialogue that would include Buddhist or Hindu monastics as members of the commission, 2) implementing an intra-monastic exchange program between Asian monasteries of different religious traditions, 3) training Asian Christian monastics for this type of dialogue, and 4) developing inter-contemplative dialogue between monastics and their corresponding lay contemplatives. This section will explore these themes more explicitly with various examples.

Developing Intra-Monastic Exchange between Different Asian Monasteries

In 2012, at the DIMMID annual European conference, Pierre de Béthune proposed that in the future DIM had to "move beyond the present level of dialogue to a deeper research into the spiritual values which underlay . . . monastic experience. The aim of such a project would be the renewal of monasticism in our various faith traditions by reaching beyond what was purely geographical and cultural."[89] He spoke about more interior dialogue through monastic experience and said that dialogue must not be limited by geographical and cultural boundaries. However, one wonders whether transcending specific geographical and cultural contexts is possible. For example, monasticism is a phenomenon of the great religions, and at the same time, it has developed differently in each cultural context. If Western monastics seek monastic renewal through dialogue with other monastic spiritualities,

---

89. Pierre-François de Béthune, "DIM/MID Annual European Conference" (June 2012), https://www.turveyabbey.org.uk/MID-GBI/news/MEB_01_13.pdf.

including Asian monasticism, beyond their local level, what role will *Asian Christian* monastics play in this dialogue within their own geographical and cultural contexts?

In the global monastic climate, this section will explore intra-monastic dialogue through a lens of intra-religious dialogue and contemplative dialogue, and the need of the development of intra-monastic dialogue in an Asian context by DIMMID and Asian Christian monastics.

Intra-Religious Dialogue and Intra-Monastic Dialogue

The prefix "intra" means *inside* or *within*. Intra-religious dialogue can mean either dialogue at the *interior* level or dialogue *within* the same culture or region.

Raimon Panikkar was the first to use the expression "*intra-religious dialogue*" to refer to interior dialogue, defining it as "the internal dialogue triggered by the thou who is not in-different to the I."[90] The first step of this dialogue, he said, takes place in "the depths of the person."[91] One example of intra-religious dialogue would be a Christian who assimilates elements from the Buddhist tradition into his or her own spiritual life and in so doing experiences a profound inner transformation.

This internal dialogue, according to Panikkar, is neither a monologue nor a meditation on another religion, but the acceptance of that religion's teaching in the search for salvation. Along with this acceptance, there is an effort "to assimilate the transcendent into [one's] immanence."[92] To achieve inner transformation through intra-religious dialogue, one has to enter the arena of genuine interreligious dialogue with a self-critical attitude. As Panikkar noted, "Interreligious dialogue is undoubtedly a preparation for . . . a stepping stone to . . . intrareligious dialogue where living

---

90. Raimon Panikkar, *The Intrareligious Dialogue* (New York/Mahwah, NJ: Paulist Press, 1999), xvi.

91. Ibid., xvii.

92. Ibid.

faith constantly demands from us a total renewal, or—in Christian terms—a real, personal, and ever-recurring *metanoia*."[93]

Intra-religious dialogue is different from interreligious dialogue. Christian Jochim, for example, uses "'interreligious' to refer to dialogues in which there are formal exchanges regarding religious thought and practice *between* members of two traditions," and "'intrareligious' to refer to 'dialogues' *within* the minds and hearts of people who have interests in two different traditions."[94] In order for interreligious dialogue to become authentic dialogue, it must be accompanied, supported, and challenged by intra-religious dialogue. In this reciprocal relationship between *inter-* and *intra-religious* dialogue, new insights can arise "in one's *intra*-religious [encounter that can] influence and shape one's *inter*-religious exchanges, which, in turn, stimulate further *intra*-religious dialogue."[95] In this dialectical process, new insights may create a new dimension of spirituality between different religious traditions and in one's inner self, as well as in one's own spiritual tradition.

Although intra-religious dialogue can certainly be spiritually enriching, it also involves challenges and risks. Without a deep spiritual maturity within one's own tradition, intra-religious dialogue may pose a threat to one's religious identity and a challenge to one's faith. For example, in "A Pathway to Inner Transformation," the document crafted by the participants in the conference organized by Les Voies de l'Orient (The Ways of the Orient) in Brussels in May 2014, the authors noted:

93. Ibid., 83 (emphasis in original).

94. Christian Jochim, "The Contemporary Confucian-Christian Encounter: Interreligious or Intrareligious Dialogue?," *Journal of Ecumenical Studies* 32, no. 1 (Winter 1995): 39 (emphasis added).

95. Kenneth P. Kramer, "Extra-, Inner-, Intra-, Inter-Religious Voices," *Journal of Ecumenical Studies* 30, no. 2 (Winter 1993): 203 (emphasis in original). In the exchange between one's inherited religious belief and the new religious beliefs learned from other religions, intra-religious dialogue could facilitate new horizons by adapting aspects of the other tradition into one's own interiority.

> While one's initial involvement with intrareligious dialogue
> may be experienced as an exciting adventure, it also gives rise
> to deep and sometimes painful questioning. . . . In some
> Church circles, [it] provokes misunderstanding and even sus-
> picion. At the same time, [it] challenges Christians to reflect
> more deeply on the major themes of the Christian faith, a chal-
> lenge especially directed to the theologian.[96]

Since Christian interreligious dialogue should not draw one away
from communion with the whole Church, intra-religious dialogue should address fundamental questions about the Christian
faith, such as the role of Christ and the action of the Holy Spirit.
However, intra-religious dialogue is not primarily theological
dialogue; it is spiritual dialogue within each participant who has
attempted to attain or has attained spiritual maturity through contemplative experience in their own tradition. Confidence in one's
own faith achieved through transcultural maturity, so strongly
emphasized by Merton, will enable Christians involved in intra-
religious dialogue to overcome the risk of weakening or losing
their faith.

Panikkar focuses on the inner spiritual life of individuals in his
development of the concept of "intra-religious dialogue," but the
term can also be used in reference to dialogue that takes place
within a certain group. For example, an *intra*net is a network of
computers that only connects persons within the same group.
Panikkar stressed that interreligious dialogue, which traditionally
refers to dialogue between different cultural and religious traditions, has to be complemented by intra-religious dialogue at the
interior level. Taking that one step further, we can say that today,
intra-religious dialogue, in the sense that Panikkar speaks of it,

96. Les Voies de l'Orient, "Interreligious Dialogue: A Pathway to Inner Trans-
formation" (May 2014), http://www.dimmid.org/vertical/sites/%7BD52F3ABF
-B999-49DF-BFAB-845A690CF39B%7D/uploads/Voies_de_l
Orient_INTERRELIGIOUS_DIALOGUE_A_PATHWAY_TO_INNER
_TRANSFORMATION.pdf.

needs to be complemented by a geographical sense of dialogue. Intra-religious dialogue at the local level would be a way to help initiate interreligious dialogue and also to develop possibilities for religious cooperation between different religions within the same culture or context.

These two dimensions (interiority and regional locality) of intra-religious dialogue can be applied to intra-monastic dialogue. Monastics and contemplatives internalize their religious identity through various spiritual disciplines. Those who are pursuing or have attained self-transformation through contemplative experience can encounter other contemplatives through silence and spiritual communion. They can also share their spiritual experience with other monastics or with lay contemplatives of different religious traditions. In this regard, what Merton referred to as contemplative dialogue, which can also be characterized as internal dialogue, may already embrace intra-monastic dialogue. For instance, in his dialogue with Zen Buddhism, he drew Buddhist *sunyata* (emptiness) and Christian *kenosis* (self-emptying) into a personal internal dialogue, and then was "plunge[d] right into the middle of contradiction and confusion in order to be transformed by what Zen calls the 'Great Death' and Christianity calls 'dying and rising with Christ.' "[97] His contemplative dialogue was always directed to his inner transformation through engagement with the profound spiritualities of Asian contemplative traditions. As Kenneth P. Kramer points out, "One can almost hear the interior dialogue just behind those writings in which Merton emerged from his *intra*-religious reflection."[98] While monastic interreligious dialogue takes place *between* monastics of different religious traditions, intra-monastic dialogue takes place *within* the inner self of monastics and is occasioned by the self-reflective

97. ZBA, 51.
98. Kramer, "Extra-, Inner-, Intra-, Inter-Religious Voices," 204 (emphasis in original).

and attentive interior dialogue between and *within* monastics of different traditions.

We can also say that intra-monastic dialogue can and indeed should be developed between different monastic traditions within the same culture or region. In the fifty years following Merton's death, inter-monastic encounters have taken place across cultures (Eastern and Western), across religions (Christianity and Asian religions), and across ethnic groups (Western and Asian). It now needs to give greater attention to local or national contexts.

This proposal is not new. Intra-monastic dialogue, in the sense of a regional approach to dialogue, was already called for in the 1970s, and in 1980 by the then Abbot Primate Victor Dammertz, who wanted Asian Christian monastics to take primary responsibility for engaging in inter-monastic dialogue in their regions. At that time, however, Asian Christian monastics were not fully aware of the need for this kind of dialogue.[99] In 1994, when DIMMID became an independent secretariat, the members of DIMMID intended that the organization would be creatively developed at both the international and *national* or *local* levels.[100] In order to pursue intra-monastic dialogue, many local monasteries will have to develop their own network of relationships with local Buddhist and Hindu monasteries, and even with Muslim mosques and Jewish synagogues. These contacts will allow for many types of exchanges at a deep spiritual level and can contribute to the breaking down of barriers of prejudice at the local level.

These different types of dialogue among interreligious dialogue, intra-religious dialogue, inter-monastic encounter, and intra-monastic dialogue can be summarized as follows:

---

99. See Blée, *The Third Desert*, 65–66.

100. See Mitchell, "The Gethsemani Encounter on the Spiritual Life," 208; Blée, *The Third Desert*, 106.

Term	Feature
Interreligious dialogue	Dialogue *between* individuals and communities of different religious traditions "which are directed at mutual understanding and enrichment, in obedience to truth and respect for freedom"[101] (e.g., between East and West, between Christianity and non-Christianity). A stepping stone to intra-religious dialogue.
Intra-religious dialogue	The interior dialogue *within* the minds and hearts of those who have interests in different religious traditions. The first step of this dialogue requires a spiritual maturity in one's own tradition, and the goal of the dialogue is a total renewal or self-transformation.
Inter-monastic encounters (exchanges)	Contact *between* monastics of different religious traditions through sharing monastic life, spiritual practices, and contemplative experience. It is similar to "inter-monastic dialogue" but focuses more on the mutual exchange through actual meetings.
Intra-monastic dialogue	Inter-monastic/contemplative dialogue at the interior level and at the local level. It includes contemplative dialogue at the intimate verbal level between monastics of the same culture and region as well as dialogue *within* the individual monastic participants.

Table 1: Interreligious Dialogue, Intra-Religious Dialogue, Inter-Monastic Encounters, and Intra-Monastic Dialogue

Intra-monastic dialogue must be developed in reciprocal relationship with inter-monastic dialogue. In a globalized world,

---

101. Pontifical Council for Interreligious Dialogue, "Dialogue and Proclamation," 1160.

there is no longer a pure Asian culture in Asia, just as there is no longer a pure Western culture in Europe and North America. All monastics in the great religious traditions need to recognize "both the limits of the culture which has hitherto been associated with their faith, and the values proper to other cultures."[102] Cooperation between Eastern and Western monastics cannot be separated from cooperation with Eastern monastics and with Western monastics in their own contexts. Inter/intra-monastic dialogue is "imperative in today's modern, multireligious context."[103] A new culture or a new spirituality could come into being through the mutual influence and integration of these two types of monastic dialogue.

Inter/Intra-Monastic Encounters within Asian Monastics

DIMMID has partially promoted inter/intra-monastic encounters on the existential, experiential, spiritual, and local levels. DIM in Europe and MID in North America have realized the value of intra-monastic dialogue (although they do not yet use this term) on the local level and they are seeking the way of dialogue through annual meetings of the commissions. For example, the gatherings of "Nuns in the West" and "Monks in the West" between Buddhist and Christian nuns or monks who live in the U.S. and have taken part in the Gethsemani Encounters can become examples of intra-monastic dialogue on the interior and local levels. Furthermore, in his annual report in 2016, Skudlarek stated, "As the demographics of Christian monasticism shift to the *south* and *east*, the future of Monastic Interreligious Dialogue will more and more depend on the involvement of monastic men and women from *those same regions*."[104] For the future of inter-monastic dialogue, Asian Chris-

---

102. Leclercq, "Introduction: The Second Meeting of the Monks of Asia," 87.

103. Kenneth P. Kramer, "A Silent Dialogue: The Intrareligious Dimension," *Buddhist-Christian Studies* 10 (1990): 128.

104. William Skudlarek, "Annual Report of the Secretary General of DIMMID" (December 2016), http://mid.nonprofitoffice.com/vertical/sites/%7BD52F3ABF -B999-49DF-BFAB-845A690CF39B%7D/uploads/2016_Year_end_report.pdf (emphasis added).

tian monastics who live in the East have to develop this type of dialogue in their own ways and in their own cultural contexts.

Each Buddhist tradition has its own customs. Indian, Chinese, Korean, Japanese, Tibetan, and Vietnamese traditions have developed "different spoken images and conceptual systems" stemming from their own cultural backgrounds and languages.[105] Thus, Christian monastics who are engaged in Buddhist-Christian dialogue have to be aware of these differences and acknowledge their own Christian limitations. They also need to undertake a reflective consideration of the many-branched facets of these two religions to obtain the big picture needed for fruitful dialogue.

Western Christians have sought various ways to reduce the limits imposed by historical and cultural contexts. For example, Hans Küng suggests that Christians who are involved in dialogue with Buddhists have to include "*any of the historically developed great Buddhist religious forms*" and have to take a critical approach to determine how each branch of Buddhism traces its origin to Gautama Buddha.[106] In addition, Lai and Brück claim that since intellectual discourse is limited, dialogue has to go beyond the conceptual approach and encourage "participation in the spiritual praxis of the other [in] promoting interreligious communal life."[107] In this regard, intra-monastic dialogue at the local level can be suggested as another way of relating to the diversity of Buddhism or Hinduism in Asia.[108] If Asian Christian monastics, who know their own cultures and religions, are in direct contact with local Buddhist or Hindu monastics, they can overcome this limitation of inter-monastic dialogue. Intra-monastic dialogue can also help overcome the difficulty of monastic interreligious

105. Whalen Lai and Michael von Brück, *Christianity and Buddhism: A Multicultural History of Their Dialogue*, trans. Phyllis Jestice (Maryknoll, NY: Orbis Books, 2001), 243.

106. Küng, "Foreword," x (emphasis in original).

107. Lai and Brück, *Christianity and Buddhism*, 253.

108. See Morris J. Augustine, "Monastic and Contemplative Encounter Group," *Buddhist-Christian Studies* 8 (1988): 199.

dialogue between Western and Asian monastics that is the result of the particular situation that exists in Asian cultures and religions. According to Blée, there are many reasons why monastic inter-religious dialogue could not fully develop in Asia: 1) the weakness of a Christian monastic presence in Asia, 2) the foreignness of Western Christianity, 3) the lack of recognition of Christian spiritual depth from non-Christians in Asia, and 4) the strong bond between culture and religion in Asia.[109] Through encounters *between* Asian monastics, Buddhist or Hindu monastics or contemplatives could recognize the presence and the spirituality of Christian monasticism within the same culture, language, and ethnic group to which they belong.

The development of inter/intra-monastic encounters in Asia requires that Asian monastics assent to their responsibility in this regard. They need to recognize the value of monastic dialogue and become acquainted with other spiritual traditions and disciplines.[110] Like Western monastics during the 1970s and the 1980s, Asian Christian monastics tend to resist other religions and are suspicious about inter-monastic dialogue. For instance, in South Korea, some Catholic monastics still have a tendency to consider the practice of Buddhist rituals such as prostration before the statue of Buddha a taboo. They are also reluctant to stay with Buddhist monastics in their cloister and believe that they do not need to learn from them since their rich Christian spirituality provides all they need. Not all monastics are interested in inter/intra-monastic dialogue, nor are they open to monastics of different traditions. Since intra-monastic dialogue refers first of all to ongoing conversations and conversions within one's own inner

---

109. See Blée, *The Third Desert*, 25–27.

110. As James A. Wiseman points out, "Even experts who have been committed to interreligious dialogue over a long period of time and have given themselves to much study of other traditions have been struck by the difficulties involved." See James A. Wiseman, "Christian Monastic and Interreligious Dialogue," *Cistercian Studies* 27, no. 3 (1992): 261.

self as well as one's monastic tradition, it can contribute to the development of a level of spiritual maturity that can cultivate mind-to-mind and heart-to-heart inter/intra-monastic dialogue. Béthune argues that "when someone whose heart has become vulnerable meets an authentic witness from another religious tradition, he or she can be profoundly moved and be led to an 'intra-religious' dialogue."[111] If they are to be able to engage in interreligious dialogue, Asian Christian monastics have to make spiritual maturity a goal in their own monastic traditions. Then they can share their experience of prayer and contemplation, ways of searching for the Absolute, and their interpretation or expressions of religious experience with other monastics who live within their region.

Although Panikkar's theory of intra-religious dialogue was developed outside a monastic context, it has influenced inter-monastic encounters and contemplative dialogues. Since the inter-monastic exchange programs of DIMMID seem to be stalled, Panikkar's approach may inspire monastic interreligious dialogue in Asia to develop as a form of intra-monastic dialogue. Merton's legacy, contemplative dialogue in particular, can also become a source and model for the education of Asian Christian monastics. In addition, we can learn from the past activities of DIMMID. For instance, at the Conference of Benedictines of East Asia held in South Korea in 1999, Béthune pointed out that Asian Benedictines may have better practical knowledge about how to promote inter-monastic exchanges than Western monastics. Nonetheless, an understanding of such exchange programs in Europe and North America would be beneficial for the development of monastic interreligious dialogue in Asia.[112]

The establishment of a commission of DIMMID in East Asia would be most helpful for fostering intra-monastic encounters. The Indo-Sri Lankan Benedictine Federation (ISBF) and the

---

111. Béthune, "Monastic Inter-Religious Dialogue," 43.

112. See Pierre-François de Béthune, "The Work of Commissions of Monastic Interreligious Dialogue," 코이노니아 (*Koinonia*) 25 (2000): 56.

Benedictines of East Asia and Oceania (BEAO) do not consider inter/intra-monastic dialogue to be their principal concern, but they do have it as one of their objectives. Asian Christian monastics have to realize the need for a contextual approach to Asian Buddhist or Hindu monastics, rather than the type of centralized dialogue that was adopted by Western monastics. In 1980, Asian monastics already attempted to hold an inter-monastic gathering of Asian monastics. At the end of the third pan-Asiatic Congress in Kandy, Sri Lanka, Christian monastics who were born in Asia held a special meeting to determine their way of engaging in inter-monastic dialogue. Béthune argues that the meeting was "an expression of the desire of Asian monks to take charge of monastic interreligious dialogue in Asia and to work together towards this end."[113] Although the meeting influenced the creation of the new commissions of AIM in Asia and Oceania some years later, inter/intra-monastic dialogue still needs to be developed by additional organizations in the East. In fact, today, the religious and cultural climates in Asia have changed. The close bond between culture and religion and the powerful spirituality of Asian religions have been weakened because of increasing materialism and Westernization in Asia. For this reason, intra-monastic dialogue in the countries of Asia promoted and coordinated by a local DIMMID commission or subcommission, could become a shot in the arm for the Asian world, which is faced with a spiritual crisis.

Another possibility would be to initiate contact with Asian monastics who experienced inter-monastic exchange programs or the Gethsemani Encounters and to invite them to begin intra-monastic dialogue on their local level. They know their culture and other religions and are much better suited to initiate encounters with other monastics who live in their own region. Their encounter should be not limited to short visits or meetings but should be

---

113. Béthune, "Monastic Inter-Religious Dialogue," 38.

accompanied by a lived experience in the monastic milieu of the contemplative practice of each tradition.

Developing the Legacy: Examples of Intra-Monastic Exchange in South Korea

For the development of intra-monastic dialogue within an Asian context, three examples will be explored in the section: St. Joseph's Monastery, Samsohoe, and Monastery Stay and Temple Stay programs. They will be helpful for promoting the development of ways of adapting Christian monastic life in its own cultural context, paths of intra-monastic dialogue on the national level, and methods for a spiritual network between monastics and lay contemplatives at the interior and local level.

Adaptation of Monastic Life in Its Own Cultural Context

Intra-monastic exchange is not only the interior dialogue that takes place when one encounters another monastic tradition. It also includes a willingness to adopt into one's own monastic culture the practices and symbols of another monastic culture. For example, some Indian Benedictine monks wear saffron-colored habits rather than the black or white habit of Western monastics. Korean Benedictine nuns dress in gray when doing physical work, as do Buddhist monks and nuns, since gray in Korea is a symbol of humility and poverty.

This adaptation into one's own cultural and religious tradition practices and symbols of another tradition is not unique to contemplative monastic life. In this regard, "*Ad Gentes*: On the Mission Activity of the Church" of the Second Vatican Council said that:

> Institutes of the contemplative life . . . are requested to establish houses in missionary territories, as quite a few have already done, so that by *living their life there in a manner adapted to the genuinely religious traditions of the people*, they might bear

an outstanding witness among non-Christians to the majesty
and love of God, and to union in Christ.[114]

Following the teaching of this decree, in the mid-1980s, St. Benedict Waegwan Abbey in South Korea, which belongs to the St.
Ottilien Missionary Benedictine Congregation, began to consider
the foundation of a Korean-style Benedictine monastery. Korean
monks have realized that their fundamental vocation is to the
contemplative life rather than to ministry in parishes and hospitals.
Abbot Deokgeun M. Lee and some pioneering monks planned
that this new community would become a place for interreligious
dialogue as well as a school for inculturation by accepting the
monastic practices of other religious traditions. In particular, from
the beginning they proposed that the new Benedictine community
would follow a Korean lifestyle in Korean-style buildings in order
to dialogue with Buddhist monastic life.[115] They also looked for
ways to adapt to Korean traditional culture.

In 1987, about ten monks began to live in the new community,
St. Joseph's Monastery, at the foot of the Bulam mountain in
Namyangju near Seoul. The monks gathered in the chapel seven
times a day for prayer, meditation, and the Eucharist, and worked
together in a pear orchard. Their lifestyle was simple, poor, and
rough, and they introduced some practices from Korean culture
and Buddhist monasticism, such as the traditional Korean way of
bowing, using the *zafu* (meditation cushion) as opposed to Western
choir stalls, and invoking the Buddhist-style gong in the chapel.
After two decades of trial and error, the monastery became an
independent priory in 2014. The monks are dedicated to deepening their monastic life as Christians, Benedictines, *and* Koreans.

---

114. "*Ad Gentes*: Decree on the Mission Activity of the Church," #40, in
Interreligious Dialogue, 61 (emphasis added).

115. See Deokgeun Lee and Sungeon Kang, "About Foundation of New Seoul
Community of St. Benedict Waegwan," 코이노니아 (*Koinonia*) 11 (1986): 14.

Intra-Monastic Encounter in the Same Culture

"Samsohoe" (三笑, a group of three smiles) is the name for the gathering of the different religious women in South Korea: Nuns of Zen Buddhism, Christianity, and Won-Buddhism (an indigenous form of Korean Buddhism). It is another example of intra-monastic encounter within the same region and the same ethnic group.[116] These nuns have been meeting together for prayer and work since 1988. The gathering began not for the purpose of comparing their doctrines but to engage in social activities, since they all work for the poor, children from developing countries, and the disabled. Since 2001, they have been praying and meditating together monthly in one another's monasteries for mutual sharing and learning. In 2006, they went on a pilgrimage to sacred places and temples of different religious traditions. During the pilgrimage, they met world religious leaders such as the Dalai Lama, Pope Benedict XVI, and Quaker leaders.[117] Their pilgrimage increased their mutual understanding and respect. For instance, the Reverend Ji-jeong Kim, one of Samsohoe's founding members, reports, "We thought we were mature enough to solve spiritual conflict through our collective wisdom. . . . But after spending 18 days eating, sleeping and traveling together, and meeting spiritual leaders from other faiths, we realized the genuine need for

116. "Samso" (三笑) derives from an old legend about a venerable Buddhist monk, Hewon, who never left his temple. He wanted only to meditate in the ascetic compound of his temple. But one day he ventured out to meet a couple of old acquaintances: a Confucian poet, Tao Yuanming, and an expert on Taoism, Lu Xiujing. Just as the monk crossed a stream to reach his friends, a tiger roared from deep within the forest. The three wise men burst into laughter (Huxi three laughs, 虎溪三笑) at the unexpected significance of the moment. Ever since, Samso has been used to describe friends with different religious backgrounds. See Hyeon Cho, " 'Another Vocation': Accompanying Christian and Buddhist Nuns" (December 21, 2007), http://well.hani.co.kr/media/5541.

117. See Chosun Ilbo, "Dalai Lama 'Happy' to Meet Ecumenical Korean Group" (February 11, 2006), http://www.phayul.com/news/article.aspx?id=11810.

respecting other people's faith."[118] They hope that their spiritual encounter in South Korea can contribute to reconciliation between religions and their collaboration for the good of the world. They have now entered on a three-year project to promote the education and personal development of Ethiopian young girls and women.[119]

The Samsohoe shows that cooperation for social engagement, spiritual exchange, and monastic pilgrimage could become paths for intra-monastic encounter. The gathering may need to stay at each different monastery a little longer for mutual understanding as well as spiritual exchange through a living experience. In the near future, the model of Samsohoe could be followed by Christian and Buddhist monks.

Development of Monastic Experience Programs for Lay Contemplatives

The Christian "Monastery Stay" program and the Buddhist "Temple Stay" program in South Korea are examples of programs for contemplative dialogue between monastics and lay contemplatives. Both programs provide spiritual growth and healing for lay contemplatives through monastic experience and contemplative practices. Interestingly, there are many similarities between the two programs.

In South Korea, Benedictine hospitality is embodied in the Monastery Stay experience. St. Benedict Waegwan Abbey began this program in 2002 in the hope of bringing spiritual growth and heal-

---

118. Soo-Mee Park, " 'Three Smiles': Lessons in Faith and True Spiritual Understanding" (November 16, 2007), http://mengnews.joins.com/view.aspx?aId =2882806. Sr. Beata, a Catholic Benedictine nun, stated, "In a way, we were very naive before the pilgrimage. During the five years when we met and prayed, we didn't tackle these practical issues at all. To be honest, we didn't expect there would be such issues. We didn't know that Buddhist nuns would have problems reading aloud a prayer that ends with the word 'God' in every verse. They didn't think seriously enough that Catholic nuns could get in trouble for bowing in front of a Buddha statue." See ibid.

119. See Samsohoe, "Introduction and Activities of 'Samsohoe' Inter-faith Association" (February 14, 2010), http://www.franciscans.org.uk/wp-content/uploads /2015/01/Samso-Leaflet.pdf.

ing to young lay people. Participants in the experience live as the Benedictine monks do, completely isolated from their everyday lives, without access to family, cell phone, the internet, and other technological devices for a period of a few days or weeks. During their stay at the monastery, participants wake up at dawn and spend their day praying, meditating, participating in the Eucharist, working at simple tasks, eating their meals in silence, attending some lectures, and learning to sing Gregorian chant. Table 2 provides the daily *horarium* for those taking part in a Monastery Stay.

Time	Activities	Time	Activities
04:50	Wake up	13:10	Afternoon work (monastic workplace)**
05:15	Vigils & Morning Prayer	17:30	Meditation (Visits to the Blessed Sacrament)
06:00	Meditation (Centering Prayer)	18:00	Evening Prayer
06:30	Eucharist (Sunday 10:30)	18:30	Holy reading (*Lectio Divina*)
07:20	Breakfast (in silence)	19:00	Supper (in silence)
08:30	Morning work & Lecture*	19:30	Conversation with monks
11:30	Meditation (Centering Prayer)	20:00	Compline & Confession (Counseling)
11:45	Midday Prayer	22:00	Sleep (Great silence)
12:10	Lunch (in silence)	Final night: gathering with the whole monastic community	
* Lecture	Topics include monasticism, Benedictine spirituality, vows, Centering Prayer, *lectio divina*, Gregorian chant, interaction with the Abbot, and others.		
** Workplace	Farming, dishwashing, house cleaning, nursing of the elderly, writing icons, making rosaries and candles, and others.		

Rules for all	Wearing the monastic habit; no access to family, cell phone, the internet; receiving a new name and calling each other by it; eating every meal in silence with Scripture reading, and so forth.

Table 2: Daily Contents of the Monastery Stay Experience

Through my eight years as director of the Monastery Stay program, I saw that many young people wanted to repeat this experience because they had experienced spiritual growth and change in their lives. Some found their religious vocation through this experience and decided to enter the monastery. Moreover, by recently extending the Monastery Stay program to all people, the spiritual development fostered through this experience has provided a way to make the contemplative life available to both Christians and non-Christians. The monastic experience can bring spiritual healing and a new view of the contemplative life that is applicable to many facets of a retreat participant's life and can also strengthen the vocation of the laity. Over the past fifteen years, more than one thousand people have participated in this program, which is now open to anyone, regardless of age, religion, or gender. It is also open to family groups.

The Temple Stay of Zen Buddhism began at the Temple of Jikji-sa in 2002, the same year the Monastery Stay program was inaugurated, but it is much more developed than the Catholic program.[120] As of 2017, 128 Buddhist temples participate in the Temple Stay Program. The number of participants has constantly risen by about 30 percent annually, and about four million visitors (including 2,400 foreigners) have participated in the program as of 2016.[121] Temple Stay carries out for rest, for an experience of traditional culture and ecology, for asceticism, and for groups who

120. See Uri Kaplan, "Images of Monasticism: The Temple Stay Program and the Re-branding of Korean Buddhist Temples," *Korean Studies* 34, no. 1 (2010): 132.

121. See Korean Ministry of Culture, Sports and Tourism, "The Popular Korean Templestay" (June 1, 2017), https://www.mcst.go.kr/web/s_notice/press/press View.jsp?pSeq=16067#.

want an experience of Buddhist monastic life. It typically has three types: One-day Temple Stay, Experience-oriented Temple Stay, and Rest-oriented Temple Stay.[122]

Types	Activities
One-day Temple Stay	"A program designed for those who have a busy lifestyle, but want to experience Korean templestay within a short period of time. Normally, one-day templestay program takes about two or three hours including a temple tour, meditation, and tea ceremony. If you do not have a whole day if you are a foreign tourist who [does] not have much time, one-day templestay would be the perfect choice."
Experience-oriented Temple Stay	"If you are looking for an opportunity to experience the Korean monastic life, here is the program. Typically, done on the weekends with one overnight stay, major traditional Korean Buddhist ceremonies include attending the morning chanting, 108 prostrations, Buddhist meals with traditional bowls, and meditation. And it also provides some cultural activities such as making a lotus lantern or prayer beads. The specific contents of the program may vary with the temples, the season, and the interests of the participants, but it aims to help people center themselves so that they could eventually find their inner peace."
Rest-oriented Temple Stay	"Do nothing but relax. The temple will become a shelter for your fatigued mind and body and will give you renewed energy. With the rest-oriented templestay program, a stress-free vacation for your mind, you can have a chance to center yourself. Away from your busy daily routine, breathe in nature and restore your life force through meditation and Buddhist ceremonies."

Table 3: Three Types of the Temple Stay of Buddhism in South Korea

122. See Cultural Corps of Korean Buddhism, "What is Templestay" (2016), http://eng.templestay.com/page-templestay.asp#.

The timetable of the Temple Stay is very similar to that of the Monastery Stay: both programs include an entrance ritual, learning monastic etiquette, wearing the monastic habit, seeing the inside of the temple or monastery, the practice of prayer and meditation, communal ceremonial service, meals according to the custom of the place, self-examination, spiritual conversation, and simple work.

A Temple Stay	A Monastery Stay
Ritual of entrance and learning temple etiquette	Ritual of entrance and learning monastic etiquette
Wearing the garb of a postulant	Wearing the monastic habit
Seeing the inside of the temple	Seeing the inside of the monastery
Zen Meditation	Centering Prayer (Meditation)
Buddhist meals with traditional bowls	Monastic meals in silence
Buddhist ceremonial services (with Buddhist chanting)	The Eucharist and Divine Office (with Gregorian chant and organ accompaniment)
Writing of confession and conversation with monks	Confession and spiritual direction lecture
The tea ceremony	Conversation with other participants
108 bows	*Lectio divina* (sacred reading)
Making a lotus lantern and a rosary	Making a rosary and drawing an icon
A walk through a forest	Manual work in the monastery's garden

Table 4: Comparison between the Temple Stay and the Monastery Stay

Lay contemplatives who want to increase their commitment, or who just want some peaceful relaxation time, may take part in a

Temple Stay regardless of their religion. According to Youn-Jo Chung, the level of satisfaction of the participants in the Temple Stay is not significantly different between Buddhists and non-Buddhists.[123] This survey shows that the Temple Stay program can provide spiritual rest and growth for anyone. Moreover, this program can contribute to psychological and community healing. On the tenth anniversary of the Temple Stay, Yong-gyu Park, secretary-general of the corps, stated:

> The program has been successful as people seek monastic experiences in nature for psychological healing amid the hustle and bustle of urbanization. . . . We will diversify the programs tailored for the needs of participants such as students, foreigners, and office workers while contributing to social integration in addition to the role of serving the public good.[124]

We thus see that the effects of the Temple Stay are not different from those of the Monastery Stay, namely, individual and communal spiritual growth and healing through monastic experience. Although there are significant differences in the worldview, theology, and soteriology of Buddhism and Christianity, the monastic practices of both religions are similar because the human condition is the same for all.

Both programs help the participants find their new identity in depth and thus attain a new outlook on their lives. Moreover, not only are they able to lead a daily life that is transformed; they may also renew their communities. In order that this new perspective may be maintained, both programs stress extending some of the practices of the monastic experience to one's ordinary life. Furthermore, repeated participation in the program helps make

---

123. See Youn-Jo Chung, *The Leisure-Psychological Model of the Temple Stay Experience* (Seoul, Korea: Dongguk University, 2009), 73–74.

124. Ah-young Chung, "Templestay Marks a Decade" (October 17, 2012), http://www.koreatimes.co.kr/www/culture/2012/10/135_122459.html.

continuous practice easy and promotes the holistic transformation of the participants. Hence, despite religious differences, a Temple Stay with Buddhists and a Monastery Stay with Catholics can contribute to an individual's spiritual growth and healing in South Korean society. Both programs can offer an example of inter-contemplative dialogue between Buddhist and Christian monastics and the laity.

The encounter between monastics and lay contemplatives in a monastic milieu—Merton's legacy—must be further developed in the next stage of inter-monastic/contemplative dialogue. Merton did not strictly distinguish monastic interreligious dialogue from contemplative dialogue and monastic contemplatives from lay contemplatives. All his interreligious dialogue was anchored in contemplation and spiritual awareness, and monasticism was considered a proper tool for dialogue. Still, many of those who live outside the cloister imagine that monastic life is a unique kind of life, different from their lives. Through a new perspective of contemplation, Merton discovered that monastics were not all that different from the rest of humanity, but that they simply lived in a different sort of way—in a monastery. Blée points out that "together, monks and lay people need to create space for sharing and reflection."[125] In the monastic space beyond religious boundaries, inter-contemplative dialogue between monastics and lay contemplatives at a more existential level can fill in the gap between them.

Conclusion

DIMMID developed Merton's legacy for inter-monastic/contemplative dialogue in the East-West Spiritual Exchange and Monastic Hospitality programs, and directly at the Gethsemani Encounters. During the 1970s and the 1980s, Merton's legacy contributed to understanding the relationship between mission and

125. Blée, *The Third Desert*, 191.

dialogue, between East and West, and between the secular world and the monastery. In the process, Christian monastics realized that interreligious dialogue was their new vocation in and for the globalized and pluralistic world. This awareness led them to the establishment of an independent structure for monastic interreligious dialogue, DIMMID. This autonomous organization works for the further development of inter-monastic encounters across the whole world. The future tasks of DIMMID are the extension of the monastic exchange programs in hospitality between Buddhist and Christian monastics to *other* monastic traditions as well as to lay contemplatives, and the development of regional exchange programs at the local level.

Today, Asian Christian monastics need to develop their own paths for inter/intra-monastic dialogue in their own cultures. As Asian Buddhists have developed various monastic forms in different cultural contexts, Christian monastics have to adapt to the specifics of their own culture and develop Asian Benedictine life in their own contexts. Inter/intra-monastic dialogue within Asia could promote this development. As Merton did through his encounter with Buddhist monastics or contemplatives, Asian Christian monastics may also discover that there are other ways of understanding the divine reality and better ways of speaking about spiritual experience in other religions. Griffiths stated, "We are challenged to rethink our religion, not only in the light of Western thought, but also that of the East. Doing so, we will discover another dimension of Christianity."[126] Inter/intra-monastic dialogue between Asian monastics may open up a new dimension of Asian Christianity and Asian spirituality.

The examples of St. Joseph's Monastery, Samsohoe, and the Temple Stay and Monastery Stay programs show that the time is ripe for inter/intra-monastic dialogue in lived experience and spiritual depth within Asia and between Asian monastics or con-

---

126. Bede Griffiths, "Dialogue interreligieux monastique," *Bulletin de la Commission Francophone d'Europe* 8 (March 1993): 1 (this part is translated by William Skudlarek).

templatives. As I stated in the introduction to this book, as an Asian Benedictine monk I was privileged to participate in the centennial celebration of his birth organized by the International Thomas Merton Society in Louisville in 2015 and the Gethsemani Encounter IV in 2015, and the meeting of the European DIMMID subcommissions in 2016 and 2017. My presence at these events led me to understand that Merton's legacy continues to grow and remains worthy of development in Asia. For example, when I suggested intra-monastic dialogue in Asia, the Buddhist nun Ven. Guang Guo agreed and expressed interest in this type of dialogue with Korean Benedictine monastics. Her mother monastery, Wu Sheng (無生) in Taiwan, has about one hundred nuns and twenty monks and ten thousand lay disciples. It has inspired, and continues to inspire, many who are dedicated to the monastic life and to inter/intra-monastic dialogue, including me and my own nascent efforts to build up such dialogue in South Korea. This monastic exchange on the local level is inseparable from that taking place on the universal level and is an expression of "unity from diversity."[127]

For the future of inter/intra-monastic dialogue for the world, DIMMID should assist local monasteries in becoming spiritual platforms for inter/intra-contemplative dialogue between monastics and lay contemplatives beyond religious boundaries. Many Buddhist and Christian monastics have developed a profound relationship with lay contemplatives through sharing their monastic life. As Corless points out, "Monks and nuns are the eyes of the Church and the *Sangha*. . . . Sometimes laypeople see as much or more than monks, but because they are professionally involved in looking (*contemplatio, vipaśyanā*), monks are more likely to see."[128] The collaboration of monastics and lay contemplatives and their intra-contemplative dialogue in local monasteries could become a witness for those who are longing for spiritual awareness and for the world in need of peace between religions.

---

127. Blée, *The Third Desert*, 174.
128. Corless, "The Dialogue of Silence," 83–84.

Conclusion

Thomas Merton's spiritual journey began with a question: "What is contemplation?" His longing to find the true self through contemplative awareness led him to a new question: "What is a truly human life?" Without contemplative awareness, he noted, human life "has lost the spiritual orientation upon which everything else—order, peace, happiness, sanity—must depend."[1] He saw that a human person was an unachieved being on the journey toward the attainment of the real human person through self-transformation or enlightenment. He realized that the contemplative life was a profoundly human life and a way to become one's true self. He believed that God planted seeds of contemplation in the deep inner self of all human persons, and that through a contemplative life the seeds could grow, blossom, and be fruitful.

This new perspective of contemplation was influenced by various elements in his own spiritual life. He had a profound knowledge of Christian contemplation thanks to his monastic life, his mystical experiences, and his philosophical and theological preparation for ordination to the priesthood. His great desire for solitude and union with God deepened over the years and was tested by complex self-contradictions and dissatisfaction with the quality of his inner life. Paradoxically, his struggles with his false ego led him to self-renewal and self-transformation through an increasing sense of the mystery of God.

---

1. Thomas Merton, "The Contemplative Life in the Modern World," in *Thomas Merton: Selected Essays*, 226.

Through his intensified experiences of the divine mystery, he realized that human beings could be restored to their original essence so as to live as *New Persons* in union with God and to share this divine love with others in universal communion. His contemplative wisdom was stretched by his study of non-Christian contemplative traditions. In particular, through an understanding of Zen Buddhism, his views of contemplation became more anthropological, *reconfirming* his conviction that contemplative experience is open to all human persons who seek truth, love, and beauty in their daily lives. He also gained an understanding of contemplation that was universal, going far beyond the traditional restrictive concepts of contemplation. The contemplative texts he authored between his early and later writings are evidence of the development of his understanding of experience-based contemplation. Moreover, through his developed view of contemplation, Merton believed that *new* seeds of contemplation, which are planted in everyone's heart no matter what their religious tradition, could transform "the mentality of the world and . . . let loose the force of radical action."[2]

His discovery of the anthropological and universal dimensions of contemplation raises a new question: "How can Christian monastics engage in interreligious dialogue with Asian traditions through contemplation?" His dialogue with other contemplative traditions, especially Buddhism, showed him that he could learn from them how to become "a better and more enlightened monk."[3] Merton stated, "I am entirely occupied with these [Asian] monastic encounters and with the study and prayer that are required to make them fruitful."[4] Béthune points out that "[t]he journal entries [Merton] made in Asia evoke the many ways he resonated with Buddhist teaching and experience, their meeting of minds, but he never says how his Christian faith was changed by these

2. Joan D. Chittister, "Thomas Merton: Seeder of Radical Action," *The Merton Annual* 12 (1999): 115.

3. AJ, 313.

4. Ibid., 324–325.

decisive encounters."[5] I believe that these encounters opened up new dimensions of his contemplative monastic life and worldview. Merton also realized that inter-monastic communion through contemplative dialogue between Buddhist and Christian monastics contributed to the transformation of human consciousness. Both Buddhism and Christianity agreed that many human problems were ultimately rooted in human consciousness. He believed that by creating new spiritual solidarity between contemplative traditions, Buddhist and Christian monastics could play a prophetic role in a materialized and divided world.

Merton's legacy for inter-monastic/contemplative dialogue prompted DIMMID to develop new forms of interreligious dialogue between East and West. At the present time, intra-monastic dialogue on the local level is required for the further development of monastic interreligious dialogue, especially within an Asian context.

Merton's encounter with Buddhists/Buddhism and the legacy he left for monastic interreligious dialogue can be summarized in the following points:

1. His contemplative life and experiences led him to openness to others and other religious traditions, especially Zen Buddhism, and his dialogue with Buddhists facilitated his monastic renewal as well as his discovery of a new way of understanding contemplation.

2. His discovery and search for his true self was the starting point and his self-transformation the connecting point for Buddhist-Christian dialogue.

3. His incessant search for self-transcendence showed that the recovery of one's original identity is not limited by religious structures but transcends them, and transcendent identity can help bring about a better understanding of dual religious belonging.

5. Béthune, *Welcoming Other Religions*, 22.

4. His knowledge of Buddhism was limited, but his encounter with Buddhism was not limited because he focused on the existential and experiential dialogue.

5. His inter-monastic/contemplative dialogue was aimed at the progressive recovery of humankind's original unity—moving from the discovery of one's true self, to friendship, to the bonding of the spiritual family in spiritual communion.

6. His inter-monastic/contemplative dialogue was rooted in the attainment of spiritual maturity in one's own tradition and of transcultural maturity.

7. Monastic exchange programs are the indirect heirs and the Gethsemani Encounters the direct heirs of his legacy and ongoing influence.

8. His contemplative dialogue already included intra-religious dialogue, that is, dialogue at the interior and spiritual level within the minds and hearts of those who follow different religious traditions.

9. His legacy of intra-religious dialogue can be further developed in an Asian context through three levels of intra-religious dialogue as a form of intra-monastic dialogue: a) *in* an individual Asian monastic, b) *within* Asian monastic communities of the same religious tradition, and c) *between* Asian monastics of different religious traditions at the interior, existential, experiential, and local levels.

10. His inter-monastic/contemplative dialogue ought to extend to dialogue between monastics and lay contemplatives in a monastic or sacred milieu that goes beyond religious boundaries.

Merton was involved in four levels of dialogue: 1) interreligious dialogue on the spiritual level, 2) inter-monastic dialogue on the existential and experiential levels, 3) contemplative dialogue on the universal level, and 4) intra-monastic dialogue on the local and global levels.

First, he discovered that Eastern and Western religions are compatible at the deep spiritual levels of multireligious prayer and meditation, religious experience, spiritual communion (dialogue of silence), and the fruits of contemplation for the world. In fact, interreligious dialogue with Buddhists will be different from that with Confucians, Hindus, Jews, or Muslims. Since every religion has its own character, Christians cannot approach Abrahamic religions the same way they approach Asian religions or nontheistic religions. Furthermore, the differences among various religious sects within one religion need to be taken into account when entering into dialogue with them. All this notwithstanding, Merton discovered that there was common ground for interreligious dialogue at the spiritual level with many different traditions, in particular with Asian traditions. For example, through his encounter with Buddhists/Buddhism, he realized that spiritual disciplines, especially that of meditation, were essential to interreligious dialogue with Buddhists. For this reason, he wanted to learn about Zen and Tibetan meditation techniques and their other spiritual practices. His dialogue about spiritual disciplines facilitated dialogue at a mystical level. For example, his *satori*-like experience before the Buddha statue in Polonnaruwa demonstrated that interreligious dialogue at the profound level of mystical experience was possible. Moreover, his encounters with Buddhists at the spiritual level demonstrated the possibility of spiritual communion and cooperative social engagement with them since they shared the conviction that the life of an awakened person is revealed through openness, compassion, and love for others.

Second, Merton discovered inter-monastic dialogue at the existential and experiential level through sharing the life of a monastic milieu different from his own. Although he could not have a prolonged experience of Buddhist monastic life in Asia, he attempted to visit Buddhist monastic communities and to share monastic and contemplative experiences with Buddhists, doing so as a monastic pilgrim-student. He saw that inter-monastic exchanges offered better conditions for mutual understanding and mutual spiritual enrichment than another path of dialogue since it could include the dialogue of life, spirituality, and experience. Existential and experiential dialogue contributed to his discovery of a new way to revelatory spiritual exchanges between Buddhist and Christian monastic traditions, namely, monastic hospitality programs.

Third, Merton's inter-contemplative dialogue was dialogue at the universal level, dialogue that went beyond one's own cultural and religious boundaries. This new consciousness of dialogue was rooted in his universal awareness and his transcultural maturity. He saw that contemplatives who attained universal consciousness through unity with One or the experience of enlightenment could transcend clinging to their own culture or religion. He noted that the awakened person's "consciousness was disposed to encounter 'the other' with whom it is already united anyway 'in God.' "[6] Thus, the awakened person could see that everything is interdependent with all things since the Transcendent is also immanent in everything. God cannot be limited to Christianity but can be present in religious traditions that are not Christian and can even transcend all boundaries. From the perspective of universal consciousness, Merton's contemplative dialogue with different traditions involved sharing their experiences of the Transcendent, which they expressed differently or interpreted in relation to their specific culture or religion. In this regard, his transcultural maturity was not ignorance of specific cultures but awareness of the immanence of the Transcendent in every culture. For example, Merton noted that "Asia in its purity . . . is clear, pure, complete. It says everything, it needs nothing. And because it needs nothing it can afford to be silent, unnoticed, undiscovered. It does not need to be discovered. It is we, Asians included, who need to discover it."[7] Aloysius Pieris, an Asian theologian and Buddhist scholar,

6. ZBA, 24; see more, Finley, *Merton's Palace of Nowhere*, 121–151.
7. AJ, 236.

points out that "it was really not in Asia that Merton discovered the East; there he only recognized and named what he had already sought and found in his own monastic cell."[8] On the cosmic and universal level, Merton realized that inter-contemplative dialogue could lead to a richer understanding of the divine mystery and the recovery of the human original *unity-in-diversity*.

Finally, Merton's inter-contemplative dialogue with Asian contemplative traditions influenced the development of intra-monastic dialogue on the local level. For example, after the second Gethsemani Encounter, North American nuns and monks initiated "Nuns in the West" and "Monks in the West," separate gatherings of Buddhist and Catholic nuns and monks for monastic and spiritual dialogue. In 2003, thirty Buddhist and Catholic nuns who live in the U.S. gathered at Hsi Lai Buddhist Temple in Hacienda Heights, California. The main topics they addressed were 1) the inner life of training, 2) the balance between inner contemplative work and outer social engagement, and 3) community and the role of authority. The gathering proved helpful for Christian nuns, who need a more contemplative life, and Buddhist nuns, who need more social engagement.[9] Nuns in the West again met at Hsi Lai Temple in 2005 and at St. Mary Monastery in Illinois in 2008.

After learning of the nuns' positive experience at their gathering, the board of directors of MID decided to begin something similar for monks. The first gathering was held in 2004 at the City of Ten Thousand Buddhas in northern California. Subsequent gatherings took place in 2006 at St. John's Abbey in Minnesota and in 2012 once again at the City of Ten Thousand Buddhas in California. The themes of these gatherings were the challenges of living the monastic life in an increasingly secular and materialistic

---

8. Aloysius Pieris, *Love Meets Wisdom: A Christian Experience of Buddhism* (Maryknoll, NY: Orbis Books, 1988), 12.

9. See Mary Margaret Funk, "Nuns in the West: May 23–26, 2003" (May 2003), http://www.urbandharma.org/nunsofwest.html.

Western culture and the meaning and practice of celibacy in the monastic life.[10]

The separate gatherings of monks and nuns in the U.S. can serve as models for intra-monastic dialogue in Asia. However, it should be obvious that Asian conditions are different from those in the United States. In Asia, there are many countries and various languages as well as different religious and social situations. DIM-MID should consider finding a way to initiate intra-monastic dialogue in the various Asian contexts. I suggest that it would be better to begin at the national level in countries like South Korea or Vietnam, where there are monastic communities of different religious traditions.

My study of Merton's encounter with Buddhism, his monastic interreligious dialogue, and his legacy leads me, as a Korean Benedictine monk, to suggest three lines of development for future inter/intra-monastic dialogue in South Korea: 1) the development of spiritual solidarity between Buddhist and Christian monastics, 2) the development of Korean style Christian monasticism, and 3) the development of the concept of *"Jeong"* (정, 情—feeling, affection) of the Korean people for monastic hospitality programs.

For the development of spiritual solidarity among Korean monastics, they should first attain spiritual maturity, which for Merton was a key component of this type of dialogue. Spiritual maturity through contemplative experience can lead monastics to be open to others and, at the same time, can facilitate entering into spiritual friendship with other monastics or contemplatives. Openness and friendship at the deep spiritual level also can lead to existential

---

10. See Thomas Ryan, "Buddhist and Catholic Monks Talk about Celibacy," *Buddhist-Christian Studies* 27 (2007): 143–145; William Skudlarek, "Monks in the West III" (October 8–11, 2012), http://www.dimmid.org/index.asp?Type=B _BASIC&SEC=%7BDBEE2BF4-6669-428C-BD7A-D5AA5302BAE1%7D. Following Monks in the West II, Skudlarek wrote *Demythologizing Celibacy: Practical Wisdom from Christian and Buddhist Monasticism* (Collegeville, MN: Liturgical Press, 2008).

and experiential dialogue beyond intellectual debate and to the bonding of the spiritual family between Buddhist and Christian monastics as spiritual brothers and sisters. Korean Catholic monastics need to recognize that monastics of different religious traditions are not pagans or rivals but co-contemplatives who are on the same spiritual journey, seeking the Truth and sharing love and compassion with others.

For arriving at spiritual solidarity, it would be helpful to set up a locally based spiritual network among Korean monastics. According to statistics in 2015, about 56,905 Buddhist monastics live in 944 Buddhist temples, while 7,186 Catholic religious men and women are members of 109 different religious orders throughout South Korea (among them there are 1,172 monks and nuns who live in seven monasteries).[11] The number of monasteries and monastics is not insignificant in a country as small as Korea. Building up a monastic network of Buddhist and Christian monasteries at the local level may allow for finding new types of exchanges at a spiritual level. It could also lead to an intra-monastic exchange program in the near future and become a spiritual network for Korean society.

Second, Korean Christian monastics should develop their own kind of monasticism. Christian monasticism in Korea has been shaped by the Western form of monastic life, theology, and spirituality, which is not always compatible with Korean culture and spirituality. Merton and Leclercq emphasized that through monastic interreligious dialogue, Western monasticism should move beyond Hellenistic categories and Platonic concepts.

11. See Statistics Korea, "Results of the 2015 Population and Housing Census" (December 19, 2016), http://kostat.go.kr/portal/eng/pressReleases/1/index.board?bmode=read&aSeq=361147; Ministry of Culture, Sports and Tourism, "The Present Condition of Traditional Temple in South Korea" (January 7, 2015), http://www.bulgyofocus.net/news/articleView.html?idxno=76958; Catholic Bishops' Conference of Korea, "Statistics of the Catholic Church in Korea: 2015" (March 29, 2016), http://www.cbck.or.kr/bbs/bbs_read.asp?board_id=K7200&bid=13011951&page=1&key=&keyword=.

Korean Christian monastics have recognized the need for a de-Europeanized and inculturated form of monasticism. I believe that intra-monastic exchange with Buddhist monastics may help to achieve this aspiration. In such an exchange, Korean Christian monastics would have a chance to live in a Buddhist monastic milieu. If they do, they must avoid interpreting and evaluating the Buddhist form of monastic life through Western lenses. Rather, they ought to attempt to look at Christian religious experience and monastic life through the lens of Korean Buddhists.[12] In addition, they must recognize that their spiritual exchange will be "a much quieter movement" within a church that is working toward spiritual communion with Buddhists, and that the development of new Korean monasticism "in *the long term* may bear the most fruit."[13]

Finally, for intra-monastic exchange from mind to mind and heart to heart, Korean monastics would do well to develop their traditional concept of *"Jeong,"* which is deeply embedded in Korean culture. *Jeong* is the Korean people's way of referring to human affection and deep-seated love. It can be experienced with family, friends, lovers, teachers, coworkers, guests, strangers, and even with places and objects, but it is difficult to explain in Western terms. Jean-Marie Gustave Le Clézio, a French-Mauritian writer and winner of the 2008 Nobel Prize in Literature, frequently visited South Korea. He once said, "The concept of affection [*Jeong*] is quite mysterious and unique. Even if you search in a French or English dictionary, there isn't a thing to translate."[14] The

---

12. Shannon claims that "the confusion has been accentuated by the introduction into the West of Eastern religions, which have brought with them a mysticism that, unlike Western mysticism, [was] unrelated to dogma or sacraments." See Shannon, "Mysticism," 314.

13. Stephen Batchelor, *The Awakening of the West: The Encounter of Buddhism and Western Culture* (Berkeley, CA: Parallax Press, 1994), 219 (emphasis added).

14. Cited in Wonchan Song, "Jeong of Korean People and Jeong of the 21st Century," in *The Cultural Gene of Korean People 1*, ed. Advanced Center for Korean Studies (Seoul, Korea: Amormundibook, 2012), 72.

disposition of Korean *Jeong* can be extended to one's encounter with different religious traditions in Korea since the concept of *Jeong* includes hospitality. Many Korean Buddhist and Christian monastics have given a warm-hearted welcome to guests and strangers, and this welcoming can be further developed by sharing one's own religious life and spiritual disciplines with monastics of another spiritual tradition. Developing Korean *Jeong* in the context of inter-monastic hospitality may help to soften the hearts of some Korean Christians who are hostile to other religions. A monastic development of this concept can also contribute to the proper understanding and practice of *Jeong*, which has sometimes been misused to function as a sort of a bribe.

For future studies of Merton's encounter with Asian traditions and his legacy, I offer a few suggestions. First, this book focuses on Merton's encounter with Zen and Tibetan Buddhism. His understanding of Theravada Buddhism, Taoism, Confucianism, and Hinduism needs further study for a better understanding of his contemplative dialogue with Asian traditions.[15] Second, reports on spiritual and practical exchanges in Christian or Asian monastic traditions should be collected and analyzed in order to further the development of contemplative dialogue. It should be pointed out, however, that there are as yet very few reports about the meaning of Buddhist meditation and Hindu yoga for Christian spirituality, or about the practice of Christian spiritual disciplines by non-Christian contemplatives. Finally, for the development of Merton's contemplative dialogue with various religions, including Islam, DIMMID may need to give more attention to the contemplative

---

15. Before his Asian journey, Merton was actually integrating the teachings of other religions into his spiritual disciplines, and his teachers were Christian Desert Fathers, along with Zen Buddhist masters and lamas, Taoists, Hindu sadhus, and Jewish Hasidics. He returned to original Christian sources and drank "from ancient sources of monastic vision and experience" in other religions, and then discovered something new to which his contemporaries might not yet have access. See AJ, 313.

dimension of monastic interreligious dialogue. Many Christians tend to think that inter-monastic dialogue with Muslims is impossible since there is no monasticism in Islam. But we need to be aware that Muhammad, the founder of Islam, intended that all Muslims become contemplatives.[16] In addition, research on encounters involving monastics, lay contemplatives, and scholars will offer an example of an integrated form of contemplative dialogue. The Buddhist-Christian Monastic and Contemplative Encounter Group, which had its first meeting at the Graduate Theological Union in Berkeley, California, in 1987, is one example of such encounters that need to be taken into consideration.

This book began with some questions regarding Merton's declaration: "Zen and Christianity are the future." Having explored his journey of interreligious dialogue, I am convinced that he discovered the *contemplative core* of future interreligious dialogue through the lens of Zen.[17] Through his encounter with Asian traditions, especially Zen, Merton realized that contemplative dialogue was possible. He believed that Zen, as transreligious consciousness, expresses the *contemplative core* in all Asian religious traditions, including Christianity. Although religions may understand the experience of contemplation or enlightenment differently and have different ways of expressing it, such as Zen *satori*, Hindu *samadhi*, Taoist *wu-wei*, and Christian union with God, their primary objective is to bring about ultimate self-transcendence or self-transformation. For this reason, Merton stressed dialogue with other religious traditions at the contemplative level for the

16. Reza Shah-Kazemi, a Sufi, gave several lectures on the spirituality of Islam at the meeting of the European Commission of DIMMID in Norway in 2016. I asked him about the existence of monasticism in Islam and the possibility of inter-monastic dialogue. He replied that there is no monasticism in Islam from the Christian perspective, but all Muslims are contemplatives.

17. It would be better to use the term "contemplative core" rather than a Zen core, which many can immediately associate with Buddhism since it has been used by Buddhists for a long time.

transformation of human consciousness and spiritual liberation. He foresaw that the *contemplative core* of many religious traditions is what can support interreligious dialogue at a deep spiritual level. Moffitt, who recalled Merton's declaration that "Zen and Christianity are the future," claims that "[Zen] avoids any conceptualized picture of ultimate reality, whether intellectual or devotional. . . . Hence, in mentioning only one religion Merton was in effect including both. If he had been a Hindu, he might have said with equal propriety, 'Hinduism and Zen are the future.' "[18]

Finally, I would like to relay a personal note. Thomas Merton changed my academic, spiritual, and monastic life. In 2012, I encountered Merton's writings for the first time. As a Benedictine monk, I could easily understand and empathize with Merton's life journey. I could relate to his struggles with his monastic journey due to my similar frustrating experiences in my own monastic life, such as my youthful clericalist attitude toward the laity, my conflicts with the Abbot and brothers, and my confusion between contemplation and action as a missionary Benedictine (I belong to the Congregation of St. Ottilien). One day, while reading his notes on the Louisville Epiphany, I was suddenly overwhelmed with an ineffable light, and felt that Merton spoke to me: "You love all people, and none of them could be totally alien to you. I love you not because you are a monk, but because you are my friend. I am only another member of the human race, and you are too!" This experience helped me to remove my superior attitude as a priest and monk, my past mistakes and faults, and to be aware that God has deeply been with me. Through this experience, I attained new understanding about a human life and a monastic life, and my frustration became one of progress toward union with God. Since this spiritual experience, my study of Merton's Buddhist-Christian dialogue led me to the realization of my new vocation for monastic interreligious dialogue. Moreover, writing this book became not

18. Moffitt, "Memories of Thomas Merton," 77.

only for my own academic interest and spiritual renewal but also a preparation for inter-contemplative dialogue in my Asian context.

Now, following the lead of Thomas Merton, I would say, "Contemplation is the future for interreligious dialogue." Contemplative dialogue must be at the heart of all interreligious dialogue with the great world religions if we are to live together in peace, as one spiritual family.

Bibliography

Primary Sources

Thomas Merton

A Search for Solitude: Pursuing the Monk's True Life. Edited by Lawrence Cunningham. San Francisco, CA: HarperSanFrancisco, 1996.

A Thomas Merton Reader. Edited by Thomas P. McDonnell. Garden City, NY: Image Books, 1974.

An Introduction to Christian Mysticism: Initiation into the Monastic Tradition 3. Edited by Patrick F. O'Connell. Kalamazoo, MI: Cistercian Publications, 2008.

"Comments about the Religious Life Today: Transcript of a Recording Made by and Edited by Father Louis Merton for Special General Chapter Sister of Loretto, 1967." *The Merton Annual* 14 (2001): 14–32.

Conjectures of a Guilty Bystander. Garden City, NY: Image Books, 2014 (first published in 1966).

Contemplation in a World of Action. Notre Dame, IN: University of Notre Dame Press, 1998 (first published in 1971).

Contemplative Prayer. Garden City, NY: Image Books, 1969.

Dancing in the Water of Life: Seeking Peace in the Hermitage. Edited by Robert E. Daggy. San Francisco, CA: HarperSanFrancisco, 1997.

Dialogues with Silence: Prayers & Drawings. Edited by Jonathan Montaldo. San Francisco, CA: HarperSanFrancisco, 2001.

Disputed Questions. New York, NY: Farrar, Straus and Cudahy, 1960.

Entering the Silence: Becoming a Monk and a Writer. Edited by Jonathan Montaldo. San Francisco, CA: HarperSanFrancisco, 1995.

Faith and Violence: Christian Teaching and Christian Practice. Notre Dame, IN: University of Notre Dame Press, 1968.

Introductions East and West: The Foreign Prefaces of Thomas Merton. Edited by Robert E. Daggy. Oakville, ON: Mosaic Press, 1981.

Learning to Love: Exploring Solitude and Freedom. Edited by Christine M. Bochen. San Francisco, CA: HarperSanFrancisco, 1998.

Life and Holiness. New York, NY: Herder and Herder, 1963.

Love and Living. Edited by Naomi B. Stone and Patrick Hart. San Diego, CA: Harcourt Brace Jovanovich, 1985.

Mystics and Zen Masters. New York, NY: Farrar, Straus and Giroux, 1967.

New Seeds of Contemplation. New York, NY: New Directions, 2007 (first published in 1962).

No Man Is an Island. New York, NY: Harcourt, 1955.

Passion for Peace: The Social Essays. Edited by William H. Shannon. New York, NY: Crossroad, 1997.

Pre-Benedictine Monasticism: Initiation into the Monastic Tradition 2. Kalamazoo, MI: Cistercian Publications, 2006.

Run to the Mountain: The Story of a Vocation. Edited by Patrick Hart. San Francisco, CA: HarperSanFrancisco, 1996.

Seeds of Contemplation. Norfolk, CT: New Directions, 1949.

Seeds of Destruction. New York, NY: Farrar, Straus and Giroux, 1964.

Spiritual Master: The Essential Writings. Edited by Lawrence Cunningham. New York/Mahwah, NJ: Paulist Press, 1992.

The Ascent to Truth. New York, NY: Harcourt, 1951.

The Asian Journal of Thomas Merton. Edited by Naomi Burton, Brother Patrick Hart, and James Laughlin. New York, NY: New Directions, 1973.

The Cistercian Fathers and Their Monastic Theology: Initiation into the Monastic Tradition 8. Collegeville, MN: Liturgical Press, 2016.

The Climate of Monastic Prayer. Washington, DC: Consortium Press, 1973 (first published in 1969).

The Hidden Ground of Love: The Letters of Thomas Merton on Religious Experience and Social Concerns. Edited by William H. Shannon. New York, NY: Farrar, Straus and Giroux, 1985.

The Inner Experience: Notes on Contemplation. Edited by William H. Shannon. San Francisco, CA: HarperCollins, 2003.

The Intimate Merton: His Life from His Journals. Edited by Patrick Hart and Jonathan Montaldo. San Francisco, CA: HarperSanFrancisco, 1999.

The Labyrinth [unpublished manuscript]. Louisville, KY: Thomas Merton Studies Center, Bellarmine University.

"The Monk Today." In *Contemplation in a World of Action*. Garden City, NY: Doubleday, 1973.

The New Man. New York, NY: Farrar, Straus and Cudahy, 1961.

The Other Side of the Mountain: The End of the Journey. Edited by Patrick Hart. San Francisco, CA: HarperSanFrancisco, 1998.

The Road to Joy: The Letters of Thomas Merton to New and Old Friends. Edited by Robert E. Daggy. New York, NY: Farrar, Straus and Giroux, 1989.

The School of Charity: The Letters of Thomas Merton on Religious Renewal and Spiritual Direction. Edited by Patrick Hart. New York, NY: Farrar, Straus and Giroux, 1990.

The Secular Journal of Thomas Merton. New York, NY: Farrar, Straus and Cudahy, 1959.

The Seven Storey Mountain. New York, NY: Harcourt, 1998 (50th-anniversary edition).

The Sign of Jonas. New York, NY: Harcourt, 1953.

The Way of Chuang Tzu. New York, NY: New Directions, 1965.

"The Zen Revival." *Continuum* 1 (Winter 1964): 523–538.

Thomas Merton: The Monastic Journey. Edited by Patrick Hart. Garden City, NY: Image Books, 1978.

Thomas Merton: Selected Essays. Edited by Patrick F. O'Connell. Maryknoll, NY: Orbis Books, 2013.

Turning Toward the World: The Pivotal Years. Edited by Victor A. Kramer. San Francisco, CA: HarperSanFrancisco, 1997.

What Is Contemplation? Springfield, IL: Templegate, 1978 (first published in 1948).

Witness to Freedom: The Letters of Thomas Merton in Times of Crisis. Edited by William H. Shannon. New York, NY: Farrar, Straus and Giroux, 1994.

Zen and the Birds of Appetite. New York, NY: New Directions, 1968.

———— and Jean Leclercq. *Survival or Prophecy?: The Letters of Thomas Merton and Jean Leclercq*. Edited by Patrick Hart. New York, NY: Farrar, Straus and Giroux, 2002.

Monastic Interreligious Dialogue

Barnhart, Bruno, and Joseph Wong, eds. *Purity of Heart and Contemplation: A Monastic Dialogue between Christian and Asian Traditions*. New York, NY: Continuum, 2001.

Blée, Fabrice. *The Third Desert: The Story of Monastic Interreligious Dialogue*. Translated by William Skudlarek and Mary Grady. Collegeville, MN: Liturgical Press, 2011.

Béthune, Pierre-François de. *By Faith and Hospitality: The Monastic Tradition as a Model for Interreligious Encounter*. Leominster, UK: Gracewing, 2002.

———. "Contemplation and Interreligious Dialogue: References and Perspectives Drawn from the Experience of Monastics." In *The Attentive Voice: Reflections on the Meaning and Practice of Interreligious Dialogue*, edited by William Skudlarek, 143–164. Brooklyn, NY: Lantern Press, 2011.

———. "DIM/MID Annual European Conference." (June 2012). https://www.turveyabbey.org.uk/MID-GBI/news/MEB_01_13.pdf.

———. *Interreligious Hospitality: The Fulfillment of Dialogue*. Collegeville, MN: Liturgical Press, 2010.

———. "Interreligious Monastic Hospitality." *Monastic Studies* 16 (1985): 227–236.

———. "Monastic Inter-Religious Dialogue." In *The Wiley-Blackwell Companion to Inter-Religious Dialogue*, edited by Catherine Cornille, 34–59. Malden, MA: Wiley Blackwell, 2013.

———. "The Work of Commissions of Monastic Interreligious Dialogue." 코이노니아 (*Koinonia*) 25 (2000): 56–62.

———. *Welcoming Other Religions*. Translated by William Skudlarek. Collegeville, MN: Liturgical Press, 2016.

Chodron, Thubten. "The Second Gethsemani Encounter." (18 April 2002). http://thubtenchodron.org/2002/04/conference-reflections.

DIMMID. *Strangers No More*, DVD. Directed by Lizette Lemoine and Aubin Hellot. Paris, France: Les Films du Large, 2016.

Funk, Mary Margaret. "Nuns in the West: May 23–26, 2003." (May 2003). http://www.urbandharma.org/nunsofwest.html.

Leclercq, Jean. "Introduction: The Second Meeting of the Monks of Asia." *Cistercian Studies* 9, nos. 2/3 (1974): 81–89.

Michaud, Margaret. "Gethsemani Encounter IV." (May 27–31, 2015). http://monasticinterreligiousdialogue.com/index.php/27-31-may -2015-gethsemani-encounter-iv.

Mitchell, Donald W. "The Gethsemani Encounter on the Spiritual Life." *Buddhist-Christian Studies* 17 (1997): 205–208.

Mitchell, Donald W., and James A. Wiseman. "An Interview with Donald Mitchell and James Wiseman." *Buddhist-Christian Studies* 23 (2003): 197–201.

————, eds. *Finding Peace in Troubled Times: Buddhist and Christian Monastics on Transforming Suffering*. Brooklyn, NY: Lantern Books, 2010.

————, eds. *The Gethsemani Encounter: A Dialogue on the Spiritual Life by Buddhist and Christian Monastics*. New York, NY: Continuum, 1997.

Mitchell, Donald W., and William Skudlarek, eds. *Green Monasticism: A Buddhist-Catholic Response to an Environmental Calamity*. Brooklyn, NY: Lantern Books, 2010.

Moffitt, John. *A New Charter for Monasticism: Proceedings of the Meeting of the Monastic Superiors in the Far East, Bangkok, December 9 to 15, 1968*. Notre Dame, IN: University of Notre Dame Press, 1970.

O'Mahony, Anthony, and Peter Bowe, eds. *Catholics in Interreligious Dialogue: Studies in Monasticism, Theology, and Spirituality*. Leominster, UK: Gracewing, 2006.

Panikkar, Raimon. *The Intrareligious Dialogue*. New York/Mahwah, NJ: Paulist Press, 1999.

Pignedoli, Sergio. "Dialogue Interreligieux Monastique." *Bulletin of AIM* 17 (1974): 61–63.

Ryan, Thomas. "Gethsemani II: Catholic and Buddhist Monastics Focus on Suffering." *Buddhist-Christian Studies* 24 (2004): 249-251.

Skudlarek, William. "Annual Report of the Secretary General of DIMMID." (December 2016). http://mid.nonprofitoffice.com/vertical/sites /%7BD52F3ABF-B999-49DF-BFAB-845A690CF39B%7D /uploads/2016_Year_end_report.pdf.

————. "Monks in the West III." (October 8–11, 2012). http://www .dimmid.org/index.asp?Type=B_BASIC&SEC=%7BDBEE2BF4 -6669-428C-BD7A-D5AA5302BAE1%7D.

————. "Refashioning the Likeness, Playing with the Differences: Monastic Interreligious Dialogue at the Abbey of Gethsemani." *The Japan Christian Review* 63 (1997): 81–92.

Standaert, Benoît. *Sharing Sacred Space: Interreligious Dialogue As Spiritual Encounter*. Translated by William Skudlarek. Collegeville, MN: Liturgical Press, 2009.

Weakland, Rembert. "Final Remarks." *Cistercian Studies* 9, nos. 2/3 (1974): 320–323.

Wiseman, James A. "Christian Monastic and Interreligious Dialogue." *Cistercian Studies* 27, no. 3 (1992): 257–271.

Secondary Sources

About Thomas Merton

Arcement, Ephrem. *In the School of Prophets: The Formation of Thomas Merton's Prophetic Spirituality*. Collegeville, MN: Cistercian Publications, 2015.

Bailey, Raymond. *Thomas Merton on Mysticism*. Garden City, NY: Image Books, 1976.

Barbour, John D. "The Ethics of Intercultural Travel: Thomas Merton's Asian Pilgrimage and Orientalism." *Biography* 28, no. 1 (Winter 2005): 15–26.

Barid, Mary Julien. "Blake, Hopkins and Thomas Merton." *Catholic World* 183 (April 1956): 46–49.

Cameron-Brown, Aldhelm. "Thomas Merton and the Contemplative Tradition." *The Merton Journal* 4, no. 2 (Advent 1997): 2–14.

Carr, Anne E. *A Search for Wisdom and Spirit: Thomas Merton's Theology of the Self*. Notre Dame, IN: University of Notre Dame Press, 1988.

————. "Merton's East-West Reflections." *Horizons* 21, no. 2 (1994): 239–252.

Chittister, Joan D. "Thomas Merton: Seeder of Radical Action." *The Merton Annual* 12 (1999): 103–116.

Coff, Pascaline. "The Universal Call to Contemplation: Cloisters beyond the Monastery." *The Merton Annual* 16 (2003): 197–220.

Conn, Walter E. *The Desiring Self: Rooting Pastoral Counseling and Spiritual Direction in Self-Transcendence.* New York/Mahwah, NJ: Paulist Press, 1998.

———. "Merton's Religious Development: The Monastic Years." *Cistercian Studies* 22 (1987): 262–289.

Conner, James. "The Experience of God and the Experience of Nothingness in Thomas Merton." *The Merton Annual* 1 (1988): 103–114.

Corless, Roger. "In Search of a Context for the Merton-Suzuki Dialogue." *The Merton Annual* 6 (1993): 76–91.

Cunningham, Lawrence. *Thomas Merton and the Monastic Vision.* Grand Rapids, MI: Eerdmans, 1999.

Dadosky, John D. "Merton's Dialogue with Zen: Pioneering or Passé?" *Fu Jen International Religious Studies* 2, no. 1 (Summer 2008): 53–75.

———. "Merton as Method for Inter-Religious Engagement: Examples from Buddhism." *The Merton Annual* 21 (2008): 33–43.

Dear, John. *Thomas Merton, Peacemaker: Meditations on Merton, Peacemaking, and the Spiritual Life.* Maryknoll, NY: Orbis Books, 2015.

Fader, Larry A. "Beyond the Birds of Appetite: Thomas Merton's Encounter with Zen." *Biography* 2, no. 3 (May 1979): 230–254.

Finley, James. *Merton's Palace of Nowhere: A Search for God through Awareness of the True Self.* Notre Dame, IN: Ave Maria Press, 1978.

Forest, Jim. *Living with Wisdom: A Life of Thomas Merton.* Maryknoll, NY: Orbis Books, 2008.

Furlong, Monica. *Merton: A Biography.* New York, NY: Harper & Row, 1980.

Goulet, Jacques. "Thomas Merton's Journey toward World Religious Ecumenism." *The Merton Annual* 4 (1991): 113–129.

Grayston, Donald. "In the Footsteps of Thomas Merton: Asia." *The Merton Seasonal* 33 (Winter 2008): 21–28.

Hart, Patrick, ed. *The Message of Thomas Merton.* Kalamazoo, MI: Cistercian Publications, 1981.

———, ed. *The Legacy of Thomas Merton.* Kalamazoo, MI: Cistercian Publications, 1986.

Higgins, Michael W. *Thomas Merton: Faithful Visionary*. Collegeville, MN: Liturgical Press, 2014.

Inchausti, Robert. *Thomas Merton's American Prophecy*. Albany, NY: State University of New York Press, 1987.

Keuss, Jeffrey F. "A Spirituality for the Advent City: Thomas Merton's Monasticism without Walls." *The Merton Journal* 10, no. 2 (Advent 2003): 2–3.

King, Robert Harlen. *Thomas Merton and Thich Nhat Hanh: Engaged Spirituality in an Age of Globalization*. New York, NY: Continuum, 2001.

Lipski, Alexander. *Thomas Merton and Asia: His Quest for Utopia*. Kalamazoo, MI: Cistercian Publications, 1983.

Lord, Andy. *Transforming Renewal: Charismatic Renewal Meets Thomas Merton*. Eugene, OR: Pickwick Publications, 2015.

Nicholls, William, and Ian Kent. "Merton and Identity." In *Thomas Merton: Pilgrim in Process*, edited by Donald Grayston and Michael W. Higgins, 106–120. Toronto, ON: Griffin House, 1983.

MacCormick, Chalmers. "The Zen Catholicism of Thomas Merton." *Journal of Ecumenical Studies* 9, no. 4 (Fall 1972): 802–818.

MacNiven, Ian S. "More Than Scribe: James Laughlin, Thomas Merton and The Asian Journal." *The Merton Annual* 26 (2013): 43–53.

McDermott, Rachel F. "Why Zen Buddhism and not Hinduism?: The Asias of Thomas Merton's Voyages East." *The Merton Annual* 23 (2010): 29–46.

McInerny, Dennis. *Thomas Merton: The Man and His Work*. Spencer, MA: Cistercian Publications, 1974.

Moffitt, John. *Journey to Gorakhpur: An Encounter with Christ beyond Christianity*. New York, NY: Holt, Rinehart and Winston, 1972.

———. "Memories of Thomas Merton." *Cistercian Studies* 14, no. 1 (1979): 73–80.

Mott, Michael. *The Seven Mountains of Thomas Merton*. Boston, MA: Houghton Mifflin, 1984.

Pennington, M. Basil. *Thomas Merton, Brother Monk: The Quest for True Freedom*. San Francisco, CA: Harper & Row, 1987.

———, ed. *Toward an Integrated Humanity: Thomas Merton's Journey*. Kalamazoo, MI: Cistercian Publications, 1988.

Raab, Joseph Q. "Insights from the Inter-Contemplative Dialogue: Merton's Three Meanings of 'God' and Religious Pluralism." *The Merton Annual* 23 (2010): 90–105.

———. *Openness and Fidelity: Thomas Merton's Dialogue with D. T. Suzuki and Self-Transcendence.* PhD diss., Toronto School of Theology, 2000.

Rice, Edward. *The Man in the Sycamore Tree, The Good Times and Hard Life of Thomas Merton.* New York, NY: Doubleday & Company, 1970.

Ryan, Gregory J. "Merton, Main, and the New Monasticism." *Monastic Studies* 18 (1988): 109–122.

Shannon, William H. *Silent Lamp: The Thomas Merton Story.* New York, NY: Crossroad, 1992.

———. *Thomas Merton's Paradise Journey: Writings of Contemplation.* Cincinnati, OH: St. Anthony Messenger Press, 2000.

Shannon, William H., Christine M. Bochen, and Patrick F. O'Connell, eds. *The Thomas Merton Encyclopedia.* Maryknoll, NY: Orbis Books, 2002.

Simmer-Brown, Judith. " 'Wide Open to Life': Thomas Merton's Dialogue of Contemplative Practice." *Buddhist-Christian Studies* 35 (2015): 193–203.

Steindl-Rast, David. "Man of Prayer." In *Thomas Merton, Monk,* edited by Patrick Hark, 81–90. Garden City, NY: Image Books, 1976.

Thompson, William M. "Merton's Contribution to a Transcultural Consciousness." In *Thomas Merton: Pilgrim in Process,* edited by Donald Grayston and Michael W. Higgins, 147–169. Toronto, ON: Griffin House, 1983.

Thurston, Bonnie B., ed. *Merton & Buddhism: Wisdom, Emptiness, and Everyday Mind.* Louisville, KY: Fons Vitae, 2007.

———. "Thomas Merton: Pioneer of Buddhist-Christian Dialogue." *Catholic World* 233 (May/June 1989): 126–128.

———. "Why Merton Looked East." *Living Prayer* (November/December 1988): 43–49.

Tworkov, Helen. "The Jesus Lama: Thomas Merton in the Himalayas, An Interview with Harold Talbott." *Tricycle: The Buddhist Review* 4, no. 1 (Summer 1992): 14–24.

Waldron, Robert. *The Wounded Heart of Thomas Merton.* New York/ Mahwah, NJ: Paulist Press, 2011.

Wilkes, Paul, ed. *Merton by Those Who Knew Him Best.* San Francisco, CA: Harper & Row, 1984.

On Interreligious Dialogue

Aitken, Robert, and David Steindl-Rast. *The Ground We Share: Everyday Practice, Buddhist and Christian.* Boston, MA: Shambhala, 1996.

Augustine, Morris J. "Monastic and Contemplative Encounter Group." *Buddhist-Christian Studies* 8 (1988): 195–202.

———. "The Buddhist-Christian Monastic and Contemplative Encounter." *Buddhist-Christian Studies* 9 (1989): 247–255.

Balthasar, Hans Urs von. *Des Bords du Gange aux Rives du Jourdain.* Paris, France: Saint Paul, 1983.

———. "Meditation als Verrat." *Geist und Leben* 50 (1977): 260–268.

———. *The Glory of the Lord: A Theological Aesthetics*, vol. 5. San Francisco, CA: Ignatius Press, 1982.

Barnes, Michael. "Theological Trends: The Buddhist-Christian Dialogue." *Way* 30, no. 1 (January 1990): 55–64.

Corless, Roger. "Sense and Nonsense in Buddhist-Christian Intermonastic Dialogue." *Monastic Studies* 19 (1991): 11–22.

———. "The Dialogue of Silence: A Comparison of Buddhist and Christian Monasticism with a Practical Suggestion." In *The Cross and the Lotus: Christianity and Buddhism in Dialogue*, edited by G.W. Houston, 81–107. Delhi, India: Motilal Banarsidass, 1985.

Dadosky, John D. "The Church and the Other: Mediation and Friendship in Post–Vatican II Roman Catholic Ecclesiology." *Pacifica* 18 (October 2005): 302–322.

———. "Towards a Fundamental Theological *Re*-interpretation of Vatican II." *The Heythrop Journal* 49, no. 5 (2008): 742–763.

Dunne, John S. *The Way of All the Earth: Experiments in Truth and Religion.* New York, NY: Macmillan, 1972.

Fredericks, James L. *Buddhists and Christians: Through Comparative Theology to Solidarity.* Maryknoll, NY: Orbis Books, 2004.

———. "Off the Map: The Catholic Church and Its Dialogue with Buddhists." In *Catholicism and Interreligious Dialogue*, edited by James L. Heft, 127–144. New York, NY: Oxford University Press, 2012.

Griffiths, Bede. "Dialogue interreligieux monastique." *Bulletin de la Commission Francophone d'Europe* 8 (March 1993).

———. "The Monastic Order and the Ashram." *American Benedictine Review* 30, no. 2 (June 1979): 134–145.

Gross, Rita M. "Buddhist-Christian Dialogue." In *Monastic Tradition in Eastern Christianity and the Outside World: A Call for Dialogue,* edited by Ines Angeli Murzaku, 261–284. Leuven, Belgium: Peeters, 2013.

Ingram, Paul O. " 'Fruit Salad Can Be Delicious': The Practice of Buddhist-Christian Dialogue." *Cross Currents* 50, no. 4 (Winter 2000/2001): 541–549.

———. *The Process of Buddhist-Christian Dialogue.* Eugene, OR: Cascade Books, 2009.

Johnston, William. *Christian Zen.* New York, NY: Harper & Row, 1971.

———. *Mystical Journey: An Autobiography.* Maryknoll, NY: Orbis Books, 2006.

———. *The Mirror Mind: Zen-Christian Dialogue.* New York, NY: Fordham University Press, 1990.

Kramer, Kenneth P. "A Silent Dialogue: The Intrareligious Dimension." *Buddhist-Christian Studies* 10 (1990): 127–132.

———. "Extra-, Inner-, Intra-, Inter-Religious Voices." *Journal of Ecumenical Studies* 30, no. 2 (Winter 1993): 203–212.

Les Voies de l'Orient. "Interreligious Dialogue: A Pathway to Inner Transformation." (May 2014). http://www.dimmid.org/vertical/sites/%7BD52F3ABF-B999-49DF-BFAB-845A690CF39B%7D/uploads/Voies_de_lOrient_INTERRELIGIOUS_DIALOGUE_A_PATHWAY_TO_INNER_TRANSFORMATION.pdf.

Mohammed, Ovey N. "Buddhist-Catholic Dialogue." *Celebrate* 31, no. 6 (1992): 13–16.

———. "Catholicism in Dialogue with World Religions: The Value of Self-Denial." *Toronto Journal of Theology* 20, no. 1 (2004): 33–50.

Nhat Hanh, Thich. *Being Peace.* Berkeley, CA: Parallax Press, 2005.

———. *Going Home: Jesus and Buddha as Brothers.* New York, NY: Riverhead Books, 1999.

Pontifical Council for Interreligious Dialogue. *Interreligious Dialogue: The Official Teaching of the Catholic Church from the Second Vatican Council to John Paul II (1963–2005)*. Edited by Francesco Gioia. Boston, MA: Pauline Books & Media, 2006.

Ratzinger, Joseph. "Letter to the Bishops of the Catholic Church on Some Aspects of Christian Meditation." (October 15, 1989). http://www.vatican.va/roman_curia/congregations/cfaith/documents/rc_con_cfaith_doc_19891015_meditazione-cristiana_en.html.

Raverty, Aaron. "Monastic Interreligious Dialogue: Tibet, Nepal, and Northern India." *Cistercian Studies* 32, no. 2 (1997): 245–263.

Sherwin, Byron L., and Harold Kasimow, eds. *John Paul II and Interreligious Dialogue*. Maryknoll, NY: Orbis Books, 1999.

Teasdale, Wayne. *Catholicism in Dialogue: Conversations across Traditions*. Lanham, MD: Rowman & Littlefield Publishers, 2004.

———. "Interreligious Dialogue since Vatican II: The Monastic Contemplative Dimension." *Spirituality Today* 43, no. 2 (Summer 1991): 119–133.

———. "The Ocean of Wisdom as Human and Spiritual Presence." In *Understanding the Dalai Lama*, edited by Rajiv Mehrotra, 97–112. New York, NY: Hay House, 2008.

The XIV Dalai Lama [His Holiness Tenzin Gyatso]. *Kindness, Clarity, and Insight*. Edited by Jeffrey Hopkins and Elizabeth Napper. Ithaca, NY: Snow Lion, 2006.

Tracy, David. *Dialogue with the Other: The Inter-Religious Dialogue*. Louvain, Belgium: Peeters, 1990.

Additional Works

Arasteh, A. Reza. *Rumi the Persian: Rebirth in Creativity and Love*. Tucson, AZ: Omen Press, 1972.

Batchelor, Stephen. *The Awakening of the West: The Encounter of Buddhism and Western Culture*. Berkeley, CA: Parallax Press, 1994.

Catholic Bishops' Conference of Korea. "Statistics of the Catholic Church in Korea: 2015." (March 29, 2016). http://www.cbck.or.kr/bbs/bbs_read.asp?board_id=K7200&bid= 13011951&page=1& key=&keyword=.

Cheng, Hsueh-Li. "Confucianism and Zen (Ch'an) Philosophy of Education." *Journal of Chinese Philosophy* 12 (1985): 197–215.

Cho, Hyeon. " 'Another Vocation': Accompanying Christian and Buddhist Nuns." (December 21, 2007). http://well.hani.co.kr /media/5541.

Chosun, Ilbo. "Dalai Lama 'Happy' to Meet Ecumenical Korean Group." (February 11, 2006). http://www.phayul.com/news/article.aspx ?id=11810.

Chung, Ah-young. "Templestay Marks a Decade." (October 17, 2012). https://www.koreatimes.co.kr/www/culture/2017/05/293_122459 .html.

Chung, Youn-Jo. *The Leisure-Psychological Model of the Temple Stay Experience*. Seoul, Korea: Dongguk University, 2009.

Cornille, Catherine. *The Im-Possibility of Interreligious Dialogue*. New York, NY: Crossroad, 2008.

Cultural Corps of Korean Buddhism, "What is Templestay." (2016). http://eng.templestay.com/page-templestay.asp#.

Drew, Rose. *Buddhist and Christian?: An Exploration of Dual Belonging*. New York, NY: Routledge, 2011.

Fox, Matthew. *A Way to God: Thomas Merton's Creation Spirituality Journey*. Novato, CA: New World Library, 2016.

Fujiyoshi, Jikai, and Kadowaki Kakichi. "Interaction between Buddhism and Catholicism (I)." *Young East* 7, no. 1 (1981): 3–17.

Gannon, Thomas M., and George W. Traub. *The Desert and the City; An Interpretation of the History of Christian Spirituality*. New York, NY: Macmillan, 1969.

Hart, Addison H. *The Ox-Herder and The Good Shepherd: Finding Christ on the Buddha's Path*. Grand Rapids, MI: Eerdmans, 2013.

Hawkins, Anne Hunsaker. *Archetypes of Conversion: The Autobiographies of Augustine, Bunyan, and Merton*. Lewisburg, PA: Bucknell University Press, 1985.

Jochim, Christian. "The Contemporary Confucian-Christian Encounter: Interreligious or Intrareligious Dialogue?" *Journal of Ecumenical Studies* 32, no. 1 (Winter 1995): 35–62.

Kaplan, Uri. "Images of Monasticism: The Temple Stay Program and the Re-branding of Korean Buddhist Temples." *Korean Studies* 34, no. 1 (2010): 127–246.

Kardong, Terrence. "Thoughts on the Future of Western Monasticism." In *A Monastic Vision for the 21st Century: Where Do We Go from Here?*, edited by Patrick Hart, 57–72. Kalamazoo, MI: Cistercian Publications, 2006.

Kilcourse, George. *Ace of Freedoms: Thomas Merton's Christ*. Notre Dame, IN: University of Notre Dame Press, 1993.

King, Winston L. "Buddhist-Christian Dialogue Reconsidered." *Buddhist-Christian Studies* 2 (1982): 5–11.

———. "Interreligious Dialogue." In *The Sound of Liberating Truth: Buddhist-Christian Dialogues in Honor of Frederick J. Streng*, edited by Sallie B. King and Paul O. Ingram, 41–56. Surrey, UK: Curzon, 1999.

Kirchner, Thomas L. "Dialogue, Intermonastic: Buddhist Perspectives." In *Encyclopedia of Monasticism*, edited by William M. Johnston, 380–381. Chicago, IL: Fitzroy Dearborn, 2000.

Komarovski, Yaroslav. "Buddhist Contributions to the Question of (Un) mediated Mystical Experience." *Sophia* 51 (2012): 87–115.

Korean Ministry of Culture, Sports and Tourism. "The Popular Korean Templestay." (June 1, 2017). https://www.mcst.go.kr/web/s_notice /press/pressView.jsp?pSeq=16067#.

Knitter, Paul F. *Introducing Theologies of Religions*. Maryknoll, NY: Orbis Books, 2002.

———. *Without Buddha I Could Not Be a Christian*. Croydon, UK: Oneworld, 2009.

Küng, Hans. *Christianity and the World Religions: Paths of Dialogue with Islam, Hinduism, and Buddhism*. Garden City, NY: Doubleday, 1986.

Lai, Whalen, and Michael von Brück. *Christianity and Buddhism: A Multicultural History of Their Dialogue*. Translated by Phyllis Jestice. Maryknoll, NY: Orbis Books, 2001.

Lee, Deokgeun, and Sungeon Kang. "About Foundation of New Seoul Community of St. Benedict Waegwan." 코이노니아 (*Koinonia*) 11 (1986): 7–16.

Lonergan, Bernard. "Mediation of Christ in Prayer." In *Philosophical and Theological Papers 1958–1964*, edited by Robert C. Croken, Frederick E. Crowe, and Robert M. Doran, 160–182. Toronto, ON: University of Toronto Press for Lonergan Research Institute, 1996.

Meister Eckhart. *Selected Writings.* Translated by Oliver Davies. London, UK: Penguin Books, 1994.

———. *The Essential Sermons, Commentaries, Treaties, and Defense.* Translated by Edmund Colledge and Bernard McGinn. New York/ Mahwah, NJ: Paulist Press, 1981.

Miller, Lucien. "Merton's *Chuang Tzu.*" In *Merton & the Tao: Dialogue with John Wu and the Ancient Sage,* edited by Cristóbal Serrán-Pagán y Fuentes, 47–83. Louisville, KY: Fons Vitae, 2013.

Ministry of Culture, Sports and Tourism. "The Present Condition of Traditional Temple in South Korea." (January 7, 2015). http://www .bulgyofocus.net/news/articleView.html?idxno=76958.

Pramuk, Christopher. *Sophia: The Hidden Christ of Thomas Merton.* Collegeville, MN: Liturgical Press, 2009.

Panikkar, Raimon. *Blessed Simplicity: The Monk as Universal Archetype.* New York, NY: Seabury Press, 1982.

Park, Jaechan. "A Christian Contemplative Approach to the Ten Ox-Herding Pictures of Zen Buddhism: Interreligious Dialogue as Mutual Self-mediation." *Dilatato Corde* 5, nos. 1/2 (2015): 132–157.

Park, Soo-Mee. " 'Three Smiles': Lessons in Faith and True Spiritual Understanding." (November 16, 2007). http://mengnews.joins .com/view.aspx?aId=2882806.

Pieris, Aloysius. *Love Meets Wisdom: A Christian Experience of Buddhism.* Maryknoll, NY: Orbis Books, 1988.

"Pope Francis, Catholics, Meet with Buddhists at Vatican." (June 25, 2015). https://www.lionsroar.com/pope-francis-catholics-meet-with -buddhists-at-vatican.

Pope Francis. "To All Consecrated People: On the Occasion of the Year of Consecrated Life." (November 21, 2014). http://w2.vatican.va /content/francesco/en/apost_letters/documents/papa-francesco _lettera-ap_20141121_lettera-consacrati.html.

Principe, Walther. "Toward Defining Spirituality." *Studies in Religion* 12, no. 2 (1983): 127–141.

Ratzinger, Joseph. *Truth and Tolerance: Christian Belief and World Religions.* San Francisco, CA: Ignatius Press, 2004.

Ryan, Thomas. "Buddhist and Catholic Monks Talk about Celibacy." *Buddhist-Christian Studies* 27 (2007): 143–145.

Samsohoe. "Introduction and Activities of 'Samsohoe' Inter-faith Association." (February 14, 2010). http://www.franciscans.org.uk /wp-content/uploads/2015/01/Samso-Leaflet.pdf.

Siegmund, Georg. *Buddhism and Christianity: A Preface to Dialogue*. Tuscaloosa, AL: University of Alabama Press, 1980.

Sharf, Robert H. "Whose Zen? Zen Nationalism Revisited." In *Rude Awakenings: Zen, the Kyoto School and the Question of Nationalism*, edited by J. W. Heisig and J. C. Maraldo, 40–51. Honolulu, HI: University of Hawaii, 1994.

Shippee, Steven R. "Trungpa's Barbarians and Merton's Titan: Resuming a Dialogue on Spiritual Egotism." *Buddhist-Christian Studies* 32 (2012): 109–125.

Siauve, Suzanne. "Experience and Love of God in the Vaishnava Vedanta." *Cistercian Studies* 9, nos. 2/3 (1974): 129–136.

Song, Wonchan. "Jeong of Korean People and Jeong of the 21st Century." In *The Cultural Gene of Korean People 1*, edited by Advanced Center for Korean Studies, 52–73. Seoul, Korea: Amormundibook, 2012.

St. Benedict. *RB 1980: The Rule of St. Benedict in English*. Edited by Timothy Fry. Collegeville, MN: Liturgical Press, 1982.

St. John of the Cross. *Dark Night of the Soul*. Translated by E. Allison Peers. Garden City, NY: Image Books, 1959.

Statistics Korea. "Results of the 2015 Population and Housing Census." (December 19, 2016). http://kostat.go.kr/portal/eng/press Releases/1/index.board?bmode=read&aSeq=361147.

Stoeber, Michael. "Exploring Progresses and Dynamics of Mystical Contemplative Meditation: Some Christian-Buddhist Parallels in Relation to Transpersonal Theory." *European Journal for Philosophy of Religion* 7, no. 2 (Summer 2015): 35–57.

———. "The Comparative Study of Mysticism." *The Oxford Research Encyclopedia of Religion*. (September 2015). http://religion.oxfordre .com/view/10.1093/acrefore/9780199340378.001.0001/acrefore -9780199340378-e-93.

Suzuki, Daisetz T. *Essays in Zen Buddhism, III*. London, UK: Rider and Company, 1970.

Tholens, Cornelius. "Une Enquête auprès des monastères d'Occident pour la poursuite du dialogue inter-religieux." *Bulletin de l'A.I.M.* 19 (1975): 49–51.

Trungpa, Chögyam. *Collected Work of Chögyam Trungpa III.* Edited by Carolyn Rose Gimian. Boston, MA: Shambhala Publications, 2003.

Watts, Alan. *The Way of Zen.* New York, NY: Pantheon, 1957.

Yagi, Seiichi, and Leonard J. Swidler. *A Bridge to Buddhist-Christian Dialogue.* New York/Mahwah, NJ: Paulist Press, 1990.

Index

activism, 98, 99, 127
actualization, 45
aesthetic illumination, 25, 42–43
aggiornamento, 128
Aide a l'Implantation
  Monastique (AIM), xxxi, 24,
  25, 181, 183–189, 190, 192–
  194, 202, 230
anatta (no-self), 29, 76
angya (pilgrimage), 173
apology, 200
apophatic mysticism, theology,
  64, 78, 79–83, 200
Arasteh, Reza, 156
archetype, 6, 126, 133, 134, 135
Aristotelianism, Aristotelian
  philosophy, 91, 121
Ascent to Truth, The, 31, 33, 36
asceticism, 9, 36, 236
Asian Christian monastics, Asian
  Benedictines, 187, 218, 219,
  220, 224, 227–230, 241
Asian tradition, 2, 10, 26, 32, 56,
  59, 66, 80, 120, 137, 140, 143,
  156, 171, 173, 178, 190, 193,
  200, 213, 244, 247, 253, 254
Atman (the Self), 29, 48, 51, 96,
  151, 158
Augustine, Morris J., 197, 198

Augustine, St., 8, 192
Australian Monastic Encounter
  (AME), 189

Balthasar, Hans Urs von, 81,
  201–202
Bangalore Congress, 181, 184–
  187, 190, 191, 193
Bangkok Congress, xxiii, 25, 69,
  72, 150, 157, 170, 177, 181,
  183, 184–187, 190, 191, 192,
  194
baqa (reintegration), 51, 96, 158
Barnes, Michael, 54, 102
Basilica of Sts. Comas and
  Damian, 10
being peace, 97–98
Benedict, St., 172, 192, 195,
  206
Benedictine Confederation, 25,
  182, 184, 189
Benedictine Interfaith Dialogue
  (BID), 189
Benedictines of East Asia and
  Oceania (BEAO), 230
Béthune, Pierre-François de, 94,
  125, 162, 166, 167, 175, 182,
  188, 189, 197, 201, 204, 205,
  206, 219, 229, 230, 244

Blake, William, 10
Blée, Fabrice, 64, 125, 160, 166,
    173, 182, 185, 186, 191, 192,
    199, 200, 202, 218, 228, 240
bodhisattva, 43, 44, 51, 85
Bowe, Peter, 125, 134, 145
Brahman (the Universal Ground
    of Being), 48, 51
Bramachari, Mahanambrata, 8
brotherhood, 119, 148, 206
Brück, Michael von, 114, 227
Buddhism (in general), xi, xii,
    43, 93, 95, 110, 153, 160, 227
    Mahayana Buddhism, 66, 68,
        71, 75, 97, 98, 106
    Theravada Buddhism, xiii, 25,
        68, 107, 141, 253
    Tibetan Buddhism, xiii, 62,
        68, 73, 86, 101, 107, 115,
        120
Buddhist monasticism, viii,
    65, 130, 138, 144, 151, 173,
    176–177, 232
Buddhist nonduality, xxv, 2, 4,
    53, 67, 79, 80, 92, 97
Buddhist-Christian dialogue,
    xxix, 52–54, 62, 70, 74,
    75, 79, 89, 93, 94, 99–104,
    107–115, 124, 125, 178, 213,
    227, 245
Buddhist-Christian dual-
    participation, 109
Burns, Dom Flavian, 24
Byzantine mosaic (fresco), 10,
    11, 45

Calcutta, viii, xiv, 25, 68, 69,
    144, 149, 191

Carr, Anne E., 28, 29, 109, 158
Cartesianism (Cartesian
    philosophy), 59, 76–77
Carthusian monk, 16, 18
cataphatic theology, 83
Catholicism, 3, 4, 14, 15, 55,
    155, 197
Centering Prayer, 199, 235, 238
Ch'ing-yuan Wei-hsin, 89
chadō (tea ceremony), 147, 153,
    195, 237, 238
changing stability, xiii, xvi
channels, 175
charism, 127–128, 131
Chatral Rinpoche, xxix, 45, 70,
    72–73, 87, 117, 118, 140,
    153–154, 175
China (Chinese), 43, 65, 68, 74,
    75, 106, 227
Chodron, Thubten, 216
Chögyam Trungpa Rinpoche, 68,
    168, 169
Chokling Rinpoche, 69–70
Christ, Jesus, 11, 22, 34, 36, 40,
    78, 83, 84, 90, 98, 119, 129,
    150, 216, 223
Christian monastics, 115, 120,
    128, 138, 141, 144, 166, 172,
    174, 176, 189, 191, 211, 218
Christian theistic mystical
    experience, xxv, 2, 52, 53
Chung, Youn-Jo, 239
Cistercian monk (Order), 16,
    172, 182, 184, 189, 198, 207
Climate of Monastic Prayer, The,
    33, 36–37
co-contemplatives, 214–215, 251
Coff, Pascaline, 162, 175, 197

communication, 109, 132, 149–
154, 161, 162, 203
communion, 5, 39, 62, 149–154,
162
Eucharist Communion, 15, 199
intermonastic communion,
xxiv, xxvi, 37, 124–126,
161, 195, 214, 245
spiritual communion, xxvii,
xxix, xxxi, 25, 95, 104,
109, 118, 120, 144, 146,
162, 179, 191, 223, 246
universal communion, xxxi,
37, 126, 148, 153, 210, 244
compassion, 20, 22, 42, 43, 44,
49, 83, 84–86, 96–99, 147,
247, 251
Confucianism, 75, 76, 253
Consiglio, Cyprian, 211
contemplation, xxiv, xxvii, 1–2,
17, 22, 26–38, 46, 50–52, 63,
73, 91, 98, 121, 127, 132, 133,
145, 176, 211, 243–245, 256
acquired contemplation, 31, 34
active contemplatives, 34
contemplation and action, 18,
20, 21, 40, 67, 127, 255
contemplative charism,
131–135
contemplative core, 254–255
contemplative dialogue, vii,
viii, xiv, xxiv, xxviii, 27,
37, 57, 117–118, 125,
137–140, 141–145, 158,
212–213, 223, 229, 246,
248, 256
contemplative experience,
xxiv, xxix, 2, 16, 24, 27–

30, 34, 35, 46, 56, 57, 76,
95–96, 134, 163, 196
contemplative prayer, 31, 36,
52, 53
infused (pure) contemplation,
30, 31, 34
lay contemplatives, xxvi, 121,
133, 144, 159, 172, 174–
176, 185, 207, 217, 218,
231, 234–240, 242
masked (hidden) contemplation,
133–134, 154, 163
*Contemplation in a World of
Action*, 33, 37–38
conversion (*metanoia*), viii, xiii,
1, 3–4, 8, 11, 14, 16, 40, 120,
129, 131, 193, 221, 228
Corless, Roger, 100, 105, 169,
177, 242
Corpus Christi Church, 12
cross-cultural religious
experience, xxix, 41–46
cross-religious encounters, xv

Dadosky, John, 42, 100, 101,
105, 106, 107, 215
Dalai Lama, His Holiness, xiii,
25, 49, 61, 68, 70–72, 87, 98,
115, 116, 117, 135, 149, 163,
198, 205, 207, 212, 217, 233
Dammertz, Victor, the Abbot
Primate, 224
de-Benedictinized monasticism,
192
de-Europeanization
(de-Westernization), 192, 193,
252
de-Hellenization, 192

Descartes, 77

Desert Fathers and Mothers, 36, 58, 65, 127, 253

detachment, 72, 76, 78, 132, 134, 148

dhyana (meditation), 72, 74–75

Dialogue Interreligieux Monastique (DIM), 182, 188, 190, 194, 201, 203, 219, 226,

Dialogue Interreligieux Monastique/Monastic Interreligious Dialogue (DIMMID), xxiv, xxviii, 62, 171, 172, 178, 181, 182, 183, 189, 203, 219, 224, 229, 240–242, 245

dialogue of action (socially engaged dialogue), 62, 94, 96–99, 103, 163

dialogue of religious experience, 55, 62, 93–96, 195

dialogue of theology (intellectual dialogue), xxix, 62, 90–93, 102, 108, 159, 170, 222

discipline, 15, 50, 71, 94, 98, 120, 123, 129, 130, 134, 138–143, 148, 160, 165, 171, 178, 202, 216, 223, 228, 247

Disputed Questions, 18

divinization (*theosis*), 58, 84–86, 96, 99

doctrine, xi, xxix, 72, 82, 92, 93, 124, 160, 208, 233

Doren, Mark Van, 8

Drew, Rose, 112

dual religious belonging (double belonging), 90, 109–115, 245

dual religious participation, 110–111

dualism (duality), 16, 77, 78, 92, 99

dukkha (suffering), 209

Dunne, John, 44

dzogchen (great perfection), 23, 45, 70, 72, 73, 74, 86–89, 116, 140, 141

East-West Spiritual Exchange, 188, 194, 195–197, 240

Eckhart, Meister, 36, 80–82

ecumenism, 22

ego (ego-self), 6, 23, 51, 58, 76, 77, 78, 79, 148, 243

empirical ego, 77

emptiness, 6, 7, 35, 36, 42, 56, 64, 79–83, 88, 98, 114, 150, 151, 158, 216

emptiness and fullness, 26, 43, 56, 83

enlightenment, xxiii, 35, 36, 42, 44, 45, 46, 51, 56, 57, 68, 70, 74, 77, 84, 85, 89, 103, 104, 115, 117, 120, 134, 143, 148, 196

eschatology, 157

exclusivism, 37, 63, 154

existential dialogue, 35, 54, 99, 102, 116–117, 137–138, 202, 203

experience of life, 156, 194

experiential dialogue, xxix, 3, 54–56, 58, 75, 93–96, 101, 108, 109, 116, 136, 137–139, 203, 205, 246, 248, 251

Fader, Larry A., 107
fana (annihilation), 51, 96
final integration, xxix, 3, 37–38,
    49, 146, 147, 151, 156, 158
Fitzgerald, Michael L., 108
Flower Sermon, 152
Ford, George B., 12
Fox, Dom James, 24
Francis, Pope, 61, 123, 124
Franciscan Order, the, 14
Fredericks, James L., 102, 103,
    214
Friendship House, 14
fulfillment, 46, 79, 83, 88, 93,
    108, 139, 142, 154, 214

Garrigou-Lagrange, Réginald,
    17
Gautama Buddha, 90, 152, 216,
    227
George, James, 154
Gethsemani, Abbey of, vii, xxiii,
    xxvi, 7, 14, 18, 26, 65, 110,
    115, 127, 137, 140, 146, 148,
    169, 174, 195, 207, 217
Gethsemani Encounter, vii, xv,
    xxiv, xxvi, xxxi, 115, 135,
    162–163, 167, 175, 195, 199,
    207–218, 226, 230, 240, 242,
    246, 249
Gilson, Étienne, 9
Graham, Aelred, 76
Grayston, Donald, 44
Greek Fathers, 34, 27
Griffiths, Bede, 145, 168, 173,
    241
Gross, Rita, 93, 94

Halsey, Columba, 129
Hasidism, 132
Havana, 2, 13, 47
heart-to-heart transmission,
    152–153
Hellenism, 59, 91, 92, 192, 251
heresy, 64
hermitage, 21, 22, 45, 72, 87,
    155, 159, 174, 176
Hinduism, xiii, 26, 48, 51, 121,
    141, 144, 146, 227, 253, 255
Holy Spirit, 22, 47, 78, 151,
    222
home, xiii, 5, 6, 19, 45, 86, 136,
    146–148, 173, 203, 204, 206
homo universalis, 158
Hopkins, Gerard Manley, SJ, 12
Hui Neng, 75
Huxley, Aldous, 9, 64, 66, 144

incarnation, 70, 78, 98
inclusivism, 154, 214
India, 25, 68, 70, 87, 131, 145,
    168, 174, 185, 198, 199, 213
Indo-Sri Lankan Benedictine
    Federation (ISBF), 182, 229
inner experience, xxvi, xxviii–
    xxix, 3, 27, 29, 38, 46, 47,
    53–55, 117, 154
*Inner Experience: Notes on
    Contemplation, The*, xxvii,
    33–35, 41, 63–64, 66
inner-mystical experience, 2–4,
    46, 47, 57
inner peace, 98
inner self, 35, 50, 62, 74, 77, 95,
    96, 103, 119, 221, 223, 243

inner transformation, 49, 97, 99,
    127, 129–130, 132, 165, 186,
    220, 223
integrated encounter, 101, 103
integration, 3, 5, 21, 26, 40, 67,
    112, 119, 139, 142, 145, 157,
    226
inter/intra-monastic encounter,
    226, 228–230, 241, 250
interdependence, 22, 58, 97, 114,
    148, 153, 163, 210, 211
intermonastic communion, xxiv,
    xxvi, 37, 124, 125, 150, 153,
    161, 162, 245
inter-monastic exchange
    (dialogue), xxx, xxxii, 38,
    115, 121, 123, 124, 125–126,
    135–138, 141, 144, 146, 168,
    170, 173, 183, 187, 203, 218,
    225, 229, 230, 247
inter-monastic pilgrimage, 159,
    172–174
inter-monastic/contemplative
    dialogue, 123, 144–146, 149,
    151, 153, 158, 159–165, 170,
    174, 225, 240, 246
International Thomas Merton
    Society (ITMS), xxiv, 44, 242
interreligious dialogue, ix, xxvi,
    22, 30, 38, 58, 61, 67, 86, 107,
    124, 126, 137, 141, 166, 176,
    178, 191, 203, 218, 221, 225
intra-monastic dialogue, 179,
    182, 183, 223–225, 227, 231,
    246, 249, 250
intra-religious dialogue, 182,
    220–222, 225, 229, 246
Islam, xiii, 121, 132, 145, 253–254

Jain, 133, 185
Japan (Japanese), 43, 74, 75, 87,
    105, 106, 110, 132, 174, 194,
    196, 197, 204
Jeong (정, 情), xxxii, 250, 252–253
Jewish, 53, 113, 224, 253
Jikji-sa, 236
Jochim, Christian, 221
John Cassian, St., 79
John of the Cross, St., 30, 31, 36,
    44, 65, 80, 82, 151
John Paul II, Pope, 160, 172,
    178, 196
John XXIII, Pope, 41, 213
Johnston, William, SJ, 77, 106

Kakichi, Kadowaki, 197
karuna (compassion), 84, 85–86,
    88
Kazi, Sonam, 86, 87, 140
Keenan, John, 100, 105, 106,
    107–108, 109
Kempis, Thomas à, 8
kenosis, 44, 56, 78, 79, 83, 120,
    223
Keuss, Jeffrey F., 167
Kim, Ji-jeong, 233
King, Robert H., 100
Kirchner, Thomas L., 178
Knitter, Paul, 111, 154
koans, 65, 105
Korea, xxv, xxxii, 74, 110, 183,
    228, 231–237, 240, 250, 251,
    252–253
Kramer, Kenneth P., 223
Küng, Hans, 110, 213, 227

Lai, Whalen, 114, 227

Lax, Robert, 9
Le Clézio, Jean-Marie Gustave, 252
Leclercq, Jean, OSB, 25, 185, 186, 192, 251
lectio divina, 215, 235, 238
Lee, Deokgeun M., 232
Lhalungpa, Lobsang Phuntsok, 118
Lipski, Alexander, 48, 49, 168
Lonergan, Bernard, 215
Louisville epiphany (experience), xxvi–xxvii, 2, 4, 18, 38–41, 47, 57, 65, 84, 99, 255

MacCormick, Chalmers, 74, 104, 105
Madhyamika (middle way), 70, 87, 88, 89
Mahakasyapa, 152
manual labor, 17, 204
Maritain, Jacques, 17
Marxism, 26, 72, 157
Massignon, Louis, 145
meditation, 53, 71, 74, 75, 98, 103, 107, 111, 115, 118, 200, 201, 202, 247
meta-religion, 74, 111
mission, 240
Mitchell, Donald W., 208, 209, 217
Moffitt, John, xxiii, 185, 255
Monastery Stay Program, 183, 234–240
monastic archetype, 126, 134
monastic ecology, 178
monastic exchange programs, 179, 182, 183, 194–195, 195–207, 241

Monastic Hospitality program, xxxi, 188, 194, 197–199, 250
monastic interreligious dialogue, xxviii, 73, 113, 125, 145, 159, 161, 162, 179, 186, 188, 189, 193–194, 219, 240
Monastic Interreligious Dialogue (MID), 181, 189
monastic vocation, 14, 18, 19, 38, 127, 164, 174, 179, 187
monasticism, xii, xxx, 26, 124, 126–131, 133, 138, 145, 158, 159, 161, 163, 168, 177, 186–187, 191–193, 219
monastics (monks and nuns), 129, 166, 179, 194, 226, 251
monkhood, 131–35
Monks in the West, 226, 249
mutual enrichment and challenges, xxx, 54, 55, 109
mutual self-mediation, vii, 107, 215
mutual transformation, 102, 109, 120, 161, 187, 208
mysticism, 9, 22, 27–30, 53, 64, 82
mystical experience, 10–14, 18, 19, 27, 42, 57, 109

negative way (*via negativa*), 82
new monasticism, 131
New Seeds of Contemplation, 33, 35–36
ngondro (foundation ritual practices), 72, 140
Nhat Hanh, Thich, 41, 66, 97, 98, 102, 110, 148
Nicholls, William, 114

nirvana, 56, 67, 84–86
No Man Is an Island, 32, 40
non-Christian monastics, 128,
   178, 185, 186, 187
non-Christian religions, 27, 93,
   155, 178
nonduality (nondualism), 4, 38,
   40, 53, 67, 80, 92, 97, 144
nontheist religious experience, 52
nonviolence, 20, 97, 98
North American Board for East-
   West Dialogue (NABEWD),
   164, 181, 187–188, 190, 197,
   199, 202
no-self, 48, 76–79, 95
Nostra Aetate, 67, 143
nothingness, 35, 79, 80–83
Nuns in the West, 226, 249
Nyingma, 69, 73, 74, 86, 118

obedience, 17, 128, 134
openness, xxviii, 4, 22, 26,
   38–41, 46, 62, 63, 85, 86, 128,
   129, 143, 151
Oriental traditions. *See* Asian
   tradition

Pallis, Marco, 66, 86, 113
pan-Asian Congress, 185, 191
pancultural monasticism,
   190–192
Panikkar, Raimon, 133, 182, 220,
   222, 229
Park, Yong-gyu, 239
Parliament of the World's
   Religions, 141, 207
Patnaik, Deba P., 148

peace, 6, 12, 21, 61, 97, 98, 128,
   164
peacemaker, 9, 20
Pennington, Basil, 11, 24, 29
Pentecost, 186
phowa, 70
Pieris, Aloysius, 99, 249
Pignedoli, Sergio, Cardinal, 187
pilgrim-student, 247
pioneer, xxv, 20, 62, 98, 99, 100,
   101, 103, 104, 124, 178, 193,
   203
Platonism, Platonist, 20, 91
pluralism, 112, 154, 155, 161,
   190
Polonnaruwa experience, xxvii,
   xxix, 2, 4, 25, 26, 41–46, 47,
   68, 114, 170, 247
Pontifical Council for
   Interreligious Dialogue, xxvi,
   90, 93, 201
practical dialogue, 137, 139–141
Prajna (intuitive wisdom), 72,
   75, 81–82, 86
Prajna-paramita (wisdom gone
   beyond), 88–89
praxis, 62, 89, 102, 208, 227
prophetic role, 54, 135, 159,
   166–168, 207, 216, 245
Protestant, 22, 113
Protestant Reformation, 126
Pseudo-Dionysius, 36, 65
psychology, 3, 5, 6, 22, 34, 44,
   47, 49, 56, 57, 156, 239
pure contemplation, 17, 31, 34
Pure Land Buddhism, 43
purity of heart, 79–80, 133, 134

Raab, Joseph Q., xxvi, 44, 45, 100, 108, 155

Raja Yoga, 132

rangjung sangay (naturally arisen Buddha), 72

Ratanasara, Havanpola, 167

Rato Rinpoche, 171

Ratzinger, Joseph, Cardinal, 91, 200, 202

Raverty, Aaron, 203

Reality, 35, 37, 48, 49, 50, 52, 53, 55, 57, 85, 90, 105, 151, 154, 157

religious experience, xxvii, xxix, 3, 5, 12, 13, 14, 20, 22, 27, 29–30, 38, 41, 46, 49, 53, 54, 56, 91, 95, 107, 120, 139, 229, 252

religious identity, 110–114, 221, 223

renewal (of monasticism), xxx, 124, 126–131, 170, 177, 219, 245

resistance and doubt, 199–207

responsibility, 17, 58, 96, 97, 99, 164, 165, 190, 224, 228

return to sources, 127–128, 130

revelation, 21, 23, 31, 76, 155

Roman Catholicism, 155

romantic view (romanticism), 23, 168, 169, 171

samadhi, 71, 254

Samsohoe, xxxii, 233–234, 241

Sangha, 152, 242

satori (enlightenment experience), 29, 42, 92, 114, 254

Saux, Henri Le (Abhishiktananda), 145, 168

Second Vatican Council, 63, 67, 128, 142, 143, 170, 184, 189, 213, 214, 231

Secular Journal, The, 13

Seeds of Contemplation, 32, 35, 113

self-emptying, xv, 36, 45, 49, 64, 65, 79, 98, 120, 151

self-transcendence, xv, 1, 24, 25, 46, 49, 51, 52, 57, 65, 79, 84, 85, 86, 95–96, 112–114, 196, 245, 254

self-transformation, xxix, 2, 3, 4, 20, 40, 48, 95, 103, 117, 130, 139, 156, 243

Seven Storey Mountain, The, 1, 4, 13, 15, 16, 56

shamatha diagrams, 212

Shannon, William, 7, 11, 15, 21, 22, 30, 45, 47, 56, 64, 83, 147, 155, 252

Sharf, Robert, 100, 105

Siauve, Suzanne, 186

Sign of Jonas, The, xiii, 17, 20, 31

silence, 14, 15, 17, 21, 50, 134, 143, 152, 203, 207, 223, 235

Simmer-Brown, Judith, 69, 70, 89, 142, 153

Skudlarek, William, ix, 208, 210, 216, 226

social movement, 1, 5, 20, 96, 98

Society for Buddhist Christian Studies, xi, 214

solitude, 6, 14, 15, 17, 18–20, 21, 84, 96, 134, 175, 203, 243 spiritual communion, xxvii, xxix, 25, 104, 109, 118, 120, 124, 126, 146–154, 161–163, 195, 246, 247

spiritual elite, 159, 165–166

Spiritual Exchange program, xxxi, 188, 194, 195–197

spiritual family, xxiv, 37, 109, 126, 146–149, 161, 164, 177, 206, 207, 214, 251

spiritual freedom (liberation), xxiv, 37, 43, 58, 71, 118, 148, 255

spiritual growth, 1, 23, 24, 67, 76, 108, 167, 208, 234, 239, 240

spiritual healing, 57, 236

spiritual materialism, 69, 168, 169

spiritual maturity, 2, 23, 38, 116, 119, 143, 146, 149, 161, 165, 171, 178, 211–212, 221, 229

spiritual platforms, 242

spiritual rebirth, 57, 78, 99, 119, 156, 158

spiritual solidarity, 117, 151, 159, 163, 164, 171, 174–176, 191, 245, 250

St. Anne's hermitage, 45

St. Bonaventure University, 14

St. Joseph's Monastery, xxxii, 183, 231, 232–233, 241

St. Ottilien Congregation, 204, 232, 255

stability, xiii, 147, 172

Standaert, Benoît, 94

Steindl-Rast, David, 73, 107

subject-object relationship, 77–79

suffering, 65, 90, 97, 165, 168, 178, 209, 210, 216

Sufism, 25, 51, 96, 132, 139, 156

sunyata (emptiness), 29, 44, 72, 79, 80, 82, 83, 88, 90, 151, 158, 223

superiority, 1, 41, 141, 155, 176

Suzuki, D.T., xxvii, 41, 65, 66, 79, 80, 81, 82, 99, 105, 106, 124, 147, 153

syncretism, xv, 3, 29, 119, 200, 155, 200, 215

Talbott, Harold, 71, 87, 88, 117, 118, 120, 140, 171

Taoism, 22, 34, 75, 76, 121, 253

Teasdale, Wayne, 164, 206

Temple Stay Program, 183, 234, 236–240

Ten Ox-Herding Pictures, 211, 212, 215

Teresa of Avila (Jesus), St., xii–xiii, 28, 53

Theisen, Jerome, 189

theism, 4

theist religious experience, 52

Theravada Buddhism, 25, 43, 68, 107, 110, 141, 253

Thich Nhat Hanh. *See* Nhat Hanh, Thich

Tholens, Cornelius, 191, 194

Thomas Aquinas, St., 31, 121

Thurston, Bonnie, xi–xvi, 29, 63, 66, 99

Tibetan Buddhism, 43, 68, 86–89, 115–118, 120, 141

todo y nada, 44

transcultural consciousness (maturity), xxviii, 21, 37, 38, 125, 126, 154–158, 170, 191, 222, 248

transformation of consciousness, xxiv, 2, 129, 130, 155, 158, 160, 163, 165, 191, 210, 245, 255

true self, 50, 51, 57, 65, 74, 76–79, 84, 95, 146, 211, 243, 245

Truth, 67, 157, 214, 251

Tsering, Kunchok, 198

union with God, 2, 15, 21, 39, 49, 51, 84, 91, 92, 98, 119, 130, 134, 143, 176, 243

unity-in-diversity, viii, xxviii, 124, 249

universal approach, 178

universal consciousness, 37, 47, 49, 73, 109, 112, 157, 158, 248

Vajrayana, xiii, 43

Viens, Joachim, 134

Vipassana, 53, 71, 141

Waegwan Abbey, 232, 234

Waldron, Robert, 23

Walsh, Dan, 8

Weakland, Rembert, 186, 188, 190, 193

What is Contemplation?, 30, 33

Wisdom of the Desert, The, 66

witness, xxiv, xxvi, 22, 29, 34, 99, 118, 128, 149, 168, 198, 229, 232, 242

Wolf, Notker, 204

Won-Buddhism, 233

wordless dialogue, 197

Wu-wei, 158, 254

Zazen, 105, 141

Zen, xxiii, xxiv, xxvii, 29, 30, 43, 53, 54, 55, 65–67, 73–76, 79, 80, 93, 103, 111, 202, 254, 255

Rinzai Zen, *105*

Soto Zen, 103, 105

Zen Buddhism, xiii, 33, 34, 38, 106, 119, 197, 207, 208, 211, 219, 223, 236, 253

Zen core, 54, 76, 254

Zen monasticism, 140, 169, 173, 198